THE LONG WAY HOME

Also by Callan Pinckney

Callanetics

Callanetics For Your Back

Callanetics Countdown

Super Callanetics

Quick Callanetics – Stomach

Quick Callanetics – Legs

Quick Callanetics – Hips & Behind

AM/PM Callanetics

Complete Callanetics

Callanetics Fit Forever

New Callanetics

From the creator of **Callanetics**®

Callan

THE LONG WAY HOME

THE TRAVEL MEMOIRS OF
CALLAN PINCKNEY

WITH BENJAMIN DAVIS

PreciousPeach

LONDON

PreciousPeach
LONDON

First published in Great Britain in 2024
by Precious Peach Ltd
42/2 Hopkins Street, Soho, London W1F ODP

A CIP catalogue record for this book is available at the British Library.

ISBN 978-1-0686174-2-3

Cover art designed by Benjamin Davis

For information about CALLANETICS classes and Instructor Trainings
please visit **www.callanetics.com**

ACKNOWLEDGMENTS

This book would not have been possible without the generous
support and trust of the Estate of Callan Pinckney.

Thanks to Brenda Dempsey, Olivia Eisinger and Zara Thatcher for
their help and expertise in compiling this book.

Special thanks to Victoria Plaistowe for words of encouragement
and reminders that anything is possible.

Extra special thanks to Gay Davis, not only for her moral support,
but also for her expertise in deciphering handwriting
and bringing these words to life.

Travel photos by whoever could aim the camera
and push the button.

To all the Callanetics instructors and students, past, present
and future, thank you for your never-ending love and enthusiasm.

DISCLAIMER

This book contains letters written in the 1960s and 1970s
and reflects the language and social attitudes of the time.
Some readers may find this content offensive.

Footnotes have been added for additional context and clarity.

CONTENTS

Benjamin
you have been
wonderful.
Thank
You.
Callan

INTRODUCTION

Vogue magazine hailed her as the "high priestess of the new fitness" but Callan Pinckney's journey to that esteemed title wasn't an easy one. At a time when America was obsessed with leg warmers and leotards and high impact aerobics, the voice of this 5'1 Savannahian was drowned out by the deafening beats of the 1980s' ghetto blasters and fitness instructors parading as drill sergeants. Callan had devised a completely different language of movement. It was a way of shaping and toning the body without all the stress and strain of the workouts common to that era. No one took her seriously. No one understood what she was doing. Out of sheer frustration, Callan made it her mission to single-handedly take on the fitness industry and challenge what everyone believed they knew about getting 'fit'.

The revolutionary CALLANETICS workout that she created was slow to catch on. She managed to get a book published in 1984 but it failed to get noticed and the publisher cancelled the second print run. So, in true Callan style, she took to the road and ventured across America visiting every possible bookstore and TV station along the way. She refused to give up and did everything she could to get her voice heard. Her determination to spread the word paid off, and a year later her book became a No 1 bestseller.

Callanetics took the entire world by storm. No one had experienced anything like it before. Callan had developed a unique way of moving that not only toned and shaped the body incredibly fast, but also appeared to reverse aging and prevent the back and knee injuries that commonly occurred in gym classes. She went on to build an empire dedicated to this new method of fitness, selling millions of books and videos around the world and opening the door for credible alternatives to aerobics and weight lifting.

Nothing was more successful than Callanetics, both commercially and in the results achieved by its students. Callan's influence can be seen across the fitness world in many modern-day workouts. Pilates and barre classes will often have elements of Callanetics incorporated into their moves, either knowingly or not. Her unique exercises are as relevant today as they were 40 years ago, possibly more so. As people move toward intelligent and mindful workouts, there has been a strong resurgence in the demand for Callanetics classes and the incredible benefits it delivers for the mind and body. Even today, Callan's original work is still ahead of its time.

Born in Savannah, Georgia in 1939, Callan suffered debilitating spinal curvatures. Her feet were turned inward so severely she had to wear leg braces up to her waist until she was seven. Despite this, she was an adventurous child who dreamed of seeing the world rather than reading about it in books. Her adventurous spirit led her to be expelled from every school she attended. Frustrated by her lack of academic interest, Callan's mother put her in classical ballet classes. She excelled and continued dancing for 12 years. She also managed to complete two years of college.

But her heart was not in the Southern lifestyle she was expected to follow. So, one day in the early 60s, she threw her suitcase out the window and ran away to sea. What was originally intended to be a few months of travel ended up being a decade-long walk around the world, filled with drama and desperation, but also a lot of fun and happiness.

My first encounter with Callan was via a long-distance phone call one rainy London afternoon, in 2008. I had contacted her lawyer with an idea for a book. I wasn't expecting to hear anything back, but a few days later I received a call. On the other end, a familiar voice said, "Hello Benjamin, it's Callan."

We struck up a friendship which I'll treasure forever. Callan was warm, friendly, crazy and stubborn, all at the same time. She was the most fascinating and inspiring person I've ever met. She really was that person we all fell in love with from her videos. And so much more.

We spoke often of her wish to write a book about her travels. She tried in the past but her publisher thought no one would believe all the crazy situations she got herself into. And so, the idea was shelved.

After Callan's passing I spent time in her Savannah archives attempting to sort her mountain of Callanetics boxes. As I lifted the final box off the shelf, a bag fell on the floor. I thought nothing of it until I caught a glimpse of an old envelope inside. As I opened the bag, I couldn't believe my eyes. Carefully packed in date order were all the letters she had sent home to her parents during her travels around the world – perfectly preserved and hidden away for over 40 years! My mother, an expert at deciphering handwriting, transcribed them all into legible text for me. As I read them through I knew the time had come for Callan's wish to come true. That book she always wanted to publish was already written in her own words. Letters that documented every step of her travels. A wonderful snapshot of a period of her life that none of us knew much about. It was a journey that led her to create Callanetics and revolutionize the world of fitness.

I had wanted to help Callan write her autobiography. We sadly didn't get very far before she passed away. But I kept all the words she wrote to me and recorded all the conversations we had. Piecing them all together has created a nice prelude. The complete collection of letters that follow are presented word-for-word how she wrote them in the 1960s and early 70s. They haven't been edited or censored or altered in any way. Some reflect the language and social attitudes of that time. It's a fascinating story of a young Callan trying to figure out her place in the world.

Throughout her travels Callan would tell her mother and father she would be home 'soon'. A decade later she finally touched back down in Savannah and joked with them that she had taken "**The Long Way Home**".

Benjamin Davis
Guardian of Callanetics

Callan

To all the people around the world who were so concerned for my safety for without their kindnesses I probably would have never made it home.

GROWING UP

I was raised in the tradition of old Southern aristocracy in Savannah, Georgia and taught to do all the things proper young ladies were supposed to do. It was drilled into me from an early age to uphold the Pinckney name, and I was constantly reminded of my forbears, which included two foreign ministers, a drafter of the Articles of Confederation and the Constitution, a U.S. senator and a governor of South Carolina.

I was a true Dixie rebel and wasn't about to be forced into the lifestyle of dainty, white-gloved ladies. So, after I bolted from college, I defiantly announced to my parents that I was going off to see the world. Naturally, my very strict, fox-hunting father forbade any such thing, threatened to cut me off from the trust fund, and quickly put a stop to my allowance. My mother, however, wishing she could go with me, discreetly slipped me five hundred dollars and I was off running. I come from a very old-fashioned type of Southern family. To us, Scarlett O'Hara was white trash! I was lucky, I got the best of the old – the folded linen, the china tea cups, being taught real manners – and the best of the new, because I could get away from all that formality, and travel.

I was born Barbara Biffinger Pfeiffer Pinckney (I changed my name to Callan in the early 70s) and come from a long line of Pinckneys whose ancestors include the first Viscount of Surrey. They fought with William the Conqueror in the Norman Conquests in 1066. I found a life of well-bred tradition restricting, but not so the Pinckney fighting spirit.

And I had to fight from the beginning, for I was born with club feet, curvature of the spine caused by scoliosis and lordosis, which makes the buttocks stick out and all the organs 'go forward', especially the stomach. Throughout my childhood I was in pain. Actually, all through my life until I started doing Callanetics, which saved me from having surgery, which I'm terribly pleased about.

When I was an infant, my mother massaged my legs for three hours a day. I wore steel braces up to my waist for about seven years. I even slept in them to try and turn my feet out. I was put in ballet classes, to try to turn my feet out even more. But at that particular time, they didn't realize that by turning the feet out, it was dis-aligning my backbone structure even more. So, I always had back problems, but being brought up in the Deep South, you didn't discuss ailments. It was considered in very bad taste. So I thought everyone suffered from back problems, but no one discussed it. My right hip was higher than my left even as a child – so much so that the hems on all of my dresses and pants (including school uniforms) had to be taken up more on the left side in order to be straight. Before I learned the advantages of sitting down at a party, I would always stand with my left leg bent to ensure that my hips looked even.

It became worse as I grew older, but I wasn't aware that one of the reasons I always suffered lower back pain might be the situation with my hips. I assumed it was natural, especially because my mother and father have the same imbalance.

Then, one evening as I was preparing to go to a formal affair, a friend of mine said, "You can't wear that tight dress. It looks dreadful on you – your body is too crooked."

When I looked in the mirror, I gasped. I looked as though I had been carrying babies on my right hip for 40 years nonstop and they had a permanent resting place there. To put it mildly, I was a hysterical maniac. Instead of going to the party (I could never allow anyone to see me that lopsided!), the next day I went to the specialist who could give me the earliest appointment.

His response was the first of a long line of negative prognoses: "Nothing could correct the curvature or make your hips even at your age. You're just too old."

My feminine vanity wouldn't allow me to accept this. Somehow, I would find a way (or a person) to correct this condition, but for the time being I forgot about it. Despite my club feet and scoliosis, I was able to excel at ballet which I loved. I trained with Ebba Olesen for seven years. She danced with Balanchine. I was a clown. Serious about my work, but a clown. I was always kicked out of class. I was very resistant. I was also trained as a diver and a swimmer.

As a child, I went to every school in the city and was kicked out of each of them. I was very well known! I couldn't sit in a chair or at a desk for more than five minutes because of my back problems at that particular time. Also, I had very bad dyslexia and it was not understood or talked about in those days. So, I ran the gamut of all the schools throughout the city. Actually, it was really quite wonderful because I got to meet people from all different backgrounds and learned about everyone in the city. Even as a child, I thought there had to be something better than going to tea parties and getting married! I didn't want to be there. I was busy dreaming of being in foreign lands. I wanted to experience life and people, not read about them in books. Even when I was a baby, my mother told me they had to put a harness on me to keep me from running away.

By the time I reached my twenties, I thought I could conquer the world. Well, that world beat me up right and center. To say that I did it the hard way would be an understatement. Growing up in traditional Savannah, I was always the nonconformist, the dreamer. All my friends were getting married and settling down, and I just knew I wasn't ready to do that. I just didn't want to fit into that role. I finally thought, *I've just got to get out of here.* It was so unrealistic. Making a lifelong commitment at age 19 or 20 just didn't make sense to me. Good God, I couldn't even decide what color lipstick to wear each day. There was a big, big world out there and I wanted to experience people. I wanted to see how they lived – why they were so different, or were they? I didn't want to get married, I didn't want to go to school, and I didn't want to work, so I decided to travel. It's called the Great Escape. I escaped getting married. I escaped the stupid 60s. I escaped the drug scene. I just had to get out. I began working at Sears[1] to save money for my big escape, always

---

[1] Large department store

hoping none of my society friends would see me. Young ladies from good families simply did not work!

At the age of 22, I left the 'Old South' and headed to Europe. I was terrified of being called a 'spinster', a word which may not even be in the dictionary anymore!! I had just been kicked out of the University of Georgia and I didn't want to go to an all-female 'Yankee' school in the north, with snow and, uh... I just thought there was something better. And I'd always wanted to see the world and experience the way other cultures lived. Where I was coming from it felt that women were second-class citizens, with unequal rights. I was a rebel. My father was horrified. He told me I couldn't live three months without his support. That was the first major challenge in my life.

Then one night in 1962 – June 2, to be precise – I threw my suitcase out of the second-storey window so my daddy wouldn't catch me leaving. It crashed on the sidewalk and broke! But that wasn't going to stop me. My friends were waiting in the car and drove me to the depot where I caught a bus for Wilmington, North Carolina. There, a German freighter was leaving that night for Bremerhaven in Northern Germany. I had been to a cocktail party aboard the ship a few days earlier. It was a party for invited guests and the ship's officers. So, I became a stowaway.

They were very sympathetic. Once underway, the crew plotted how to get me safely off the ship in Germany. I didn't have a stamp on my passport. The captain washed his hands of me totally. However, the crew had a party on shore at Bremerhaven. We put my clothes in little bags and when everybody was leaving the ship to go to the party, they each carried some of my belongings in a little bag! I thought it was incredible that the Germans would do this, I really did! Because I thought they were so rules-orientated. I was still picturing them in Nazi Germany. They were young chaps, 21, 22... cute! And then once I was out, well that was it. I thought, *Oh my goodness, there are all these other countries. Oh, my goodness there are these continents. Oh my God, there's the whole world!*

ON THE MOVE

I never knew where I would be going next. I went where the roads and rides took me; I didn't care where they went. I wrote letters home. To this day I haven't read them – I don't think I ever shall. But my mother kept them, probably from sheer disbelief mixed with a bit of excitement of what her Southern Belle daughter was getting up to. Whenever I told people about the things that happened to me they didn't believe me. After my first book was a success, an editor wanted to write a book about my life. But when I started sharing the stories she said no one would ever believe them and the book was dropped before it even started.

I traveled around the world for a decade. I was the original 'bag lady'! I slept under trucks and in alleyways, any place that I could find protection. I had a survival attitude. There were five basic things that were the first things that I learned every country that I entered…

… "Please," "Thank you," "Water," "Food," and "Forgive me,"…

…just in case I insulted them or their custom and didn't realize I was doing something to insult them! I was in survival mode and lived moment to moment, hour by hour, which was nerve-shattering. I was often scared and sometimes immobilized with fear. I had been brought up to be a lady, and a Southern lady at that! I was taught never to draw attention to myself. So to survive on my own, I had to get beyond that. I would pretend I was a female John Wayne. I got a Turkish sword, small, round and lethal. I forgot I was short. I forgot I was female.

When men accosted me, I flashed my sword. They were so flabbergasted, they backed off. Three times men attacked me and three times the killer instinct in me exploded. Once, in the Sahara Desert, an Arab started to molest me. I removed his hands from my breasts and said, "How unchivalrous of you!"

He was crazy with anger and said in perfect English, "I'll rape you! I'll kill you! I'll bury you in the sand! No one will find you!"

Then he saw all my freckles. He thought I had a disease! That was the end of him and he disappeared into the night. I've been slapped by men but never cried. I felt I was fending for my life. It was my life or theirs. If I was going down, they were going to go down with me. That was the fighting attitude I possessed. I guess I have two angels looking after me, one on each shoulder. I was never raped. There wasn't a day when I wasn't afraid of being killed, maimed or raped, but I got myself out of every bad situation. I still have a fear of being destroyed, but I've lost about 70 percent of that over the years.

When I got halfway around the world, wandering became a lifestyle. My father had said I couldn't exist three months without his money. After a while, I lost all track of time; it didn't matter. To this day I don't wear a watch. Being free of the strictures of time is wonderful. It really frees you.

I was often very ill from eating different types of food. I had three terrible bouts of amoebic dysentery. Unfortunately, the five hundred dollars my mother had given me ran out in no time, so I was forced to work a variety of jobs, many of which I had no idea even existed! I shoveled coal in England, modeled clothes in Tokyo, worked the rice paddies of Southeast Asia, sold whiskey in India, and studied animal migration patterns in Africa. There were several months at a time when I lived on a budget of fourteen cents a day.

Along the way, I managed to get myself into some crazy situations that I thought I'd never get out of. I spent time in four separate Arab jails, disguised myself as a native to cross borders and avoid paying for visas which I could not afford, and gave up everything to live in a Buddhist monastery in Ceylon. It was also in the African hinterlands that I learned of President Kennedy's assassination – six months after the fact and only then by tribal drums. After a certain number of years – maybe five years – I got caught emotionally and physically and mentally hating the world, hating being alive because there was such poverty. Seeing maimed children having to beg for food. Starvation. It really got to me. In fact, to the point I became a part of that world… and emotionally I kept going down and down and down, becoming a martyr. I felt guilty eating a tiny piece of bread if I was blessed to have a piece.

Then, all of a sudden, duh, it hit me. *Wait a minute! What I have to do if I feel so strongly about this is I have to make a lot of money. Then I can come from total choice to give money to poor people if I choose or to do whatever I want to. Now I will release myself of being a victim and a martyr.* But I still wandered aimlessly around the world for a few more years. I returned to Savannah one Christmas, 1967 I think. My mother and father begged me to return home after I lost contact with them whilst in India. War broke out and I was caught in the middle of it. But after two weeks in Savannah I couldn't sit still and jumped on a plane back to Europe. There was too much more I wanted to see in the world. I wanted to learn Spanish at the University of Madrid, or to work taking pictures for National Geographic. I had dreams of the trans-Siberian train ride and journeying through South America (which sadly I never did).

When I first arrived in Germany in the summer of 1962 I had no particular itinerary. All I knew is that I wanted to see the world. For three months I traveled through Europe. I acquired a Volkswagen with a friend, Wendy, and that became my home to cut expenses. I fell in love with Majorca and stayed in a villa there for a month before going to Madrid and then England. In the fall of 1962, I hitchhiked my way to London. To this day it's still one of my favorite places in the world, although stupidly overpriced and very expensive to live there. (The food was terrible too, but on my more recent visits, I had some of the best food I've ever had anywhere in the world). But that first winter in London was not for the fainthearted. I had never felt such frigid temperatures. That winter broke all records for low temperatures. The only heat I had in my apartment, or 'flat' as the English say, was a little electric heater which kept catching fire. There was no central heating. One night I was sleeping so close to it to keep warm that my nightdress caught fire!

I had no papers and the only job I could get was shoveling snow for around $3 a day. I lived on biscuits and jam, cookies and as much starchy food as I could eat. Anything to help insulate my body in fat. I think I gained 30 pounds. I'm only five-foot-one so you can imagine how heavy I looked. Then an elderly English lady took pity on me and offered me work in her house. I'd never really worked before except at Sears. I never realized that people worked for a living. The lady asked me to hang wallpaper for her. She was so prim and proper. She was just wonderful. However, I'd never hung wallpaper in my life! I didn't know what you were supposed to do. So, she called a friend who had a wallpaper man at her house and he was telling her what I should be doing. What a disaster! I think it's one of the funniest jobs I had.

Whilst in London I heard from many people about the wonders of Africa. I couldn't get all the necessary travel permits in England so I had to hitchhike back to Hamburg to obtain them. Can you believe I got all the way from London to Hamburg and back for free?! You could never do that today. My plan was to spend the next few months in England, Scotland and Europe and then travel to Africa before winter hit again. I bought a huge rucksack in London to carry all my belongings. It was huge, as big as me!

I didn't realize at the time that I would spend the next decade hitchhiking and traveling around the world carrying my belongings in that rucksack. It became my mobile home. When I put it on, I literally had to kneel. And I'd have to put my hands on my back and wiggle the rucksack up my back. Trying to stand up straight with all this incredible weight on my back was a horrible process. But once I got up, that was it. I couldn't sit for the rest of the day because it was just too agonizing to sit down, take a breather from the rucksack, and then try to get it back on my back again and then stand up… so once the rucksack was on, that was it! It did terrible things to my back and bones. But I was off to see the world.

LETTERS HOME

1962

France

Paris

July 5, 1962

Paris, France

Paris is beautiful. I am having such a wonderful time. Germany was great, but cold. The French people are terribly dirty and they never take baths. Neither do I, I'm in style. Holland was the cleanest place I've ever been. I don't want to leave Paris but it's cold and the sun hasn't shone. Want to go to Spain next, but don't know. I've been living off $2 a day in Paris but in Germany I spent over $40 in three days. Wish y'all were here. I am fine. Kiss children for me.

⊶⊰❊⊱⊷

Andorra

Andorra

July 7, 1962

Andorra

We are in the small country between France and Spain in the Pyrenees mountains. It is so beautiful you couldn't believe it unless you saw it yourself. Had to drive to the top of the mountains at night and I said two rosaries. Was really worth it though and have been having more fun. The people here are very old fashioned, and they speak Basque, a language that no one knows where it came from. We have been sleeping next to brooks, and we buy bread, milk, and cheese, spend about $2 a day, and we get to see more than if we were on a tour. Keep this card for me. Didn't meet the two girls in Paris. Write!

⋯⋯⋯⋯⋯ ⊸◦⧉◦⊶ ⋯⋯⋯⋯⋯

Spain

Pamplona

July 12, 1962

Pamplona, Spain

Y'all this place is so fantastic and you wouldn't believe it. Everywhere we go we run into the neatest Americans. The Spanish are so great and so poor it's hard to believe. Wish y'all could be with me. Please write me. The Spaniards raise far more Pinckney hell than marines. You can't imagine how great Pamplona is. They never go to sleep, and they stay drunk all the time. People dancing in streets and there must be 1,000 small bands roaming the streets. The bull run is at seven in the morning, and everyone stays up for it. The cops wouldn't let me run. Don't get mad, but when the car is shipped, we are hitchhiking. Everyone does it. I still can't believe this place. Spain is great, to Madrid next week. Forgot to tell you, we went to Chartres Cathedral. This is the most historic cathedral in the world. It's right outside of Paris. Went out of our way to see it and Versailles, the summer palace of Louis IV, I think, and where all the treaties have been signed. Unbelievable. Spain to me is so much more wonderful than France. They're both so historically beautiful but in Spain poor people live in the most elegant old houses. They aren't run down. All of them have beautiful courtyards of stone with little fountains in the middle and beautiful marble and lacy ironwork. Just like you would imagine. The buildings are more than 500 years old and the streets are hardly wide enough for a car to go through with cobble stones, and dirty water is thrown out of windows like in one of Shakespeare's plays.

⊸⟨⟩⊶

Valencia

July 21, 1962

Valencia, Spain

Was supposed to go to Barcelona but we came here for the bull festival. I am a fantastic bullfighting fan. Have seen about 20 and I sometimes go without dinner so I can buy a ticket. The other night I dreamt I was a matador. I grow to love Spain and the Spanish more and more every day. They are so poor and so generous. They always want to pay for things, and yet they are starving and when you refuse they get insulted and go into a rage. I have finally caught up on money in Spain. You can't believe how cheap and great it is. Saw Charlton Heston and Ava Gardner in Madrid. Saw Jerry Carson in Pamplona. No matter what happens y'all have got to come here. Next, to Barcelona.

⊸⟨⟩⊶

Barcelona & Madrid

July 31, 1962

Barcelona, Spain

I am now living with a Spanish family, and my clothes are beginning to smell like Spain again. Mother, you're so funny – Spain is great to be in whereas they love Americans, and other countries hate 'em, and the Spanish go out of their way to help you. Wish we could go to southern Spain but not time. I love the bullfights.

Went to the Expiatory Temple of the Holy Family. It is without a doubt the strangest thing I have ever seen in my life. I couldn't get the background on it, so I had to buy a book because the history of it was just too educational to pass it by. Barcelona is a tourist trap, but we manage okay. Wednesday we are going to a beautiful small island called Majorca off the coast of Spain in the Mediterranean. From there to Italy. There is so much I want to tell, but honestly, I wouldn't know where to start, and besides I couldn't do Europe justice with the way I write. I have gained 12 pounds and look terrible, plus my clothes have had it, haven't learned to drink wine yet. You would love Spain so much. One can live like a king on $5 a day here. We have lived off $1.60 plus bought presents. At 6 pm we are going to the bullfight with two American boys, and they don't know a thing about it, so we can show off how much we know. Please let me know how y'all are doing and the children. I miss them so much. Honestly, I would like to write a book about Spain, I love it so much. So poor and the past is still here. Very few modern buildings. You can actually see the people of 1,000 years ago. Just wonderful. Haven't even seen screens on windows. They've never heard of them. The most dreadful thing is they have Turkish johns which are unbelievable. I love Spain so much, and I hate to leave it, especially the bull fights.

In Madrid we went to the Prado Museum (the world's greatest collection of paintings). I bought three copies of Goya, but I don't know how I'm going to manage when I ship the car. There is a bull fighter who is so fantastic. He is called the Clown of the Ring and he has been gored 30 times in the last 1½ yrs. He was gored in Valencia and we saw it. Y'all have got to come here. It is worth everything, 10 miles out of Madrid is the 8th Wonder of the World, a church built on the side of a rock, and Franco ordered it built, and 1,500 Spanish died building it. We couldn't find it.

Please keep all cards and letters for me. These are the only things I have to remember Europe.

My favorite fighter is Cordobés. He is 22 and will be a matador in October if he isn't killed. Wendy and I have become fanatics on bull fighting. The other night we went to see a movie about Cordobés' life and he played in it. The next day he fought. We are now going to see Miquelin fight, who Daddy has heard of. He is our favorite, and has been gored 30 times in the last 1½ yrs. He got gored in Valencia.

Well you certainly can't complain about my writing. I guess y'all shocked. Mother, my fur coat is at Sandi's house. I left it there in winter, please get it. The thing I miss most is mayonnaise (Kraft). They have never heard of it.

We are going to try and get a job in Germany. Having such a great time I don't know how to explain.

———— ⊲⊱⊰⊳ ————•

Costa Brava

August 10, 1962

Tossa de Mar, Costa Brava, Spain

Hey, we are about 50 miles from Barcelona. Daddy, you remember when Harry drew a circle around the eastern coast of Spain, and said it was expensive and a tourist trap? Well here we are. It is in Costa Brava. I have never seen such a beautiful place in my worldly travels. God, how corny. Seriously, you can see the bottom of sea. Oh y'all would love beautiful Spain. Its past is its present.

I sent a card to y'all with me on the front. Hope it gets to you. Wendy and I are on our way to Majorca, a small island off of Spain, then from there back to Barcelona. Honestly, the best way to tour Europe is by camping. It is so cheap and you see everything. Thousands of camping camps. This is without doubt the most beautiful place I have ever seen. We have been here a week and have gone deep-sea diving. Stopped though when I saw an octopus on the bottom! Underneath it is hard for one to imagine the beauty unless one has actually seen it for oneself. Y'all, Spain is so cheap it is unbelievable. You can live like kings for $5 a day. I'm so mad, I wish all I had brought was two dark baggy blouses and a pair of Levis (jeans) and one dress. When we get rid of the car I am throwing a suitcase of clothes away. Too much to carry. This is the only smart thing I have done in my life coming here.

In the main square a man painted me. It was terribly embarrassing because the whole circle was filled with people watching. I hope I don't lose it, it's quite good. Y'all are actually going to die when you see what Wendy and I have done for y'all – it's a surprise.

⸺⸙⸺

Palma

August 16, 1962

Palma, Mallorca

I hope by the postcards you can realize why I love Spain so much. Palma is on the island of Majorca and its packed with British, but we avoid them. A man that we met in USAF[2] had to leave and he gave us his villa for a week, plus good old American food in it! I don't know how long we will be here, because every boat is booked for weeks and the car is in Barcelona. This is the Spain I love.

Honestly, I try to say so much about everything but sometimes I actually cry because I never want to leave this country. In one small town we accidentally drove through, the picadors were testing the bulls, oh we were so thrilled – we were the only tourists there. Tomorrow we see Cordobés fight. Can't wait.

Another tragic thing I love to see is that in the section we live, women still wear all black with little shawls, carry large string baskets for bread and wine. You can't help loving them for their ancient ways, and above all they are happy.

⸺⸙⸺

[2] US Air Force. They had a base on the Puig Major mountain in Majorca.

Barcelona

August 21, 1962

Barcelona, Spain

Dear Mother and Daddy,

Left Majorca this morning and now I am back in Barcelona. Wendy is in Madrid and is coming here in four days and then we will drive to Hamburg to ship the car. Majorca was so packed with British, it was terrible, but the island itself was lovely and expensive, and the Spanish speak Majorcan and not Spanish. Sounded funny after hearing Spanish for almost two months.

Wendy and I are leaving here Friday for Hamburg and should get there August 30. I was only in Germany for four days when I first arrived in Europe. Klaus (one of the officers I met on the German ship) is going to make the arrangements for me before I arrive. I wrote Mr. Nugent an urgent letter about shipping the Volkswagen and never heard from him, so we will see him in Hamburg. Don't worry, I would never consider traveling alone. Wendy is staying with me until I leave. Mother, you really are funny. Spain is the best place to be. Like right now I am staying with a Spanish family and the wife is sitting here trying to make conversation with me and can't speak a word of English, while she is sewing all my clothes I've torn, which is practically everything. I'm kind of getting prepared for the cold weather too, since I didn't bring any winter clothes. Wendy has to go to Iceland for a week to be at a wedding and I am waiting on her in Hamburg so that will be my next address. Then we are going through Austria and Switzerland on our way to Italy and will stay there a month or two. What comes will come. I really hate leaving again, because overall the people are so much fun, and they treat me like royalty and they love freckles.

Oh, by the way, we were stuck on Majorca and couldn't get out, so I finally got a jet to Barcelona and I shall never forget it. I didn't even feel us going up, and I could see the majestic landscape of the Spain I love so much. Daddy, you would really get a kick out of the Spanish uniforms. I don't know what all of them mean because everything is so secret but some of them are gray and gold uniforms, with gray hats, and they wear swords and they look as if they just stepped out of a five-year war, the Civil War. Others wear German uniforms except they are bright green and the helmets shine. You complain about me not writing info. But so many times I have sat down and tried to explain everything I have seen but I cannot begin to do it justice. Write me about the children and when the baby is due.

"Muchas gracias, Señora." This is what the Spanish say to me, "Thank you very much, Miss."

Love Barbara.

—⊷⊶⊷—

England

London and Windsor

November 1, 1962

London, England

I am in the lounge here waiting for my sightseeing bus to show up. We went on a marvellous tour yesterday. Way out in the country to Windsor Castle and Hampton Court, passed Eton – the exclusive boys' school. The boys were walking and riding bikes and they wear formal morning coats with tails and cravats (wide ties, I guess this is the name). School had opened up day before and there were hundreds of them about the place.

I took some pictures of Windsor Castle and the guards (in red pants and crazy black fuzzy hats) and hope they all come out o.k. Had some chap take Barb– a Canadian girl that I am traveling with – and I together. There were such gangs of tourists in different parties that it was chaotic – we rented a radio with earphones and as you went from room to room they explained what you were seeing – you were always losing your party and never had time to see much. There was a doll's house but we didn't have time to see it as we chose the magnificent chapel – these tours are for the birds! I wanted to buy a book for Jane, Page and Soren of the doll's house but didn't have time! They are really crazy.

7 pm, back from the tour to Buckingham Palace – was very interesting but I have just about had it with these tours! You don't dare let your guide out of your sight, or that's the end for you! Someone is always getting left!

I am a little tired right now – we are on the 3rd floor – no screens on windows in London but only one or two flies! The toilet is three doors down and the bathroom with tub only and a chair and a crazy shower! This rubber tube is like a doctor's stethoscope – with hoses hitched to each faucet and a spray at the end on a handle. You stand with your back to the wall and spray water all over yourself. I was always forgetting and got the rug slightly wet! We had one devil of a time finding a hotel with a shower! The one we stayed in the two nights had the toilet down the hall (we were on the 1st floor) then up three steps, turn and go down the hall again, the tub was down quite a flight from there! I said *The heck with all this, we are going to look for something else!* The tiny dining room closed at 9 am and we didn't even wake up till 10.30 am! We were about to have a tizzy – so we just got out and kept walking till we found this quite nice place, run by a woman who speaks fluent Cantonese.

The first thing we asked was *Do you have a shower?* and no one has but this lady put one in because she has so many like us who would take rooms if they had showers (this shower arrangement is simple – I don't understand!). Even went to three really nice good size hotels and they were £20 to £22 per day and no private baths or showers! London prices are terribly high and the food is garbage. French fries with everything! I won't eat any more – breakfast is standard – egg, English sausage (ugh!) or bacon, awful coffee, and most people were having French fries too (chips) and toast. Cold and hard! We haven't been in any fine (real) restaurants but Barb said one time about five of them went to a real nice restaurant for dinner in the evening and they served French fries with that meal. I don't know what it is – nothing has much taste! And they cook with too much grease!

Tomorrow we go out to "Churchill Country" – should be nice, all day with lunch and later "tea". There really isn't much variety in the food so far – this evening we are going to the revolving restaurant on top of the Post Office Tower which is 619 ft. high – have a postcard, hope it won't be too expensive. If so we will just have salad and drink. Bourbon and gin are prohibitive here – you see everyone drinking beer – (of course we don't move with the Dorchester Hotel crowd – Elizabeth Taylor and Burton pay $400 per day! They do have showers!). I ran out of paper. Barb is bringing some with her, also stamps – so that's why I am using a piece of sack that came from some pamphlets that I collected today. Went into "The Old Curiosity Shop" – that was really something (but ten thousand other tourists were squeezed in there too) and you didn't know what you were looking at or what you wanted or anything and the bus driver said, "Hurry along a bit now you know, it's just around the corner, be back in 10 mins!"

I just got a couple of postcards and two boxes of notes with the shop picture on them! People were shoving and they only had two clerks and this is really a doll's house. (The doll house at Windsor Castle was a room full of dolls from way, way back!) We went to Fleet Street, St Paul's Cathedral (got a postcard), it was really something. The boys' choir was to sing in the beautiful chapel at 4 pm for evening service so we had to get on – the organ is the original and I wish we could have stayed! I will write again soon. Must start writing to Jane, Harry and Bubba [Jane is Callan's sister, Harry is Jane's husband, and Bubba is her brother (real name Francis)], Ticky, and all those who gave me gifts – tell Mary Anne I write when we get out of London. It takes forever to do anything here! Hope all are o.k.

Here it is Sunday morning and we just came up from breakfast – bought the very first newspaper since leaving Madrid, don't even know if Eisenhower is still living – didn't see any TV in Madrid or here. There is one here in the lounge but we haven't had time to look at it. I didn't go to the "Churchill Country" tour. I wanted to go down to Selfridges, the largest store in London – it would take days to go through. Gorgeous crystal chandeliers, the lifts were made of something that looked like gold leaf, very ornate carvings (a lift is an elevator) and the store smelled so good! We also made a trip down to Carnaby Street and that was really wild! Tiny little stores on narrow streets off the main streets (Oxford, Regent), the radios blaring so loud that you are screaming at the clerks who couldn't care less if you never came in! Nobody takes a bath and the sweaty odors nearly knock you down! And the prices! And the way these young people dress! Skirts up so high that you just miss seeing everything! They wear floppy hats, boots, long chains, long hair, etc.

It was a real experience. We went back to Marks and Spencer, a huge department store – real bargains and Barb made my buy two pairs of panty hose – £1.

I bought a real way-out hostess dress – looks like a lace tablecloth, real wide sleeves, long shirt and full with belt – Jane can wear it too, I know she will love it! Bought it at Harrods, the nicest store here! Went out last night about 6 pm to find a bottle of milk or O.J. and ran across a darling area with an Italian restaurant and rushed back to tell Barb we would eat there for supper. We went over (just two blocks away) and had wine and my mouth was just watering thinking of "Anna's Little Napoli" so we ordered lasagne. But when it came it was nothing but noodles with grated cheese on top! They serve boiled tomatoes with everything but didn't even use it in this dish! (They are crazy where food is concerned – we had ham for breakfast!). And we closed our eyes and chewed and there was no taste at all. I have read that you have to forget the food while in Merry Old England! It's true – but "very interesting"!

If you talk to Mary Anne tell her we couldn't live without her clothes line – it's full of things every day! If you talk to Sabre tell her I have never treasured anything like her wallet – it is stuffed and I have never let it out of my sight. When we get to Coventry I intend to write to everyone but you know Jane and Bubba will read these letters – save all of them.

Barbara called Wendy in Ireland last night and they are expecting us – she wrote Barb at the American Express[3] but we didn't go there – never thought there would be mail! Well Barb had written to Wendy saying we might go to Scotland and Ireland and Wendy answered her letter right away – they have moved into a new home and are excited about our coming. We are really excited about getting the car tomorrow, only 1/2 hrs by train from here!

Well it is now 12.30 and we want to get to the huge flea market, where hundreds of artists line up their work outside and I can't wait to get there – I don't think we can take pictures as it is raining a little but we have raincoats and an umbrella, they have stuff from all over the world like in Madrid. I don't believe my feet, I haven't had the first ache or

---

[3] American Express was an express package delivery company before it became a credit card company.

pain, I haven't had an itchy scalp, very little muscle trouble and I have been rushing around. Barb can hardly keep up with me! I carry that big satchel over my shoulder all day long – or carry it hanging down, and that bothers me very little by the end of the day. We dash into the bathroom to take a hot shower (what a luxury!), rest a little while and run out to some little place to eat and are back here early! It's really quite safe in London believe it or not. Did I tell you about the underground? I can't find out how deep it is but you get a real weird feeling that you can't get out! The escalators take you down and down and you had better know what train you have to take or that would really be the end! So different from Madrid's metro, it is very clean and very cool and everyone is so quiet – no loud talking, screaming and shoving – it's really wonderful to see people so polite on the streets. They are like ants – I have to hold on to Barb every inch of the way! If we ever got separated that would be it!

The London "Bobby" is riding up and down the streets on horseback. We went into a beautiful large two-storey china and crystal store yesterday and two women were making these beautiful small baskets of flowers that we see in some jewellery stores at home (like fine china) quite expensive though – glad we are leaving for Coventry in the morning. People live terribly here – no central heating etc. but that's what makes this all so interesting. Will write the children soon – hope you all enjoy these letters. Will write soon again.

Love to all,

Barbara.

1963

Scotland

Loch Lomond & Others

June 21, 1963

Scotland

They all call us wee lassies!

Dear Folks,

Well I'm on the move again. I decided I just couldn't work in the summer, so I am on the move again hitching all over Europe with Barb on a $1 a day. We really look a sight with our rucksacks on our backs, standing on the roads in the rain, laughing at ourselves. We stay in youth hostels and they are really a blast. I really am having the best time I have ever had in my life. We are waiting to catch a boat to Sweden and then we're going to Hamburg. Will be there around the end of June.

Scottish people are fabulous and their hospitality is terrific. Everyone that picks you up tells you the history of the clans and of the countryside we are in at the time. They invite us home for meals with their families, and we really don't spend a cent. We are learning so much about the people, and I feel this is most important. We stayed in a castle on Loch Lomond, and there were so many people there. We became very good friends with two Dutch girls and that night we went to a Highland dance. They made us dance and we laughed so much at ourselves that we could hardly dance. It was the craziest place I've ever been, and the most fun.

In the morning at the hostels you have to do a chore and at night, you have to be in by 10 o'clock. The people you meet are so much fun. This is the only way to really see a country. In Northern England a lady picked us up and took us to a hound hunt. That was the funniest thing and most interesting, and a tourist would never see this. In Scotland they take you through the cities and show you the historical places. This morning we saw a Stuart castle and a Gordon castle, and the place where the Campbells slaughtered the MacDonalds in their sleep.

—◦◦◦◦◦—

Germany/Italy

Frankfurt, Salzburg, Linz, Germany; Venice, Italy

July 13, 1963

Venice

Dear Mother and Daddy,

Well after we left Hamburg we got a ride with five U.S. boys to Frankfurt in a '61 Buick. They gave me 40 cigs and treated us to an American hamburger on a base. Gee, it was the first one for over a year! When we got to Frankfurt we had a half-hour to get to the hostel before it closed, and a man picked us up and he drove us right there, and gave me 40 Pall Mall. The next morning we started hitching at 7 am and made it to Salzburg that night. We spent all day looking at everything, and then we found out we couldn't get a place that night so at 5 pm we had to hitch to the next town that had a hostel. It was pouring and we looked dreadful. Thank goodness three American boys stationed in France picked us up in their big American car and gave us a ride to Linz and also gave me 20 Camel, and treated us to a meal. When we arrived at the town they took us straight to the hostel, to find out it had burnt down! Well there we were at 9.30 pm – they didn't want to leave us, so they bought us supper and wanted to give us money for a hotel, but we wouldn't accept it, because I think they wanted something in return. They finally left us, and we just started walking until we could find a park bench or something to sleep on. We came to a building, half way built, and we decided to sleep in there.

The next day we hitched to Venice. We arrived in Venice at 9.30 pm, and all the hostels were filled, so we had to stay in a Catholic missionary which cost $8 and it really cramped our style! Today at 7.30 am (can you imagine me getting up so early!) we caught a boat for $1.50 and rode to the other side of Venice to the hostel. We don't know if there will be enough room for us, and if there isn't we are going to sleep in a gondola. I really can't begin to say how fascinating and beautiful Venice is. You would absolutely go wild. The Viennese glass is breathtaking as is everything else. This is the most romantic city I have seen. Really, I am so in love with it. We rode on a gondola for $1.60 an hour and it broke us, but that's the only treat we have allowed ourselves. I hate so much to leave tomorrow, but we don't have but two months left for other places.

I was so happy to receive a letter from y'all today. The picture of the children is lovely, I can't believe how they have grown. I am writing this letter in St Mark's Square, and at the outdoor café across the way a three-piece orchestra now are playing, and it is so beautiful and romantic. It is hard to believe I am really sitting here. Daddy, I just can't read your writing, and don't worry what those people in Savannah say about hitchhikers. But I can honestly say I really feel sorry for the students who come over here for three months and jump from place to place in planes and trains, and get to know nothing about the real people of each country. I only wish I had done this last year. Please write to me in Athens.

I can't take pictures because I don't have a camera and if I did, I couldn't afford film, so my letters and cards are the only souvenir I have, so keep them.

Yugoslavia/Greece

Belgrade & Niš, Yugoslavia; Athens, Greece

July 23, 1963

Athens

Dear Family, well we finally made it to Athens. When we left Venice, we got several lifts with Italians to a small place, and stayed in a beautiful villa which was on the Adriatic Sea facing Yugoslavia for 2 days. We had a lovely rest, and met so many interesting people. Then we hit the Yugoslavia border and did we have a hard time getting a lift! This is without doubt the worst country for hitching because the people don't have cars and the tourists are the only ones to pick you up. We sat at the border for about an hour, an Italian picked us up and drove like a maniac over Yugoslavia mountains, and I didn't think we would come out of it. He dumped us out in the middle of nowhere, and we sat there for about an hour and half. Absolutely no cars on the highway, and finally a brand-new Mercedes picked us up, and it was an Arab, who gave us a ride to Belgrade (Barbara and I drove).

In Belgrade we stayed at the university, and they were all beautiful new buildings. Driving through you would think they had really progressed, but when we entered, we were so shocked. They were only about three years old but had no hot water, no showers, Turkish johns, plaster falling off the ceiling, and bugs were crawling out of the wood in the floors. The rooms smelt so bad, it was almost unbearable, and this is the condition the university students live in! Really terrible!

Belgrade was a joke. It looked like a town just thrown in to the middle of a desert. No flowers, no scenery, no cars and lights all over the large new streets. The Yugoslavian people seem to be very nice, but are extremely poor. They never seem to laugh, sing, or hold hands, which is a part of a happy existence, and I've never seen so many beggars and gypsies. Honestly, I don't like this country much! There was absolutely nothing to see in Belgrade so we left the next morning to try and make it to Greece as quick as we could.

We caught the bus out of town and landed in some God-forsaken place, and two Yugoslavian (communist) boys picked us up and tried to brainwash us on how great communism was. After that we sat on the highway for 45 mins and finally a car came by and two Persian boys gave us a ride to Niš, a city further down south. They were so good-looking, and were very kind. We got to Niš at 6 pm and then it was impossible to get a ride. The beggars wouldn't leave us alone, and strange men kept approaching us, and we were scared and all the strange faces looking at us, so we didn't care how much we paid to sleep just as long as we got away from those strange faces. So, we went to one of the three hotels in the town and it cost $1.50 a night. It was new, but had no showers or tubes and no hot water and it was built very poorly. The manager had holes in his uniform, and Barbara got in an argument with him in French, and she told him exactly what she thought of the poverty and state control of the country and he got so mad he handed us back our passports and said if we didn't like Yugoslavia we could leave. She apologized and he let us stay there.

The next morning at 7 am we caught a bus out of the city and sat there again for about an hour. Honestly, it is so hard to describe the people. They looked like they were living in Christ's days by their clothes and they walk miles for a pitcher of water. On the road Barbara was taking a picture of an old woman about 85, sores all over her, bare footed, and her teeth all rotten and the whole street – mostly men and young boys – ran across the street. I honestly thought they were going to kill the old woman! This was in the south of Yugoslavia – they are pro-Communist and they don't like tourists to take pictures of the poorest, as they don't want the outside world to know. We were so mad we started screaming at those men so they would pay attention to us instead of the old women.

After that, a gigantic passenger bus stopped and picked us up. There were two Turks in our bus and were just fabulous to us. There were three buses traveling together and the other two were filled with Turks. Honestly, if you could have seen us you just couldn't have believed it. Here we were sitting in this gigantic bus like we were queens. We stopped for brunch on the highway and walked on a field, all 125 of us, and they got blankets for us to sit on whilst they sat on their feet eating and they shared it with us. Oh, if only I had a picture of that, you wouldn't have believed it. They drove us to the border with Greece, and at the border the officials told Barbara and me we had to pay $50 fine because hitching was forbidden in Yugoslavia. They pretended they didn't speak English but we knew they could, and we told them where to go, and we would stay in jail before we would pay the government any money.

Well the Turks wouldn't let us talk, and they paid a fine for us! We were so upset and felt terrible that they were involved, and we asked them to please tell us how much they paid, and they wouldn't. They were fabulous. (By the way, most of the Yugoslav people hate the Russians and like the Americans.) The Turks then drove us about an hour from the border and treated us to dinner. Gosh they were funny. They don't like the way Greeks cook food, so they went in the kitchen and cooked their food. After that they dropped us off at 9.30 pm in Thessalonica and we went to the police again who took us to the hostel. By the way, when we were driving in Greece, two police were waving their arms at the bus. The two Turks thought it was a check so they stopped and the two police got in and sat down – they were hitching of all things!!

The next morning, we were on the road at 9 am and a man gave us a ride in the back of his truck and then we got a ride with two boys from Iran. They were so sweet, and the drive was beautiful. They treated us to dinner in a beautiful modern restaurant on top of some mountains overlooking the beautiful blue sea, with a castle over to the left. I could just imagine y'all sitting there. You would have loved it. We kept driving and then they treated us to supper in a small Greek tavern. We arrived in Athens at 10 pm, and it was the most beautiful sight. I don't know why, but the lights made it look like a Christmas tree, and the Acropolis was lit, and it was like we were in Ancient Greece! A wonderful feeling. They drove us right to the youth hostel and said goodbye. It was full, so we had to sleep on the floor, and then we were very lucky as someone gave up their bed for us! The next morning, we got up at 7 am and walked to the other hostel for a shower, and we went to American Express to see if we had received any mail. We had no mail so we met the two Iranian boys and sat across from the old Royal Palace drinking orange juice. It was getting very hot so Barb and I left and went back to the hostel, to get her film, and we fell asleep until 6.30 pm! It was too late to go sightseeing so we just went and had a shower, washed our clothes and went back to bed. In these Mediterranean countries it is really hard to sleep without a sheet on, because of the flies, and yet it's too hot for the sheet.

The next day we went to a beautiful beach about 10 miles from Athens with three American boys, two English girls, one Swiss and four Greeks. Honestly, I have never had so much fun, and I am so brown, Barb is embarrassed to walk with me. The water was so blue, and you could see the bottom, but it was terribly salty. We stayed there all day, and they had piped in music and showers all over the beach. It really was beautiful and clear. That night we went out with two of the Greek boys and they took us to a quaint little restaurant under the Acropolis and we ate Greek food which was really bad. Then we walked up to the Acropolis and it was gorgeous with all the bright lights shining on it. This morning, about 30 of us went to the Red Cross and gave a pint of blood and got $10. I feel fine, but Barb looks as white as a ghost.

I don't know where I will be for quite a while, so you can't write me. Tomorrow we leave for Turkey, and will stay in Istanbul two days but there is no American Express. Don't worry, there are about six of us with four boys in a car, so please don't worry. The Turks are lovely people.

I think of you all the time and I don't like to make you worry, but things always look 75% worse than they are, and I think you realize I always have been different, and it's just in me to look for adventures. I adore Athens, and Greece, but the men are men-lovers.

⊲∘§∘⊳

Greece/Turkey

Thessalonica, Greece; Istanbul, Turkey

July 29, 1963

Istanbul

Dear Family

Received your letter Mother in Athens just after I had mailed my letter to you. Again, I have no camera but postcards take care of that. Anyway, I couldn't afford film. Gosh, can you believe I'm in the Middle East! I may as well tell you now that I am planning on making a world trip, and will be home in two years, so you may as well stop worrying.

The last night in Athens, we went to a performance on the Acropolis which told the great story of Athens in English, and played beautiful music. Truly it was exciting, and we sat on a mountain across from it, and lights were shining throughout the performance. It was beautiful and when they showed it on fire, it was breathtaking. After that we caught the bus to the hostel, and got up at 6 am the next morning and walked around to the other hostel for breakfast and a shower. We were back on the road at 8.30 am.

We left Athens by bus and came to a small town about 10 miles away and a Greek boy gave me a ride on the back of his scooter to the main highway, which was about 15 minutes away, and then he went back and picked up Barbara! I talked to a policeman on the highway while I was waiting for Barbara. Gosh, didn't we look funny straddled on the back of the scooter with our packs on. We waited for about 10 minutes and a big U.S.A. station wagon drove up and we asked the gorgeous Californian if we could have a ride. He said sure, so we hopped in, and drove for about an hour when we saw a Jewish boy from N.Y. waving a small U.S. flag. I asked the Californian if we could pick him up – I could tell he didn't want to, but in the end he did. The Jewish boy was looking for someone who had gone AWOL. We drove up to a restaurant where there were three more U.S.A. trucks, so Barb and I got in one of the trucks.

Barbara got in a truck with a man of about 45, and I got in with a Private of about 22, and we made the Jewish boy get in a gigantic truck which was carrying four missiles, and he was furious with us. The group were so nice, and treated us to dinner and later to two orange drinks. They were real country bumpkins. They let us out in a small town called Larissa. An hour later we were still standing there when they drove back past us, and we had been joined by another eight hitchhikers. They pulled up and said we would never get a ride, and asked us to go out with them that night, and stay and we could get a ride in the morning. We were very hesitant, but we took a chance and they paid for a lovely room with a bath and we went out for dinner. There were four of them, and we had steak and the works! However, I had diarrhea so bad I was in agony. I kept running to the toilet and had chills and fever, so they took me back to the hotel and I went to bed, whilst Barbara went with them to a Greek bazooka club where they danced in circles, mostly men (the Greek men love each other!) and she had a blast.

The next morning, they woke us at 5.30 am and we had coffee, and one of them gave me 200 Pall Mall. They gave us a ride to the highway and just as we were getting out of the truck and saying goodbye, a car pulled over with two men – one from Jordan, and one from Syria. We asked them for a ride to Thessalonica and they said yes, but the U.S. boys were very afraid for us. Also, they wanted to give us money because they hated to see U.S. girls having it so bad, but we said no and they made us promise if we ever needed it, to write and tell them. They were really dears. (Before I forget, a small town in Yugoslavia called Skopje had an earthquake the week after we went through and 300 tourists in one hotel died.) Well, we got in, and if you saw them you would have died – they were so grubby looking! He drove like a maniac and we were a little scared.

Greece was quite lovely, but quite poor. The people seemed happy though, and not so badly off as the Yugoslavs. Other than the big cities, Greece is covered in little villages dotted in the dry hills. Their crops are olive trees and tobacco fields which line the roads and hills and can be seen for miles and miles. We saw true shepherds with sheep that looked like they came from Jesus' times. The people do all their traveling on donkeys, sitting with their legs dangling over the sides with big baskets of melons on both sides and fruit in others. The poor donkeys are so precious and always look so hot and tired. The houses are plaster shanties in white with red tiled roofs. The country people are very slow and always seem to be sitting at the side of the road with their donkeys and carts. I can't get over all the clothes they wear, long raggedy skirts and blouses and lots of scarves wrapped around their heads. The middle-aged and old women wear black from head to foot. I could just imagine Mother dressed like this! Black scarves, black stockings, skirt (usually to the ground), and black blouses that hang out and come to the wrist with a high neck.

The city people on the whole dress quite nicely. The women wear nice cotton dresses. The buildings are of the same white plaster and flat roofs. They are building many apartment buildings in Athens, and they're really lovely. The traffic is quite unruly – last year 50 New York policemen were sent to Athens to try and show the Greek police how to do a better job! They were supposed to stay six months, and left after two weeks!! The cars would rather run you over than stop.

The Greeks are nice people, willing to help and friendly, but are quite ignorant, thinking that Greece is the only beautiful place in the world. The men aren't half as bad as the Italians for bothering us, and it is not an unusual sight to see them walking down the street holding hands and caressing each other in parks or buses. We had to go back via Thessalonica to get to Turkey. It was terribly hot and dusty riding with the Syrian and Jordanian and we had to wait three and a half hours in Thessalonica on their visas for Turkey. We decided to drive to Istanbul with them because we would arrive at midnight and we didn't want to be stuck in a small village in the middle of nowhere. They treated us to a steak dinner, and it was good, and then Barbara had diarrhea!

They picked their visas up at 1 pm and then we were Turkey-bound, on the most hectic ride I have ever experienced. They drove very fast from Larissa to Thessalonica but that wasn't too bad cause the road was fairly straight. One of them asked if we could drive and we said yes so he let me drive. He sat right up beside me and watched every move I made. We were coming up behind a truck, and I was trying to pass it, when it moved into the middle of the road! He grabbed the wheel and by mistake, I put my foot on the gas, and we were going 120 K and rocks were flying and the car was skidding and I thought the day of judgment had come. When we finally passed and slowed up, I thought the Arab was going to faint. He was as white as a ghost. I was really scared at the time, but we laugh about it all the time now.

The road to Turkey was like a snake, and we were tearing round the corners on two wheels in the mountains – the squeal from the wheels was unbearable. I relaxed the whole time because I figured if we went over, I would have a better chance of surviving. We dropped the Syrian in a small town not far from the Turkish border. When we reached the border with Turkey, we had to be checked and rechecked. The Turkish roads weren't even paved and there were no signs and it was dark and we ran off the road two times. The villages were very basic, and the women still wore veils over their faces with none of their body showing except hands and eyes. They all waved at us with big smiles. Truly the Turkish people are wonderful.

We arrived in Istanbul at 11 pm and the Jordanian took us to a student hotel. We were shown our room with six beds in it, and we have it all to ourselves. We were so dirty, and we had to brush our clothes and our packs. It felt as if we had just crossed the Sahara Desert. My lips were so dry I could hardly open them. We took a shower and boy was it chilly, and went to bed. We woke up the next morning to the most beautiful view of the Baltic Sea and the city with the towers of the mosques looking like space rockets from Cape Canaveral! Gosh it was beautiful.

I looked at Barbara and she had broken out in a terrific rash. We went to breakfast and the men thought she had gotten it from bugs, so they sprayed the room with DDT. It kept getting worse and worse and the poor thing does nothing but scratch with my hairbrush until now her skin is raw. We went to the Blue Mosque and we met a little Turkish boy who had been to the U.S. and spoke beautiful English and he gave us the history. He then took us to the Black Market and there we changed our Greek money into Turkish money. It was Sunday and before we left the hotel, one of the men from breakfast gave us $5 apiece so we could buy something.

We went to two more mosques and then at 1.30 pm we went back to the Blue Mosque and sat in the middle of all the men whilst they were chanting and praying, whilst the women stand at the back and wail. Gee that was an experience of a lifetime! They sat on their feet in rows, and got up, knelt down and kissed the floor. It really was odd but interesting to watch.

We then went to the Sultan's Palace and boy, was it fabulous. It's really hard for one to imagine the wealth in the furniture and pottery. Rubies and diamonds and precious stones from all over the world in the furniture. Furniture made out of solid gold. Truly breathtaking. We went into the harem and it was indescribable. It was so beautiful. The Sultana's bedroom was a building by itself, and the bed was as big as my room! We also saw the swimming pool including a fountain that the harem swam and bathed in, and a large balcony just above it where the Sultan watched them. We also looked through a door sealed off by glass and this was a sacred room because all of Mohammed's things were in there. We didn't see everything, as Barbara and I were so exhausted and we felt like death so we went back to the hotel and slept until 7 pm.

We wanted to take a shower but there was no water! We were informed that there was a break in the main city pipe, and water has been cut off for two days! It was supposed to come on at 8 tonight, but hasn't. Everything we own is dirty, and ever since we arrived in Turkey we have had terrible diarrhea and gas pains and so has everyone else in this place. The johns are almost overflowing with it with loads of flies because they can't flush because of no water, and the odor would knock you out! Honestly, it's just terrible and we can't even wash our hands as all the bottled water is for drinking only and there is a limited supply. We are beginning to smell pretty bad – when one can smell oneself you know it must be bad!

Our room has a balcony on it and we sit out here and look at the beautiful scenery. That night we went out with two Turks to a night club, and had a blast and came in at 2.30 am. The one I had a date with looked like Dez Brown [a friend from Savannah] and was very kind. Today the little Turkish boy we met before came at 10 am and took us to the big market place – boy was it a swindle! Everything was in American prices, but was so interesting. I looked for material for Jane and Mother but they wanted U.S. prices and we just got tired of arguing. We came back and went to sleep and woke up at eight and went to supper and now I am writing and Barb is scratching. She's really getting deformed looking – thank goodness I had sense enough in London to get the jabs for malaria, yellow fever, cholera and more. But Barb didn't.

The Turkish people are lovely and I like them very much. Istanbul is lovely but extremely dingy and dirty but fascinating, and they deliver fruit to the poor on a donkey. The wife lowers a basket on a rope with money in it and yells what she wants and the man puts it in the basket and she pulls it up. Also, a lot of the poor still cling to the customs of wearing veils over their faces and in the villages, they still have more than one wife. All the traffic is American cars, and they decorate them with plastic flowers in the back and funny shiny things hanging on the ceiling. The men have been so kind to us here at the student hotel – they can't speak English but wait on us hand and foot. Turkish cigarettes are 10c for a pack of 20 and they are pretty good. While we were sitting on the balcony, a Turk started chanting in that dreadful tone, and Barbara copied him, and everyone looked out of their windows. Gosh it was funny, because it just echoed.

Tomorrow we head for Ankara and we figure it will take us three days to make it to Syria and from there to Jordan and then to Israel where we will work in the kibbutz like in *Exodus*[4] for one or two weeks and then Arabia, then Egypt, and from there I don't know, but will write you once a week. Please don't worry because we have knives and we are very careful. Follow me on the map.

—◦◦◦◦◦◦—

Turkey/Syria

Ankara, Turkey & Syrian border; Aleppo, Damascus, Syria

August 2, 1963

Aleppo, Syria

Dear Family,

We left Istanbul at 8 am in a taxi and caught a boat to the Asian side of Turkey. We met a Turk on the boat who had lived in U.S. who managed to get us a ride with a taxi cab driver and his wife, who gave us a ride 10 miles out of the city. The driver didn't speak English so didn't know what we wanted from him, so he drove about three miles to a summer resort where he knew someone who spoke English. We told a lawyer that we were auto-stopping (hitching) and he explained to the taxi driver. It is very hard to explain what hitching is and they cannot believe it when they see two girls standing in the street waving for rides. They are still very backward and keep their women in.

We were let off at a gas station and stood there for five minutes when an elderly Turk and a young girl gave us a ride all the way to Ankara. They were extremely kind and treated us to a dinner at a lovely restaurant on the highway. We had salad, milk, tea, potatoes, and steak, and cream, coffee. It was really delicious. As we were driving I had terrible gas pains but was afraid to tell them to stop. We went on and on and finally I burst out crying because the pain was so bad and I could feel it coming out. They pulled up to the next station and I flew to the outhouse which had a hole in it and all the no. 2 was piled up to the hole. I went and when I

---

[4] *Exodus* is the 1960 award-winning American epic film about the founding of the State of Israel. It is credited with ending the practice of 'blacklisting' in the US film industry.

looked, I couldn't believe it. My poo was bright yellow! Never in my life have I seen that! We drove on and they were very concerned about me. The girl spoke English and the man spoke French. My stomach was so torn up, it was almost unbearable.

As we were driving I noticed farmers going around in a circle on a little chair, being pulled by two water buffalos. The man explained to me that they crush the wheat with the wood the man sits on because it contains spikes that flatten the wheat – the grains on the bottom are torn apart, and when they are finished, the farmers take long wooden forks and throw the wheat up in the air, and the grains fall straight down as they are heavier and the chaff blows away. They sit on a little chair with a long stick to hit the water buffalo to make them go, and they go round and round and they also have a little tin (well, large) on the side to catch the poo and flies are all around it and it is right next to the man! Later on we pulled off the road and we walked across a field and he asked the farmer if we could sit on it, and we did. Did I look ridiculous on it in blue jeans and two sweaters at 3 pm in the afternoon but I had chills from the diarrhea.

We arrived in Ankara at 7.30 pm and he took us to his house and we showered while he called up different places to see if we could stay. He asked us out to dinner but I was too ill, so he took us to a lovely student hotel and we stayed the night. We had clean sheets, and another shower and I went to bed and Barbara washed her hair and clothes. The next morning, we left at 7 am and tried to get out of town and everyone kept directing us to the bus station. Again, they couldn't understand hitching. We bought some pills at a chemist (the man called up a doctor and asked him what we should get) for diarrhea and in the bus station we met a wonderful man who spoke English and he said it would take forever to get out of the city so he gave us a ride to the highway.

We sat on our packs on the highway for about 45 minutes. One man stopped and said he would take one girl and I gave him a nasty sign and told him to go to hell – you have to really be nasty and vulgar to them to make sure they understand. He drove off swearing at us and we standing there swearing and shaking our fists at him. Finally, three Mercedes Benz drove up and all these people jumped out, nine in all, and a red-headed girl said, "Do you speak English?" in a French tone which is how everyone does when they don't know, and we laughed at her and said yes. Well you won't believe what happened to us after that. She was English and called Frances, traveling with her boyfriend Bryan, who was also English. They had been hitching in Yugoslavia and Frances went up to the Mercedes Benz at a red light in shorts and asked them for a ride. They said yes, but they were going to Syria, and Frances and Bryan were going to Israel but they still agreed. But when they found out Bryan could drive he had to do all the driving, and when they picked us up, he had been driving for four days! If it hadn't been for them, I don't think we would have got the ride, but they kept telling them we were students and good.

One of them spoke a little English and he asked me what I was studying. I said psychology, praying he didn't ask me any questions! He also asked if we had any money to pay and I said I wasn't paying for any bloody rides. He liked me for saying what I thought and they had a big conference, because in these countries the people have a custom of paying for everything for a guest. Since we wouldn't pay, that meant that they had to treat us to all our meals – when we told them we would pay for our own, this offended them! So, after the conference we were accepted and I jumped in the car with the two English and Barb got in the car with two men. There was a pregnant lady also, the wife of the one who spoke English.

Frances and Bryan explained to us the little 'games' the Arabs had been playing with them. For two days they thought they were being kidnapped, because they were never allowed in the same car as their luggage and they never told them what was going on. Whenever they asked, all they would say was *Please hurry*, and as they were driving, all of a sudden, they would pull off the road and everyone would change into different cars, but the little conference was always first. Before they picked us up, Frances and Bryan got in a terrible argument with them because they kept making them switch cars, and they left and they drove off with their luggage, so Frances and Bryan had to get into another car to chase them!

We drove and drove and finally came to a place where we had dinner and I could not eat because I was still sick, so I had nothing. I had left our water jug in the Turk's car, so we were lucky Bryan and Frances had two. After dinner Barb rode with the English and I was stuck with a man whose name was Abbdice – he was real sweet, but couldn't speak a word of English. Abbdice let me drive, and said "good chauffeur"! We kept driving and driving but every 45 minutes there was another conference, and I really got tickled at this. There was Barb and two men in a caravan of Arabs!

We stopped when we came to a salt lake. Miles and miles of nothing but white salt, and we walked on it! The man who was in charge was named Abbobashaer which in Arabic means 'Abbo – father' and Bashaer is his eldest son, so he is named Abbobashaer. He never talked, but was very handsome. He reminded me of Daddy in a way. We did not know what they were going to do with us, but we didn't dare ask for fear of making them turn against us. When it was turning dark we reached the city of Adana and this was where we told them we wanted to go to at first. The man who was married and spoke German and English came up to me and said in German to give them as much money as everyone could. I told them I only had 50c in Turkish money and Barb had 10c. They kept asking me for U.S. dollars, and I kept telling them I had none. I don't know why they couldn't exchange their Syrian money into Turkish, but they needed money for gas so they picked up people and gave them lifts, and they had to pay for it.

I fell asleep in the back seat in the car Frances and Bryan were in and finally at 12 pm we stopped in a small village for supper. I felt much better cause of the pills and I ate loads. It was alright. This time, we both got in the car with the English, and after a minute Bryan was falling asleep at the wheel! Abbobashaer knew this, so we pulled over for another conference. He put Abbdice at the wheel and he took me out of the car and put me into the front seat of his car, and two hitchers (Turkish men) were in the back. We drove in the mountains for about 1one hour, and they were all moaning their songs, and I was climbing the walls, it was driving me insane.

We stopped for another conference and I was taken out of the car and put into another car with the Turk driving and the married man and woman. We drove until 4 am and came to a small town and there we let the two hitchers off, and we slept in the car for two hours. The married couple are of a certain class, so no one could sleep with them except Abbobashaer, as he is their uncle. They asked me to sleep in the car with them and I did – everyone was very impressed! I had just settled down, when all of a sudden, I heard the Muslim prayer music and songs coming over a loud speaker calling the early worshippers to the mosque. I heard Barb and Frances laughing, and I also started laughing, and they didn't appreciate it very much. At 6 o'clock they woke us up and I had blood all over me from my period and so did Barbara. They wouldn't even wait five minutes for us to wash up, so there we were. Honestly it was ghastly – we all smelt so bad.

We drove around the bloody corner and we were made to sit for an hour while they drove to the border to get some money for gas from one of their friends they had called up. We sat in a dungeon with about 10 Turkish men but they left us alone and were kind. I like the Turkish very much. In the small towns the women go even further with covering themselves and hide their whole body in black and they wear veils over their heads and they come down to the waist line in the front and back.

Finally, we were on the road again. Flies just stick to you in these countries and one gets tired of shoving the bloody things off, so you sit with about 15 flies on you. I've gotten used to it. Just before we got to the Turkish border we stopped and switched luggage and we were asked if we would take some things through customs for them… what could we say, but yes? So we put on Turkish shoes and suede jackets. We waited one hour at the Turkish border and were cleared. At the border, an Arab lawyer (friend of Abbobashaer) met us and drove back to the Syrian border with us. He spoke French to Barb, Frances and Bryan the whole time. This time I was in the front with the lawyer and Abbobashaer and Barb was in the back with all the luggage. We drove on a dirt road with barbed wire separating Turkey from Syria and I saw a large building with flags flying in the middle of this desert.

All of a sudden, I see about 20 people running towards the car. I wouldn't have believed it if I hadn't of seen it. They all ran to the first car which we were in, and Abbobashaer kept driving very slow and one by one they came up to him and kissed both of his hands and kissed him on the mouth – both men and women. He kept his face straight on the road not looking at them, and tears were in their eyes and in his, and they were his children and his brother's children. When we stopped, they all piled into the car and I was suffocating. His two wives ran up holding hands and a seven-month-old baby and kissed him over and over – he did not look at them but was crying. To me, this was the most beautiful, moving scene I have ever seen and I was crying too for the joy of these simple people. Just to see the love in their eyes for each other was worth more than $1,000,000. Someone gave me the baby and we drove a mile to the border.

Before I forget, everyone in Syria has terrible scars all over their body, and mostly on their face. It looks as if skin has been grafted and no one seems to know from what it comes from. Only children get it and the scar stays with them for life. Honestly it is terrible looking. Also, when we were traveling in the cars, whenever anyone had to go to the bathroom, they wouldn't bother to go behind bushes, they did it right in front of us, and the men instead of standing up squatted. I was shocked at first but got used to it. Anyway, we would much rather go in the open because the bathrooms are unbearable.

When we got to the border there were more of the family waiting for us. We stayed there about 1½ hours and then we were off again going on the same dirt road until we got to the customs. We stayed there two hours and when they asked us to bring in our luggage, I was terrified, as I had put on my state form I had no cigarettes and no jewellery. Of course, I had 200 cigs and a necklace I had bought for Mother in Greece, so when I was getting my things out of the car I hurriedly opened my pack and threw the cigs in a ditch and put the necklace in my bra. Gosh I was scared because one doesn't mess with these people. Someone made Barb and I put on the leather jackets and when we went in, we had to pledge on the government book that they were ours, and we did.

The customs officer was a real bastard. He wanted to see our maps and Barb showed him a beautiful map of the Middle East that she paid $2 for in London, and he took the map and scratched out Israel completely and I was furious and said I thought he was more sensible but I was wrong, because of the silly games they were playing. He told me if I didn't want to end up in jail I had better watch what I say, and then he started screaming that Israel was their enemy. We finally got back to the car and someone had hidden my cigs for me, and returned them to me. We drove and drove and finally came to Aleppo. Again, we were taken out of the car and put into a 1963 Chevrolet and were taken to a hotel of one of Abbobashaer's cousins.

Abbobashaer is an extremely wealthy man. It was not a clean hotel but there was a shower, thank God. We took a shower and Frances, Bryan, Barb and I were taken out to dinner by one of Abbo's sons and two cousins. We had a fabulous time walking in the filthy little streets looking at all the men in their Arabian costumes, and boy are they scary-looking with their scars. So many of them have one eyeball crushed in, and they sit on the street squatting as if they are going to the john, praying on their heels and some smoking Turkish pipes, with black-masked women hiding in doorways. Everywhere we went men followed us and everyone stared. I did not see one tourist thank goodness. The boys said it was too dangerous for us to walk around, so we went to his car and we drove around and got some delicious ice cream, and then we went back to the hotel and went to bed. The boys said they would pick us up at 3 to go swimming but at 10 am we were woken to be told Abbobashaer was summoning us so we took a shower. Barb became ill with fever and hives covered her whole body; it looked like 50,000 bees had stung her, so we took two hours and the boys were a nervous wreck, and kept asking us to please hurry.

When we got to Abbobashaer's office, he was sitting behind a large desk and some of his friends were with him. Gosh, did he look handsome! We sat there and Barb was getting worse so they called for a doctor but they couldn't find one because it was Mohammed's birthday and everyone was at the mosque. So, we took pictures of everyone and had the most divine scented tea, and then we went to the chemist for medicine for Barb. No one seems to know what she has, but she caught it in Turkey. Thank God I was willing to use food money in London for shots and I kept telling Barb but she said she would chance it because $10 was too much. Well, now she is paying for it.

After that we went to the police station to register again. Honestly Daddy, you wouldn't believe the stupidity of these people. They really don't have common sense. They told us we had to go back Sunday morning, but we didn't. We went back to the hotel, and rested for two hours and then we were collected by the cousins and sons to go to Abbobashaer's office again. When we reached there we got into a 1963

Ford and Abbobashaer drove down the highway and turned when he saw the police check. They started shouting for him to come back but he didn't and they gave him hell.

We then went back to the gas station and waited there for an hour, not knowing why when finally, a car drove up with the Arab who spoke French and two more men who spoke English. We drove for 10 minutes and then we changed cars again, and Abbobashaer grabbed me and put me in his car and the two speaking English. It was getting dark now and we drove to the Turkish border to a small town called Ajovroya where Abbo had a summer home.

On the way there we had to go through 11 checks by police and soldiers on the highways because of all the trouble in Syria, which you have been reading about in the papers. I had left my passport back at the hotel, and so they told me not to speak as they said I was one of their wives! Abbobashaer and his friends are of the high class, wear Western clothes and are educated. You honestly wouldn't have believed these idiots at the checks. They kept looking at Barb, Frances and Bryan's passports upside down and they were so dirty and sinister-looking. The guns they had were very small, but one could tell they could do a bloody good job with their itchy fingers on the trigger. Gosh, it was exciting!

All the villages consist of hundreds of small, dried mud huts, shaped like a beehive, with flies, donkeys, and no. 2 all over the place. The flat land is almost like a desert, not a tree in sight. Honestly, it is just like being in the movies. We went to a friend of Abbo's, ate dinner and had a lovely time. We ate meat out of cans from Europe because no animals are allowed to be killed on Mohammed's birthday. They had six servants and two cows in the garden, and it was a beautiful home. The host spoke English along with several of the guests. The wives never go out, and we were the only females. They just couldn't do enough for us.

After dinner Abbobashaer wanted us to visit his garden, but it was 12 pm and Bryan said he was tired and wanted to go back to Aleppo, because we were leaving early in the morning. They were worried about me not having my passport because curfew is at 12 pm and said it would be better for us to stay there and they would drive us back in the morning. Frances told the host that it was "dangerous for them to be here by themselves" and they took it the wrong way and thought she meant that it was dangerous for us to stay with them! She meant in the Middle East generally, but their pride was hurt and their honor had been offended because they are all honorable men, and I knew that they would never forget that. We tried to explain what she meant and they didn't believe it. Honestly, you have to be so careful what you say!

We left under strange pretences and we knew that we had lost their friendship. Barb and I and Abbobashaer and the two English-speaking men we came up with, started back to Aleppo. (Before I forget, at one of the checks going to the house, one of the checkpoint men asked them for a ride and they couldn't refuse him, because that would make them look suspicious, so he got in the back seat with his long dress and the scarf on his head – he looked like one of the biblical people except for the gun in his hand pointing at us! When he got into the car Abbobashaer said, "Do not speak," and the others started laughing so he wouldn't think he was talking to me. I broke out in a sweat because the police are very nervous people and they act before they think. He could have thought I was one of the Revolutionists – shoot first and ask questions later.) Anyway, on our way back, Abbobashaer said to the man to tell us that he thought of Barb and I as his daughters and loved us very much and wanted no harm to come to us but said the two other English-speaking men were bad people. We didn't talk about it anymore.

We came to a Roman road and boy was it fantastic, and the main highway cut right across it. The main highway is 1,500 kilometers long from Istanbul to Damascus and it was in beautiful shape. We got to Aleppo at 2 am and they told us to stay one day but Frances and Bryan left. We were going to travel with them but Bryan started telling us what we were going to do without even consulting us! You know I'm not one for taking orders, so we said goodbye to them and said we would meet them in Damascus, which we aren't going to do!

The boys came by for us at 12, and we went to Abbobashaer's for dinner. He had just got up and the eldest wife cooked a delicious dinner for all of us, including seven children plus some cousins – the children made a mess with more food on the table than on their plates! It was a mad house, plus there were people painting three rooms! After dinner we sat in the reception room and had lovely Syrian tea with spice in it, and then came in the younger wife with the baby and she started nursing it in front of all of us. Barb and I were so embarrassed and shocked and I think the boys realized it because they looked at us and then looked at each other, and then suggested that we go out on the balcony. We stood around for about 10 minutes and then we walked back in and she stood up to shake our hands, and one of her bosoms was hanging out. Gee, I just about died of embarrassment!

The boys drove us to get some ice cream, medicine for Barb and papers and soap for the both of us and they wouldn't let us pay for it. Then we went back to the hotel to write, and they picked us up at 6 pm and we went to a market underground in a cave. It had long cobble stone streets filled with donkeys, and little shops built into the dirt with Arabs sitting on the floor, weaving and carving. Gosh, it was fascinating! We went into the clothing street, and we went to the boys' uncle's stall because we wanted to buy the long dress the Arab men wear, and people were running back and forth to his stall trying to sell us things. We got one for $1.50 and they are really beautiful.

After that, we went to see the movie *Lady Hamilton* (in English) and then just as we came out of the movie, lo and behold armed police had blocked off the street, and people were jammed up against the wall, with guns everywhere! Barb has long blonde hair and these people get very excited over light skin and blonde hair. Thank goodness I look like them. We kept walking, and four police on scooters started screaming at us, and I was scared, and they shouted at us to carry on, and we did without an argument. The boys told us the police were telling the men not to follow us and to not look at weird women! But I guess we did look pretty weird, not masked up. Then we went to an outdoor garden, and met their uncle (the one who was married and spoke English, that had picked us up) and had dinner, and then we walked back to the hotel with the boys.

We got up this morning at 7 am, and the boys came at 8 am, and at 9.30 am we caught the bus to Damascus and, boy, what a bus! We did not spend one cent in Aleppo, not even for the hotel! They gave us everything. Well we are on the bus now, right jam in the middle of 50 Arabs, and boy does it smell! No one speaks English, and we don't even know if we are on the right bus! I wouldn't believe it, if I weren't sitting here. Everyone is eating nuts and they spit the seeds on the floor and since there are no racks for luggage except roped on the top of the bus, we left ours in the aisle and they are covered with watermelon seeds and shells of nuts! Plus there is a water tap and a cup, and everyone keeps climbing over our sacks and spilling water all over them. We stop about every half-hour for checks because all the Communists haven't yet been caught, and people walk on the bus and climb over our sacks selling cold orange soda and lemonade, and everyone drinks out of the same cup. We were so thirsty but I just couldn't drink after them.

We stopped at a restaurant and a young soldier bought us a Bubble Up (7 Up) and some cantaloupe. We stopped again, and he bought us a cherry soda, and something to eat. On the bus the women are nursing their babies and everyone seems to love picking their nose with their bare fingers, everyone spits, burps and farts out loud and all sorts of charming things, and the two veiled women offered us a drink of their water, and we had to say no. They just lift their veils up to drink from the cup – you never see their faces!

Barb was drawing a picture of an Arab in his clothes. The little boy across the seat from her saw, and told everyone and they all looked. I didn't want them to think we were making fun of them, so I said it was a man and pointed to him and the Arab took her paper and signed it with her pen upside down. The bus is a 1942 Mercedes and it is a dilly [unusual] but we are having the time of our lives. Gee, how lucky I am to be sitting here. Also, there are some people who dress like gypsies, but not as dirty, and they wear gold coins on the forehead, and they have two gold hooks in their nose (the women) and they have patterns tattooed on their faces. Really weird. Also, we have been seeing camels and the music on the radio is not to my taste but I guess it goes in with the scenery.

P.S. I AM HAVING THE TIME OF MY LIFE, and WISH YOU COULD SEE ME, YOU WOULDN'T BELIEVE I WAS YOUR DAUGHTER.

Syria/Jordan/Israel

Damascus, Syria; Syrian/Jordanian Border; Petra & Jerusalem; Jordan, Jerusalem; Tel Aviv, Nazareth, Israel

August 12, 1963

Damascus, Syria

Dear Family,

When we arrived in Damascus, we walked through the old section of town to try to find a cheap hotel. When we were walking through the market place, a young, clean-cut boy came up and asked us in a lovely English accent if we were students; we said yes, and that we wanted a cheap hotel. He took us to one for fifty cents apiece and we said that was too much so then he took us to a friend's house and we stayed there two nights. These were Christian Arabs and extremely nice. I think they must have had a lot of money, because the house was very large and it had an open marble courtyard with a pond in the middle. There were two brothers in their early twenties and a brother of 26 who was married and lived there with them, as is the custom in these countries. The family means more than anything but the women age so quickly because they are just like slaves.

Of course, we were treated just like queens and they washed and ironed all our clothes. The Arabic hospitality is just out of this world and they cannot do enough to please us. We had a delicious dinner on the terrace then we were given a gigantic bed and went right to sleep. The next morning, I woke with the dog licking me and the whole family was in the room! Gee, we never had any privacy because they liked to watch every move we made! After breakfast we went sightseeing in the Christian section and this is where Christ came, according to the Bible.

I'm not feeling too well, so please excuse me if I do not go into detail about all the places we saw. We then went to a cousin's house and had dinner and rested and then went back to the house and rested again and then that evening we were driven all around Damascus by a cousin in a 1962 Plymouth with a record player in the car! They really go all out for American cars. Later we went to a very exclusive nightclub, and drank beer and danced and left at 11.30 pm because of the curfew.

When we came into Damascus there were tanks all over the place and I finally realized how serious it was. We were told that 200 had been killed just in Damascus and all the way on the bus police kept checking everyone. It really became a bloody nuisance. The next morning, we ate breakfast at 8 am and they kept asking us to stay, but we just couldn't so we left, and the mother cried. They gave us a ride to the highway and they stopped a car with a family of eight and asked if we could have a ride! We could tell the people didn't want to but the others insisted. Gosh, were we cramped!

When we got to the Syrian border we were asked to see the officials and we were really scared because we thought it was the suede coats from before! It wasn't, they didn't even ask about them. It was because we had to pay for visas for visiting Syria – Barb had to pay $2.50 and I had to pay $5. Well, I burst out crying and caused quite a scene, and the official kept asking me why I was crying and I said I was a student and I could not afford to pay, so he let me go free and stamped my passport 'Paid'! Boy, I was lucky! After that we walked across to the gate and sat there for about an hour in the desert on our packs. God, it was hot. The men at the border were so kind, they kept bringing us hot tea and water. I asked everyone that passed for a ride. Three men gave us a ride to the Syrian border and the Syrian police called up the Jordan border which was about five miles away and told them to let them know if we had arrived safely.

It was things like this that made us love them so much. When we hit Jordan customs, we were taken into a special room and there Barb had to pay $3 and me nothing, thank goodness. A man and his wife were there and invited us to go to their camp. Gee, it was out in the middle of nowhere, and the flies were terrible. We had a trailer to ourselves, and one of the servants washed our dirty clothes. The next morning, we got up at 3.30 am and drove to a place called Petra which was an old civilization, built into the rocks. Couldn't buy pictures, because I had no Jordanian money. We rode a donkey and there were so many camels in the desert and we passed the King of Jordan. At one point, we had to go through a passage just wide enough for a car, and last year 25 French girls drowned in there because there was a flood.

We had dinner with the chief engineer of the project and then Barb and I rested for an hour in his cave in the mountain. There was an Arab man by the name of Saudi and he couldn't speak much English so he never talked to us. We found out later that when we were in the camp, he guarded our trailer with a gun all night long so none of the Arabs would sneak into our trailer! When we left Petra, we drove back to one of the camps that one of the men was in charge of and had dinner in one of the tents. Then lo and behold, 11 Arabs army bigwigs came and ate with us. Barb and I excused ourselves for five minutes and came back wearing the Arab men's dresses that we had bought in Aleppo, and they went into hysterics.

I have no idea what happened to the wife of the man, because she didn't come back with us. It was getting dark and Barb and I were in the car with Saudi and the man who was married. Barb was sitting in the back with the married man, and I was in the front with Saudi. The man told Saudi to drive off the road into the desert because he wanted to show us some old ruins. We drove for about 15 minutes and the man tried to kiss Barb, so she slapped him and told him to act like a gentleman. He went crazy and pulled a knife on her! He was choking her and kept screaming, "I kill you, I kill you!"

Saudi stopped the car very calmly, and I grabbed the man's arm and told him to leave her alone, and Holy Mary, he pulled a gun and pointed it to my brain, screaming, "I kill you, I kill you!" I was so scared I started laughing and Saudi calmly pushed the gunman's arm away from me so that it was no longer pointing at my head. I was practically choking him to hide from that the gunman! Saudi kept talking to him very softly and he finally came to his senses. All these people were civil engineers! Barb and I were both hysterical so Saudi put me in the back seat and asked Barb to drive. The man insisted on sitting next to her so we said yes because we didn't want to upset him. However, all the way back, Saudi held a gun at his head, and if he had even leaned towards Barb, Saudi would have killed him.

We were in the wicked man's car and Saudi told him to get out at the next town and that he would drive us to Jerusalem.[5] And the man was really sorry for what he had done and agreed to let us go. We drove and drove and Saudi was getting very tired by the time we passed the River

[5] During the 1948 Arab-Israeli war, West Jerusalem was incorporated into Israel, while East Jerusalem, including the Old City, was occupied by Jordan.

Jordan. Remember he had watched over us the night before so had no sleep! We stopped at the Dead Sea and slept three hours. Saudi slept outside on the sand with his hand on his gun.

At 6 am, we arrived in Jerusalem and met a friend of Saudi's and had a gorgeous breakfast. At 8 am, we went to American Embassy to get permission to go to Israel. It took two days to get clearance so Saudi invited us to see some friends in a town not far away. He was afraid to leave us by ourselves after what had happened. All along the way people yelled "Hello" and came up to shake his hands. I do not know to this day what he is, or was, but he's a political prisoner of Jordan and can never leave the country because he talked about the evils of a dictatorship and the Jordan King was punishing him. Poor dear, he wanted to leave so badly.

We had dinner with his friends and had a shower. Barb was caught throwing some food out of the window, because she just couldn't eat it. Saudi laughed, but the host didn't. We then went to Sebastiya with five of the host's children and saw the palace where Salome danced and where St John the Baptist was imprisoned. It was like steeping back into Christ's time – women with long dresses walking back and forth with water jugs on their heads.

We then went back and ate dinner with some more friends in a small village and then we drove the children to another village to sleep. Every 20 minutes, Saudi stopped and bought everyone drinks and candy, and always stopped to give some poor person a ride. This man truly is a saint! He then took Barb and I to a village where his sister lived and we spent the night there. She washed our clothes while we slept – no running water in the villages!

The next morning, Saudi woke us up at 7am and we had breakfast and then went to Bethlehem, which was disappointing. We then went back to Jerusalem and Saudi booked us into a hotel. We rested and as usual, he stood outside our door protecting us. Later we went sightseeing and he paid for everything. His English had improved by this time. We ran into some more friends of his and they took us to their home and fed us while Saudi did some business. He then packed us up and asked us where we wanted to go, and we said swimming in the Dead Sea. Barb drove and I talked with Saudi. He kept saying, "You are my little sisters."

When we arrived at the Dead Sea, it was completely dark and he sat on the edge watching us. It was so salty it stung our whole bodies, and it is impossible to drown. You just float, and it is the craziest sensation. He then took us to a restaurant, and I kept noticing that a man was staring at me, but I didn't pay any attention.

When we left, Barb drove and Saudi kept saying, "Please slowly," and kept looking around and was very nervous. A car drove up behind us, and Saudi told Barb to let them pass and she did. They pulled over to the side of the road, motioning us to pull over and Saudi said, "Hurry," which we did and they turned off on the road to Jericho, but Saudi was still nervous. We came to a police check and they wanted to see Barb's license which she didn't have and Saudi saw someone peeking out from behind the police house. We managed to get past that and then the same car passed us again, and motioned for us to stop. Saudi said, "Hurry, hurry!" and Barb was driving like she had just robbed the bank of New York!

They caught up and tried to force us off the road so Saudi said, "Stop!" and we did. He jumped out of the car with his gun pointed at the driver and they were screaming and hollering at each other and Barb and I were terrified. All of a sudden, Saudi got back into the car and told us to drive slowly whilst telling us what had happened. The men wanted to take us both and rape us, and they were planning on knocking Saudi out. But one of the men recognized him from school, and liked him very much so they changed their minds and apologized over and over.

They followed us to Jerusalem and pulled us over again. The driver invited us for a drink and we wanted to give him a piece of our minds so we accepted! We met him at a very nice nightclub where all the UN soldiers were and I have never seen anyone so embarrassed and ashamed when we started telling him off. We ended up as friends, and Saudi said to him, "Spit on your God if he makes you act like that." We then went back to the hotel and Saudi sat in the hall guarding us, and we slept in the room that he had paid for.

The next morning, he woke us at 6.30 am and gave me his watch and asked me to marry him! He got insulted when I told him I could not accept the watch, so I had to and told him that in two years' time I would come back to see him. He took us to breakfast and then to the gate where we walked into the Israeli side of Jerusalem. We kissed him goodbye and he grabbed my hand and I could see the tears being held back. I really hated to leave him, so did Barb.

It was the Sabbath in Israel. The minute we entered, there was a certain amount of coldness, and I felt even more out of place here than Yugoslavia. We saw a few shacks that we later found out belonged to Arabs. The people looked at us as if we were street urchins and we really felt like it, the way they were dressed up in beautiful clothes and diamond rings flashing all over the place along with beautiful expensive jewellery. As a whole, they are dressed far better than the Parisians. It was just like being in Miami Beach!

We stood in the blazing sun for about an hour till finally a man picked us up, and gave us a ride to Tel Aviv, the capital. We arrived about 4 pm and were dropped right in the middle of town. No one would tell us where the American Embassy was and we were beginning to wonder if there was one, and finally we got the hint that they couldn't be bothered!

Two boys came up and asked us if they could help and we told them we were looking for a cheap hotel. They drove us around looking for one but the cheapest was $2 a night. They said we could stay at their house so we did. It's a good thing because I got very ill, and I was throwing up and had diarrhea something fierce for two days, and they looked after me. I couldn't eat for two days, and all the strength drained out of me. They were really sweet, but were driving us crazy, so when I got better, we left, and some boy that we met on the beach said his mother wouldn't mind if we stayed at his house so we did, and we slept on the front porch on blankets. Yesterday we went to the beach, and last night to see the film *Summer Holiday*, and then we were brought to a vacant apartment with one dirty mattress on it, with roaches all over the place and this is where we slept! What a difference in hospitality! The Arabs would give you their bedroom and they would sleep here.

We feel as if we are stuck because we can't go back into an Arab country from Israel and we are waiting for a boat for Cyprus. The houses here are so modern with Oriental rugs all over the floors, and they don't buy any U.S. goods because they make everything of their own, even their cars!

Today, Wednesday 14, we made reservations for deck class on a ship to Cyprus on Friday 16 and will be in Cairo after Cyprus. We then hitched to Nazareth. I have never felt so free after we left Tel Aviv. It was so hot, our clothes were sopping wet and our backs were sunburned and the packs just killed them. We arrived in Nazareth at 4:00 and it was the most wonderful feeling seeing the Arabs again. We really felt like we were home! However, as soon as we arrived, two young boys came up to us and said for us not to speak to anyone and it was too dangerous for us to be walking the streets. We told them we had just come from Syria and Jordan and knew how to take care of ourselves!

We showed them the address of the Arab's family, the chap in the Mercedes who gave us a ride in Yugoslavia, and they took us in a taxi and waited for us while we talked to the parents and interpreted for us. They just couldn't do enough for us and were crying and kissing the floor and thanking Mohammed for us and we had grapes that were hanging off the vines over our heads. Gee, this family was poor, I really felt as if I had done someone good. They asked us to sleep at their house, but the boys said they would book us into a convent.

The boys took us to a German convent but they were full up so they brought us to a French hospital where we are now staying and they paid for it. We were not allowed to go out at night so they are bringing us dinner. We will stay in Nazareth tomorrow and on Friday 16 we have to be in Haifa at 10 am to catch the boat to Cyprus which cost ten dollars. Since we have been in the Middle East, including Turkey, I have spent only eleven dollars and I have bought presents. It's kind of hard to believe, I know!

⸻ ❦ ⸻

Israel/Cyprus

Nazareth, Sea of Galilee, Haifa, Israel; Famagusta, Nicosia, Cyprus

August 20, 1963

Cyprus

Dear Family,

I can't really remember where I stopped on the last letter but I will continue.

The next morning, I went and bought 30 postcards for everyone I haven't written to and the boys came by at 12 and took us sightseeing and then for dinner. I don't care much about seeing these places Christ visited, because they are so commercialized and it just takes the beauty away from it. Anyway, we got in the back of a truck and started out for the Sea of Galilee. The scenery was beautiful, I must admit, and we reached the sea at about 4 pm and went swimming. It was fresh water and I almost sank as it was so hard to keep afloat! We then had supper, and I promise you there were so many flies, you could hardly see the food. These flies are so bad, because they sting and when you move they cling to you and they crawl on your lips and eyes, and one dare not leave their mouth open. Really disgusting! It was sort of an oasis, and was simply beautiful, and everything the most healthy, lovely shade of green and the palm trees were so high and beautiful. I really loved this spot, and across from the Sea of Galilee one can see Jordan and Syria, and the beautiful lights of Damascus.

It was dark by now, and I walked up to a man-made dam to get some water when I heard Barbara scream! I went running back and she and the boys were hiding behind a tree, because these gigantic rocks were landing in the place we had been sitting. They were so large, they could have killed someone. Suddenly, they stopped, and we sat down again and about 15 minutes later the rocks started flying again! This time the boys tried to find out who was throwing them, and while they were gone, the rocks kept coming. They finally returned with no luck and the rocks stopped and then started again. Finally, we found out that the people throwing them were Bedouins who have tattoos on their faces, and they didn't like the idea of us being there.

I forgot to tell you that on the way to Nazareth, the driver and one of the boys got into a terrible argument but we didn't know what they were arguing about. The driver stopped the car and we sat and sat. Barb and I were afraid we would never get to Nazareth, so we jumped out when we saw a car coming to try and hitch. It was a police car but our driver promised them he would drive us straight to Nazareth. He was Jewish and wanted more money for taking us than what he had originally asked for. Anyway, we arrived in Nazareth and the driver let us out and we walked and had dinner and went back to the hostel for sleep.

August 16 We got up at 5 am and were on the road at 6am. Terrible men stopped to pick us up and we didn't like their looks, so we caught the bus to Haifa and a man paid for it. We slept on the bus and arrived in Haifa about 7.30 am and just walked around until 9.30 and then we went to the docks where we were to catch the boat. It is really hard for one to imagine the confusion and inefficiency. It took us about an hour to find out where we were supposed to go. The people just don't like to help anyone. When we finally found it, there were so many people trying to get on board at the same time as the people were leaving the ship. We stood there from 10.30 am until 3 pm, not daring to move for fear of losing our place. Barb and I couldn't take it anymore as we were packed together like sardines and people were fainting, and people's sweat was all over us, so we snuck in a back gate, but then hit another line which was even worse! You couldn't even move your hands and Barb couldn't take it. So I stood there for two hours and people were hungry and hot and restless and fights broke out all over the place – you just wouldn't believe it! Finally, we got our tickets checked and we went on the deck of the ship.

You just wouldn't have believed the confusion.

There was absolutely no room left on deck for sitting, much less sleeping! The company had booked too many people – there were about 500 on deck and some were not even allowed on board (poor people). In cabins for two, they put six or seven people and some people that had paid for cabins had to sleep on deck and they couldn't get their money back. You actually had to climb over people, and everyone was swearing but we found Frances and Bryan were also on the board! We sat and talked to people and I finally wound up between two bodies and went to sleep with a hand across my face! But anything was better than being in Israel. Slept until 3.30 am and woke up freezing, and couldn't find my backpack to get a sweater.

Cyprus, August 17 We arrived at 5.30 am and the harbor at Famagusta was beautiful. Completely surrounding the port and city is a gigantic wall and fort – this is what Shakespeare describes in *Othello*! It took about an hour to go through customs, and a port authority young Greek man said he would get us on a ship to Alexandria for free, and he told us to report to him every morning at 11 am to see what ships were leaving. We told him we would be back in two days because we were going to Nicosia to visit the English girl Barb traveled with last summer, called Jane, who is now married to an RAF man.

As usual, we started hitching and an Englishman picked us up and gave us a ride of about 10 K, and then some friends of the port authority man picked us up and gave us a ride to Nicosia. I really shouldn't tell you because you will worry, but I got the terrible pains in my stomach that I had in Damascus. I was in such pain I flaked out and when we got to the town they thought I had just fallen asleep. I told Barb what had happened and the pain was gone by then, so we went to the bus station to catch a bus to the RAF section. Lo and behold, I got them again and was actually screaming and rolling around on the floor and people were running here and there trying to get me things. Barb told someone to call a taxi to take me to an English hospital. A man from British Guiana jumped in the taxi with us and took us to the RAF hospital where he paid for the taxi!

At the hospital, they immediately put me into the officer's ward where there were no men rather than the general ward, as this was a man's hospital, and then they called the American Embassy. They gave me medicine that was like cement, and pills and orange juice but I threw it all up and had vile diarrhea and was in terrible pain. Honestly, they were so kind to me. The American naval doctor came late that evening when I was still in pain, and I couldn't even speak to him as I was so weak so Barb told him about my constant diarrhea. He told them I needed a week in bed with medical attention and said the U.S. Govt. had no hospitals and a Greek one would cost $6 a day. But the British allowed me to stay at the RAF hospital for free!

Meanwhile, the whole RAF spent one day trying to find Barb's friend Jane, as she didn't know her married name! They found her house after eight hours and left a note on her door telling her where we were, and the next morning she came to see us. I stayed in the RAF hospital for three days and then they released me because Jane and Barb promised them I would stay in bed for at least four days, and rest at least 16 hours which I needed to. They gave me the medicine to take with me to Jane's house.

After five days, I felt much better and across from my window was a beautiful modern building which housed 22 U.S. Marines. Barb and Jane had gone out shopping and some of the boys were sitting on the roof drinking beer and I yelled "Hello!" and they starting jabbering in Greek to me – they thought I was Greek! When they found out I was American, they all started yelling and told me to come over. I took a shower and got presentable and went over, and the reception I had was fabulous. They sat me down to a steak dinner (which went through me sadly!) and offered me cigs and asked me what did I smoke and I said Winstons and five minutes later I was presented with two cartons of Winstons. They were not officers but were chosen to guard the Embassy. The government built the Marine House for them and it was as pretty as Hunter's Officers' Club in Savannah! I stayed there for two hours and then went back to bed from utter exhaustion. When they got back, Jane and her husband couldn't understand why I wanted to go over there with the "animals"!!

Yesterday, August 23   I was taken to the Embassy to pick up more medicine and to see the doctor. One of the boys drove me. The doctor said I had food poisoning and an infected and sensitive stomach which was clearing up. He also looked at my left eye and said that was infected too and gave me medicine for it. He didn't charge me and I know I walked away with about $25 worth of medicine! Honestly, I have really been lucky!

The boy then drove me around the island and then we went back to the Marine House and they were all waiting to eat with me. I had steak again and kept it in this time, thank goodness! Barb came over and they were really thrilled. They organized a cocktail party for us that night and word had gotten all around the U.S. people that I looked like Liz Taylor and everyone was dying to meet me, or so the doctor told me! That night there were about 200 men – 29 were RAF – and Barb and me!! They said never had they had so many men come to see them! Honestly, I felt like a queen and they were so wonderful to us.

They got my handbag mended, gave me shampoo, a razor, 200 vitamin pills and cigs and told us if we ever ran out of money or were in trouble, to write and let them know, and they would help us. My favorite marine is a man who is 6ft. 6 named Big John. Everybody loves him! We left the party at 1.30 pm and went straight to bed.

This morning we got up at 7 am and went over to show the boys our packs, and they laughed at us but hated to see us leave. We said goodbye and they said if a ship didn't come in, to come back to Nicosia for a party tonight! We hitched to Famagusta and made it by 11 am but the port authority man said that no ships were leaving today, and that we could stay at his parents' house until one came in. We are now sitting on a lovely beach with him but are going to tell him Barb left her passport at Jane's so we can hitch there and go to the party and come back in the morning!

Cyprus is lovely but can drive you crazy if you stay here too long.

Sorry – it's later than a week with this letter but Barb didn't know what to write and I was too weak. Hope to receive a letter from you in Cairo.

Mother – please do me a big favor. Send me two brown Merle Norman eye shadow and two black mascara (Helena Rubinstein) that are waterproof and come in a little tube with a brush. Send by regular mail to 42 Belsize Square, Hampstead, N.W.3, London. Will be in London October 10.

Cyprus/Egypt

Nicosia, Famagusta, Cyprus; Alexandria, Cairo, Egypt

August 31, 1963

Cairo

Dear Family,

Just received your letter of August 24. I must say I was very happy to hear from you, but was very annoyed with Daddy's attitude. It just makes me not want to write about all that happens. You may as well get it through your heads that I am the way I am, and I shall continue to do just as I have. So please no more nasty letters. Just accept it. I cannot give dates, because it is hard for us to tell when we will arrive at our destination. It all depends on our luck.

I am writing larger, Mother, so that your eyes won't go bad trying to read my letters. Now, to continue from Cyprus, August 24, I think. My last letter was written on the beach at Famagusta with the Cypriots bothering us and we couldn't take any more of it, so Barb and I played as if she had left her passport in Nicosia and we had to go back and get it. They didn't want us to go, but we got out on the road and a taxi picked us up and gave us a ride. At about 20 K we ran into a Jordan millionaire who had hired the taxi we were in for a week! We pulled over and he asked what we were doing in his taxi, and the driver told him we had no money, so the wealthy man told him to take us to Nicosia, and he gave us $5.60 to buy cigarettes. Gee, we were floored!

We arrived at Nicosia at 6.30 pm and he drove us to the Marine House. The boys were really glad to see us and they threw another party for us and we spent the night in the house of one of the boys who worked at the American Embassy. One of the marines, Jim, had the hots for me, so he picked us up at 7 am on Sunday, and drove us to Famagusta to see if a ship had come in. When we got there, he treated us to breakfast, then I decided I wanted to go back to Nicosia, so Jim and Barb went to the port authority man's house to tell him I was sick again. He wasn't there, so Jim left him a note and told him we wouldn't be there Monday morning. Then Jim and Barb came back and picked me up at the café where we had breakfast, then the three of us went back to Nicosia. Jim dropped us off at the house where we had spent the night, and he went back to the Marine House and slept and we went to sleep.

At 4.30 pm, Jim came back with about six others and they started drinking beer. We then went to Kyrenia, which is a beach and wine place where all the marines hang out, and stayed there until 9 pm and then came home. Barb stayed up and talked to them but I went to bed because I was still a little weak. The next morning (Monday) Jim gave us a ride to the highway and there we got a ride in a nice car with a Cypriot man and arrived in Famagusta at 11.30 and went to the port authority man's office and he told us that he had found a ship for us for free. We walked to the ship, and you will not believe what it was! It was one of those babies that you see in the movies that carry marines from a battle shop to shore, and the front opens up and they all pour out. We just about died, and we decided against it.

We then went to the beach and then booked into a hotel and the Cypriot boys took us to a fabulous restaurant on the water and then we went back to the hotel (50c a night) and slept until 11 am. We then went back to the beach to ask the man if another ship would come in. When he arrived there were none, so we made up our minds that we would book on a Russian ship, the *Feliks Dzierzynski*, that was leaving on August 29. We rushed to an agency and paid $19 for the ship and then we cut out for Nicosia again.

When we arrived, I called up Jim. Big John picked us up as Jim had to work that night. Big John took Barb and I to a cocktail party, and then afterwards he took me for a steak dinner. He was so good to us and very worried about us. I suddenly felt very ill so he rushed me back to the house in a cab, and mixed my medicine for me and made me go right to bed.

The next day, Barb and I just messed around the house and I dyed my hair and Big John brought us lunch and returned about two hours later with about 20 boys! Gee, they really treated us like queens. Big John and Jim had to work that night, so I got an early night and Barb went out to dinner with one of the boys.

Tuesday, August 29 Big John arrived at the house at 7 am and took us all the way to Famagusta in a taxi. We had to be at the docks for 8.30 am. We arrived and went through about a half hour of formalities and then sat in the shade by the boat, waiting for Jim to arrive. He came about 9.15 am and the boat left at 11. I really hated to leave them, as they were so kind to us! We had such a good time with them, and we hadn't spent any money.

Sailing away from Cyprus was a beautiful sight. The water was a beautiful aqua in the harbor and just like a straight line it turned a deep blue. Gosh, it was gorgeous. The ship was fabulous, and we had a lovely cabin that we shared with two Arab women and one bratty little girl, who kept screaming and turning off the fan, until I screamed back at her!! The mother seemed grateful because she behaved herself after that! The shower was opposite our room and the ironing room which was very helpful. We had three meals, and the service was wonderful – the dining room was air conditioned and looked like it was for royalty. You were not allowed to tip, which pleased us very much. Barbara got really badly seasick and couldn't eat so threw up and slept! I sat in the bar for about half hour and the bar man (Russian) gave me two lemonades for free since we couldn't use Cypriot money. They were real nice and everyone knew I was that "ugly" American from abroad, even though I looked more like the locals. The women wore long braids on the top of their heads, and had large muscles.

We arrived in Alexandria on Friday, August 30 and did I go through hell with the Egyptian officials! They kept asking me what nationality my parents were and if I had ever been to Israel! They thought I was Jewish, and they went through my passport about 10 times looking for an Israeli stamp. If they had used their heads, they would have noticed that I had a Jordan stamp that had the date when I left, and the next stamp was a Cyprus stamp with arrival date, so that left one week that was not accounted for on my passport and where else could one go to and from Jerusalem, but Israel.

We finally got off the boat and we saw Nasser's[6] yacht in the harbor of Alexandria. Gosh, was it beautiful! We had to go through more customs

[6] Gamal Abdel Nasser Hussein was President of Egypt from 1954-1970. He became extremely popular in Egypt and the Middle East after his nationalization of the Suez Canal Company and his victory in the subsequent Suez Crisis, known in Egypt as the Tripartite Aggression.

which was complete hell, and had to fill out more forms. We got through that in about two hours, and then we walked through the city but people just wouldn't leave us alone. One man came up and asked if he could help us, and we asked him where was the main road to Alexandria, and we walked and walked. Barb then wanted to change her money on the black market, so we went up to a duty finder, and our man was trying to keep the people away from us, and got in a fight, so the three of us cut out. He took us to a restaurant on the top of the buildings for tea, and a helicopter flew by and dropped thousands of leaflets advertising a TV program, and the whole city went wild! People running crazy, knocking each other over, pushing and shoving just to get a silly piece of paper. Gee, it was really funny watching from the roof!

Alexandria is so dirty, as are the people. About nine out of every ten have an eye defect here. It's horrible to look at as the eyeball looks like it has been eaten away. We were finally taken to a road and told we could hitch from there, and we stood there for about half an hour until one man came up and told us we were going in the wrong direction and that we would never get a ride, as all the cars were full because everyone was coming to Alexandria for a festival. He took us in a cab to the bus station and all the buses were full, and then he took us to the state travel agency and then left us. The girl at the agency told us to get a bus to the desert road and she gave us 50c as we had no Egyptian money. We got on the bus and rode through the city to the outskirts.

We finally got off the bus in the desert, and we were getting a little afraid as there were hardly any cars and they were all filled with men. We sat there in the heat on our packs and at 3.30 pm we saw an international taxi coming and we got in the middle of the highway and flagged it down. The man was going straight to Cairo. He was German and very interesting and nice. He bought us a cake and didn't ask any questions unless we wanted to tell him something. It took about three hours to reach Cairo, and there was absolutely nothing, nothing, but desert. As we were driving into Cairo, we saw the three pyramids rising above the sand hills, and it was so beautiful, just as you would see in a magazine. The man drove us to the pyramids and I was so intrigued with the sight.

After that he took us to the youth hostel and drove off. However, there was a bloody note on the door saying, 'Closed for Repairs'! Gee, we were furious, as it only cost 10c a night. We didn't know what to do so we went around the corner to the American Embassy and they tried to find us a cheap place but weren't too successful. We were sitting there while the Sergeant Marine, whose name was Ken, called up different places, and I guess we looked such a mess, sitting on our torn rucksacks and my airline bag completely ripped with a towel on top to hold everything in, and my torn blouse and dirty hair, that a woman (one of the officials) came over and handed Barbara $2. We were so embarrassed and shocked because we didn't realize we looked so bad.

We gave up and went around to the Canadian Embassy, and there a nice boy drove us around to a restaurant owned by a Greek Cypriot, who got us in to one of the nicest hotels for $1.75 a night. It really is lovely and the Marine House is right behind us! It was about 9 pm by then so we went back to the restaurant and had a gorgeous dinner of Indian curry, two veal cutlets, salad, potatoes and two coffees and it was only 50c a piece! We then went back to the hotel and went to sleep.

Saturday, August 31 We woke at 11 am and went for dinner and went looking for a hotel that the youth hostel said was really cheap. Finally found it after walking through the center of the city, and it was filled with nothing but Bedouins and we got scared so left. We then went back to the hotel, and then went to American Express shop to get our mail. The Hilton Hotel is simply beautiful, but the Nile is muddier than the Savannah. I was very disappointed in that!

We came back and started our letters home. We saw marines sitting on their porch listening to music and I finally got up the nerve to yell to them. Well, that started it off. They invited us over for dinner and boy, was it good! Real steak, and we just sat around talking to them until 2 pm and then we went back to our rooms and went to sleep.

September 1 I woke up at 7.30 am, took a shower and we had breakfast at the Marine House. Pancakes with lots of butter and Log Cabin syrup. Gosh, it was really great. Then we went to the museum with one of the boys and then onto the Hilton for a drink. We then went looking for postcards, but they were 16c apiece, so I could only afford to send one. Barb changed her money and lost 20c on a dollar. Gosh, these people are crooks and this was the bank! Tonight, two boys are taking us out to the pyramids – we are going to ride on a camel, go inside the tombs, and watch a performance in English.

Tomorrow we leave for Alexandria as that is the only way we can get out of Egypt. Will be in Madrid in two weeks because we are going through Tunisia, Algeria, Libya and Morocco and then up through Spain towards London.

As I said before, I could tell you a completely different story, but I think you deserve the truth.

—◦◦◦◦—

Egypt/Libya

Cairo, Giza, Alexandria, Egypt; Egyptian/Libyan Border; Benghazi, Al Bayda, Benghazi, Libya

September 7, 1963

Benghazi, Libya

Dear Folks,

Well, I hate to say this, but you really are in for a shock. Barbara and I are being held prisoners of the Libyan government!

Giza

I shall start from my last letter and follow on up to now. We stayed in Cairo one extra day. We rested and wrote letters. Met a married couple who had two friends, nice chaps, and we went to the pyramids in Giza. We were going to climb to the top, but we lost our nerve, because it would be a long fall if we slipped, so we went inside and boy, did it smell nasty! Then we walked all around the Sphinx that guarded the pyramids and the sun was just beginning to set and the most beautiful shade of gold reflected on the desert and Sphinx and pyramids. We were dying to ride a camel so each of us hired one and I had the time of my life on that dirty, smelly beast! It was just like an exciting dream sitting on a camel, passing the pyramids and hills.

The guides were not supposed to let go of the rope but I talked my guide into letting me ride by myself. I kicked and 'switched' the camel and all of a sudden, I was tearing across the desert, that animal was really cutting out! Barbara couldn't believe her eyes and she screamed, "Barb, please come back!" I was scared at first and I know that my expression was like the first time Mother took me up on the ferris wheel at the fair. It was so much fun getting up on to a camel! They get up on their back legs first and you have to lean way back, and their front legs come up and you have to lean forward.

Well – let's get back to my charging across the desert. I realized that I was getting too far away from them and could barely hear my guide screaming, "Cleopatra, come back!" so I turned it around, and came galloping back to them and all the guides were standing together waving their arms, screaming, "Stop, stop!" and when they saw that I had no intention of stopping and was heading for them, did they run! Barb and the rest of them just sat on their camels with their mouths open. They couldn't believe what they were seeing. I passed them and went into a small village, tearing around corners. People started running when they saw this maniac coming. I didn't realize these stupid, sulky looking animals could go so fast!

I was slipping off by now and it was pretty far to the ground, so with a super human effort I slowed him down after knocking over a cart of nuts. The guide finally caught up and was completely out of breath. Gee, I have never seen anyone so nervous! He kept saying in a sad voice, "Queen of Sheba, you get me in trouble with police, why you do this?"

I said "Molish!" which in Arabic means, "never mind, it doesn't matter." Talk about *Hi, Ho, Silver* on camelback, well that was me!

Ken paid for the damage to the cart and also paid my guide for all the trouble. We bought a Coke which was hot and horrible and sat on the sidewalk (dirt) and waited for the box office to open for tickets for the performance at the pyramids in English, just like the one in Athens at the Parthenon. We sat in the second row and the people from the United Nations sat in the first row. It lasted an hour, and was all about the building of the pyramids and the lives and habits of the people. We then went back to the city to our hotel. We could have seen many more things but it was too hot, with too many flies that cling to you and sting.

After dinner we all went to a movie. When we came out and were walking along the main street, people kept putting little pins with pictures of Nasser on them onto Ken's shirt and demanding money! I took them all off and threw them in the street but one man went into a rage. Ken was flabbergasted – he has to be very careful of what he does and says, since he works for the American Embassy. The man asked why I had done it and I said that I didn't want any bloody pictures of Nasser! He ordered me to pick them up but I wouldn't – he began creating a real scene, so we ran! We walked to the Nile Hilton Hotel which was featured in *Life Magazine* a few weeks ago – it is one of the 10 best hotels in the world. We sat on the terrace and had real coffee. Barb and the others were there waiting for me – we then went down and sat on the bank of the Nile in front of the hotel, and a gigantic rat ran across my foot – I nearly had a heart attack!

Egypt is very poverty-stricken, and the people are suffering from eye disease. Egypt looked exactly as I expected it to; I was not disappointed with it. But for my letter to you from Cairo, it cost me 47c and their excuse is that the government put up the price yesterday! Even the banks cheat you! Egyptian money is worthless on the outside. The Egyptians who travel outside this false paradise are only allowed to take out $43 and the clothes on their backs, and when they return many times the government has taken over their possessions! We have seen so many different kinds of dictatorship, we are completely disgusted with them, and only hope my country never allows this to happen. The people in this type of country are prisoners and slaves to their government. Americans don't realize how precious their freedom is. To be able to say you don't agree with the government without fear of being killed, is a wonderful feeling. Egypt has extreme wealth, and extreme poverty – there is no middle class and the poor are actually starving. It makes me sick to see this. We have seen some inhuman sights. I think you will be pleased as well as shocked at my outlook on life now, that is if I make it alive!

Alexandria

When we arrived in Alexandria, we found a youth hostel. It was very dirty but at least had a shower. We walked all over Alexandria trying to find a map of North Africa, but no luck, so there we were with nothing but a small map of each country that has little pictures of all the things you can see and do in these dreadful backward countries, plus the names of the cities are in Arabic which looks like shorthand. We washed our clothes and went to bed. We were then up at 5 am and caught a trolley to the point where we had to catch a bus to go to the road to Libya. We asked the depot man when it was coming and he said at 8 am. I asked him if we were supposed to catch the bus at the No. 1 sign and he said yes – so we waited and waited. At 8.45 am I asked him where the bus was and he said it had left at 8 am and the next one would be at 9 am! I asked him where from and he showed us a completely different place! Gosh – did we blow up! Barb told him exactly what she thought of him! I asked him if he was sure we should take a No. 1 and he said he should know, he was in charge of all the bus schedules and should know their numbers. Well, lo and behold we had to catch a 31b and we would have been there all day waiting for No. 1. This is what one has to go through every day, and to think he was government!

When we finally boarded the correct bus, we nearly fainted from the odor – packed with children, no one wore shoes, and the women were completely veiled. We got into a terrible argument with the driver, because he wanted more money than the tourist office had quoted. We were screaming, he was shouting in Arabic and calling us "Pigs"! I told him the only way he would get us off was to throw us out bodily, but if he touched us we would run him through with our knives, because we had done it before. (Of course if he had, we couldn't have used them!) He left us alone after that, but kept walking up and down, cursing us, and a fellow passenger had to tell me when to get off as the driver wouldn't.

We got off at a farm and there was a police station nearby so we went in and sat for several hours – a young Arab spoke English. He turned on the portable radio in English for us and we heard about the integration demonstrations[7] in Savannah. I nearly died, hearing that name while

---

[7] The Savannah Protest Movement was a campaign led by civil rights activists to bring an end to the Jim Crow laws and racial segregation in the state. The movement began in 1960 and ended in 1963.

sitting in a desert in North Africa! A truck finally came by with other travelers, so we said goodbye to the Arabs in the station and went off on the road to Benghazi. We could only do 25 miles an hour as the road was dreadful – at 11.30 am we entered Sallum, the last Egyptian town before the border. It was right on the ocean, with desert in the back, and mountains all around. We went to the only hotel in town and was it dirty and smelly. We ordered a meal and an hour later we were still waiting; all the Arabs were being served first! We were so mad we left. We bought a melon from some Bedouin venders, one had lived in the U.S. for three years. Forgot to tell you that on the way here we stopped at a deep-water hole and three Bedouin women were pulling up water on a rope in a bucket, a mother and her two daughters. One nostril was pierced, and they wore a large gold piece – really weird, but they were pretty girls in spite of the dirt and dust.

After we left the hotel, we took a bus up the mountains. We came to an Egyptian check and they made us go back to Sallum because we hadn't been cleared by customs! We went back and found out that we had to wait three hours because the border officials and customs were having their daily siesta! We went down to the Mediterranean and washed our clothes, and almost lost half of them as the current was so strong! We went back to the customs shack and ate bread, cheese and fruit and hung our clothes all over the customs officials' cars! Finally, they opened up and half of them were still asleep; we had to fill out many forms, going from one official to the other – this interesting little game plagued us for a couple of hours.

At the Border of Egypt and Libya

We were finally on a bus and arrived at the Libyan border at 5.30 pm and went into the checkpoint station and gave them our passports. However, we had no visas! We thought we could buy one like you do at every border but they told us we would have to go back to Cairo! We nearly died cause we just couldn't afford it. They really thought they were something, those guys behind the desks; they said they could send a telegram to the doctor (who is Minister for Immigration) in Benghazi to see if he would give us permission to get visas at the border. We asked how long it would take, and they said, "Maybe tomorrow morning, maybe five days, we don't know!" Gee, Barb and I just couldn't imagine sitting there for five days with all those men around. I asked if anyone else could give us permission at the border and he said that the officer here in charge could. I asked where he was and they said they didn't know, in town somewhere, but would be back in an hour, but he never showed up. Anytime we would say anything, they would tell us to simply go back to Cairo! That was impossible, but these dreadful men staring at us gave me the creeps. We tried to explain it was very dangerous for two girls to hitch, and that the German boys with the van couldn't wait for us. They just couldn't understand and told us to come back in the morning and the officer would be there. Well the boys agreed to stay there that night but before that they said they'd go and drink beer for an hour so if the officer did come, we would have a better chance by ourselves.

We sat on the steps with the mosquito net wrapped around us and were falling asleep. One of them said we could sleep there, and we said no and they got mad, so we went along with them and pretended we would. We walked up some dingy stairs, and all the men followed. One of them opened a door and there was a dirty office room with a desk in it. He pointed to the floor and said, "You sleep there," and gave us some blankets. We went downstairs and sat and waited for the boys and officer. The boys came back, and said they met a man who said the officer wouldn't come tomorrow because it was Friday (their Sunday). When we heard this, we were very upset because we just couldn't imagine staying there with those men and no money. We couldn't cash a check because they had our passports.

We then drove on the desert away from town in the Germans boys' van and had a good night's sleep. Woke up the next morning (Friday, 6) at 9 am, and there were four Bedouins sitting on their feet just staring at us. We paid no mind, and one of the boys, Charlie, cooked breakfast again. We sat there and ate; the Arabs were looking at us, and we at them. The old man starting digging around with a steel stick and spitting in the hole he was digging, making the most dreadful noise. We thought he was crazy, but about five minutes later he pulled out a crazy small creature! It was a desert kangaroo rat. It really did look like a kangaroo, with long back legs but really short at the front. We offered them what we had left over, and they tasted it but didn't approve, and were content to eat their desert rat!

Back at the Border

We then packed up and went back to the border, and the officials were so rude to us. They wouldn't tell us anything, not even if they had telegraphed the doctor. We waited an hour and the boys said they would have to leave if they were ever going to make it on time because the roads are so bad. Barb and I just didn't want to be by ourselves with those dreadful looking men, so we both decided to go to Benghazi, where the American Embassy is, and let them help us. We decided even if we had to have a jail sentence, that would be better than being with those men. We were really worried and knew that we would have to get away from there somehow, so we told them we were going swimming and would be back at 12. We went just far enough to get out of sight and waited till it was dark and went back for our luggage which was outside the shack.

We sat on the side of the road and prayed for a car and at last one came and we thankfully boarded it, scared to death that we would be asked questions. The car stopped at a place called Cyrenia on the Med. It was an old Greek city on a cliff overlooking the greenish-blue water. The floors of the temples were still there, truly magnificent; figures of Greek Gods in mosaic. We saw the rock where Apollo sat to guard the city. We could see ruins of the city on the ocean's floor. The sun was going down and cast a glow on the water and pillars of the temple. An Arab was sitting on a rock watching the sun set and praying to Mohammed. It was a lovely peaceful sight, one that very few people ever witness.

Benghazi

Next day we reported to the American Embassy and were told that we would have to go back to the border to pick up our passports, and we were not allowed to hitchhike so would have to go by taxi. Libya has no trains or buses. The man said it would be $30 each and we nearly fainted! I told him we would stay in jail before we would or could pay that much money and he said, "Oh no you won't, because I'll wire your parents and tell them you are disgracing the American government!"

Back to the Border

We knew he would do it, and that you would believe it. He then told us that a Libyan driver for the Embassy would take us back in the Embassy car to get our passports from the border. A lunch had been packed for us so off we went. The driver lived along the route so he stopped and introduced us to his wife and seven children – what a house that was! But they were so kind – they made tea for us and gave us a dozen boiled eggs and a box of Animal Crackers (stale!). Then his wife went into the yard and killed a chicken for us to carry on our journey when we left Benghazi – he said we could pluck it and cook it when we became hungry!! If you refuse anything you are given, it is a great insult – so you just don't! I just about died on this one – because personally I just couldn't face a dead chicken hanging on my pack with all the flies on it, and me! Anyway, we finally arrived at the checkpoint at the border and were given our passports plus a visa saying we were only allowed five more days in that country, which suited us fine.

There is one charming custom in these countries that I must tell you about – one of the chores the women do is to follow camels and donkeys with a pan and catch their droppings or scoop it up off the streets. They then make it into patties, let it dry in the sun, and use it for fuel for cooking. We have seen houses made out of it. The American Embassy had a truck going back to Benghazi so we piled all our luggage (you should see it) – minus the dead chicken! – into it and off we went.

Back to Benghazi

We slept the whole way back to Benghazi except when we came to checks and we had to get under blankets, and the German boys would put their heads on it to hide us. At some stage, a flashlight was shone into the back. Another time we almost didn't make it, because we were going around a curve and there was a check which caught us off guard. However, we made it safely to Benghazi, and spent the rest of the night in the car at a showers place on the beach, and the next morning, we took a shower in the open. The boys dropped us off at the American Embassy and in we went. We asked for the consulate, and were shown into the waiting room. Barb did all the talking and I just sat there petting my nails. The consulate was quite shocked, and didn't see how we could get out of it, and he called up the British Embassy for Barb and they decided since the doctor liked the Americans better, that the American Embassy would represent her.

Benghazi

Mother, if you think you get nervous in a time of crisis, well you should have seen me going through those checks. I was 50 times worse than you! We sat at the Embassy for an hour, and then the Libyan police came and questioned us. Thank goodness we told the truth. They were looking for the boys for smuggling us into the country, and us for committing a 'crime' [entering the country illegally without the right papers (visa)] against the Libyan government. The consulate came back about speaking to the doctor for two hours! He was told that the Embassy had full responsibility of us, and that we were to be put where the boys couldn't find us and to remind us that we were "prisoners". We were taken to an apartment from which the consulate had just moved out, and the apartment was completely empty, except for three beds. That evening, the consulate picked us up and took us to dinner at his new place. We had chicken cooked in white wine and mashed potatoes with gravy, and peas and Brussels sprouts. Gosh, it was good. A friend of his (Lin) took us back, and invited us to have dinner with him the next day.

Sunday, September 8 We went around to Lin's house and had eggs and tomatoes and bacon when we arrived there at 11 am. He couldn't get out of a previous engagement, so we went back to the room and started writing this letter. The consulate came at 3 pm, and asked if we wanted to go swimming, and we said yes, although we couldn't stand him and we didn't trust him. We went to the beach, and on the way back, we saw the German boys' van parked in the same place as we had stayed in, and the consulate let us talk to them which he wasn't supposed to do. We met them at 7.30 pm around the corner. We all compared notes of what we had each said to the police. We told them that the consulate said that they were sending our passports from the border, and that we would get them Monday morning. The boys had to catch a boat from Benghazi and were told that they wouldn't get their passports until they were on the boat. The only reason the Libyan police didn't prosecute the boys was because they would have to do the same to us, and the American Embassy had intervened so they didn't stick us all in jail. At 9.30 pm Lin and a friend came by and took us out to dinner. They ordered steak for us, and then Barb went back and washed her hair, and I went to a nightclub with the two of them, and had a real nice time watching the English girls try and do Eastern dancing [belly dancing] in the floor show!

Back to the Border; Al Bayda; Back to Benghazi

September 10   Got up at 5.30 am, and the man picked us up at 6.30 am in his Volkswagen and off we went. (Just lost my other pen!) He can't speak English and has tattoos on his face and hands. This is stylish to the Bedouins, which is what he is, and he stopped and bought us six eggs apiece (hard boiled). I've never had so many eggs in my life to carry around! Then he bought us tea. We were let through the checks because they were warned we were coming. We hit the border but the telegram that should have been sent was not there! The border police said the officer was in Salkam in Egypt and they didn't know when he would be back! Our driver said he would wait half hour and so we went to the post office and asked if we could call the American Embassy collect, and we explained that we were ordered by the Libyan government to come back. He called the asses at immigration and they called the doctor and he said to give us a visa and that we were only allowed five days to get out of the country, and that suited us fine.

One of the officer's felt Barb's legs as we were walking down the stairs and wanted to go into the bathroom with her! Boy, did she ever slap him! You see, Mom, why we didn't want to stay. Poor Barbara really gets it bad, cause all these people are fascinated by blonde hair and blue eyes and light skin. They never bother me, because I look like one of them! Our driver has three wives, and is looking for a fourth, as he is tired of the three! If you really want to know some of the things that happen to me, then read the July-August 1963 issue of *Ladies' Home Journal*. It has an article in there called 'Caravan', and it is so much the life I am leading.

On the way back, the man bought us dinner, and was it really bad. He had the radio at full blast which drove me crazy. Will write you in one week's time and let you know what has happened to us with the government. The driver was very good to us and kept buying us things, and we arrived at Al Bayda at 9 pm, and went to the American Guest House and went to sleep. There was only an old Libyan there in his native uniform and I think he was really glad to see us back.

Wednesday, September 11 We woke up at 6.30 am and cooked some of the eggs and peas that had been given to us, and we snuck in the kitchen of one of the guards and stole some coffee, sugar and milk. The sheriff came at 7.30 am to give us a ride to American Embassy in Al Bayada as we need extra papers and could only get them from there. I must admit it seems that whole country knows about us! The Embassy didn't have any trucks going to Benghazi as only the ambassador was going, and we were trying to avoid him, so we got on the road, and waited. We got a ride in a Libyan army Jeep and we sat on smelly sheep skins. He let us out, and then we got a ride with a man who bought us a lemonade and then he let us out in the middle of the desert. I was so entranced in reading my book that I left my thick sweater in his car! Gee, I don't know what I'm going to do, because it will be cold in Europe. Sat in the road as the red dirt is hard to get off your clothes and finally two Western-dressed men drove up and gave us a lift. They treated us to dinner and gave me a pack of Viceroy cigs and then drove us to the Embassy in Benghazi. The exciting conclusion of this story will be continued in next week's letter, so look to the mailbox.

Love, your gypsy daughter.

Libya/Tunisa/Algeria

Benghazi, Tripoli, Benghazi, Libya; the Desert, Tunis, Tunisia; Constantine, Algeria

September 20, 1963

Algeria

Dear Family – continued from last letter of September 11, 1963 Benghazi, Libya.

In Benghazi

Wednesday, September 11 We sat in the American Embassy for about two hours waiting for the consulate. When he finally arrived, we showed him our passports and said he would notify the Libyan government the next day that we were back, because they were closed that day. We went and stayed at the same place we had stayed before, but everything was completely removed, except two beds that had the top legs on them but not the bottom. The consulate asked us out for dinner and we hate him, so we said no! We walked around to Lin's house and he took us over to the Marine House where we had dinner and talked to the marines and they really gave us the scoop on the consulate. After that we went home and had a real good night's sleep.

Thursday, September 12 We got up at 7.30 am and took a shower and packed up, and went around to the Embassy but the consulate wasn't there. We waited until 9.30 am then decided we couldn't wait any more, so we snuck out. We had orders not to hitch, but had to, for financial reasons. We walked and walked through the city, until we came to the main road leading to Tripoli. A man picked us up, and gave us a lift of about 30 kilometres then let us out. When we were sitting on the road, under the shade of large oak trees, we remembered that the Libyan government did not know we were back in town, and when they asked the Embassy where were we, they would have to say we had left, and then they would have wired all the checkpoints, and made us go back and be in more trouble. So, we sat and sat waiting for a car going back to Benghazi, and finally one came. So back to the Embassy we went, and the consulate was still not in, so we asked his Libyan secretary to call the Libyan officials, to tell them we arrived yesterday and were leaving now since we only had three days left to get out of the country.

To Tripoli then back to Benghazi

(I forgot to mention it, but between Benghazi and Al Bayda there is a town called Barce. Six months ago, there was a terrible earthquake, and the whole town was practically destroyed and Japanese scientists surveyed the country after this happened and said that within five years' time the whole Libyan coastline was going to be completely destroyed by earthquakes. The English and Americans gave millions of dollars, and the Libyan government bought tents for the thousands of homeless. I kept noticing the Bedouins' tents looked very nice, and remarked to Barbara about it, because the other tents are made out of rags and newspaper.)

Going to Tripoli to get to Tunisia

The officials asked if we had made plans for a taxi, and we said yes, and they told her to tell us to come by because we had to register, so we walked around, just praying they wouldn't ask us to drop by in the taxi before we left, because it would have cost $65 apiece to get to Tripoli by taxi! They didn't ask, thank God, and we registered and went back to the Embassy, and packed up our luggage. Just as we were walking out, the consulate walked in, and we told him we had registered, and that we were going to Tripoli. He asked us how we were getting there and we told him that we were hitching. He said that he felt responsible for us – and we later we found out that he was the one who suggested to the Libyan government that we needed the taxi to the border! He would have got into a lot of trouble if anything happened to us, as we were in the Embassy's "care". We were so mad, because we had told him we only had $60 left to get back to London!

We then stepped out into the street, and a French man with a little boy stopped in his crazy French Citroen, and asked if he could help us.

He gave us a ride out to the highway and gave us the name of a friend of his in Tripoli if we ever got in trouble. He was really a kind man, and said we were braver than he was, because he wouldn't do what we were doing. We then sat on the road for 20 minutes, and one car came by and it was the interpreter for the Embassy! He gave us a ride for about five miles. He wanted Barb to go out with him! He dropped us off and we sat by the road for a long time, and the flies were unbearable. Finally, a nicely-dressed man with two men in the back of his Mercedes picked us up. We stopped at the little town of Ghemines and he bought us dinner and bought me two packs of cigs, and then drove us out of the town to the road so the town people would leave us alone. There we sat and sat, with no trees around and the hot sun bearing down on us. I had damp towels, so Barbara and I put them over our backs and let them hang loose so that our heads could keep cool. Gee, did we look funny.

We sat for about two hours and finally, a truck came by and the man gave us a ride for about 25 miles and let us out in the desert again. Lucky enough, he dropped us off in front of a little shack that was a ruin of some kind and some Bedouins were living in it, and they made us hot tea and we dipped our towels in their well. It's so easy to get sunstroke in the desert! We continued sitting on our packs, with the dripping towels hanging from our heads and just continuously trying to pick the flies off. Finally, a mini bus taxi came by with seven men, eight children and three veiled women and they were like sardines before we even got in! Boy, were we cramped! These were true Bedouins and the children had gigantic holes in the upper parts of their ears with large rings in them and also in the earlobes, and all their teeth were rotten, wearing smelly, dirty clothes. It was funny watching the women peaking at us behind their veils. All of a sudden, I would give a big jerk towards them and they couldn't cover their eyes fast enough. They were very nice to us and we appreciated them picking us up.

We were let off at a dingy little village called Agedabia. These dirty, filthy villages really give me the creeps. I have noticed in all these countries that the women's veils and long gowns vary, but each village wears exactly the same. In Libya one village wears red, and another blue, and all the towns and villages are like this. I think the general store must buys thousands of yards and one pattern, because they get it at a discount! The veils completely cover them, and they hold it in front of their faces with their teeth. The dress that covers them goes to the floor and they put everything inside the back of their veils, even their babies and they look like little fat penguins! In Tunisia they wear white from head to toe and long pink wool stockings. In the large cities they look like nuns' dresses because they carry nothing in them and they are straight on the body. It's really unbelievable and here in Algeria they wear all black except for a white veil over their faces.

We walked and walked down the main road to get out of the village and it was so long and I had to rest, and Barb kept walking. A nice young man came up to me and asked could he help. I said no, but got talking as he had been to school in London and was getting ready to return. An old man about 80 passed by in a cart pulled by a donkey, and asked could he carry my bags to the police station, so the boy and I walked behind the cart and then we met up with Barb, and picked up her bags. When we got to the police station, the boy bought us a soft drink, and we sat and sat but no traffic. A policeman came over and started picking up our luggage, and we asked him what he was doing. He told us we had to go with the red truck across the street. We said we didn't want to, but he said he wouldn't let us go when it started turning dark, so we had no choice. We climbed in with the man who couldn't speak English. There were only two seats and the motor was in the middle and that's what I sat on – I thought I was going to be burned alive!

We drove on and on through the desert, and it really was lovely with the sun going down and the white sand and the Bedouins' tents. It was very peaceful looking. They have many sandstorms and a few times I thought we were going to get stuck as soft sand had completely covered the road. We stopped at a small town and the man bought us a drink and all the men in the village came and sat on their feet with their elbows rested on their knees and they just stared at us. We kept driving and finally came to a crossroad right in the middle of the desert and it really was strange looking. Once in a while we would see robed policemen in the distance on their camels. It turned dark, and the driver was o.k. and didn't bother us, which was a nice change! We reached an arch in the desert called Marble Arch where there was a checkpoint. By now it was 9.30 pm and the man said that trucks weren't allowed to drive at night so we would have to sleep there! Gee, we just about had a fit.

The driver drove over to a small checkpoint and he was going to sleep sitting up in the truck to give us his bed. We didn't want to sleep on the ground and he couldn't understand, so we sat on a straw mat while he cooked supper and then about five trucks drove up full of sheep and the men went crazy when they saw us! So our driver drove to the Arch and let us sleep in the truck and made us lock the doors whilst he slept on the ground with a gun, in case any of the men got fresh ideas. One guard came over and said he had a ride to Tripoli for us and we went through the Arch and there was a minibus with 10 men in it, and they were just trying their hardest to get us in the bus. We told them that we only drove with one man and they got mad and asked if we thought they were "animals or something, we gentlemen, we just try to help you!"

I got mad that they couldn't understand and gave them a piece of my mind. They then got upset but I couldn't care less. We then walked back to our truck and our driver was standing there watching everyone in case they tried anything on us. Barb and I were so tired, we didn't even feel the coldness of the desert.

On the way to Tripoli

Friday, 13, I THINK. I've lost track of dates. Woke up next morning at 5 am and left at 5.30 am. My dirty feet were right in Barb's face! We drove on and I got to sit in the seat so slept until 10 am. Then we had tea and swapped so Barb sat in the seat. We couldn't read or write as it was so bumpy. About 1 pm we stopped at a deserted village for dinner and we put all the cooking equipment in an open-door house. Our driver cooked and we looked around. From the Italian writing on the buildings and the name 'Mussolini' all over doors, we figured it was a police headquarters when the Italians occupied Libya. It took two hours for this bloody meal to cook and I saw him put meat in the stew, and I just couldn't eat it! He was insulted, but I was in no mood for more stomach pains.

We finally were reaching civilization again when we were heading towards glimpses of beautiful tall date trees and palm trees. These little places are so pretty as they are cool, shady, clean-looking with clumps of green all over the place and irrigation wells about every 10 yards with the water pulled by a cow. It's just like the pictures in the Bible. Thousands and thousands of trees. I would like to stay in a place like this for a while if I had a mosquito net and a fly swatter! At one time, we were so thirsty, that we stopped at a filling station and drank the water from the rubber tube used to put water in the tank of a car. It's very dangerous to drink from the kitchen taps, but this was the worst. We broke out in welts from it later on. Later on, when we were nearing Tripoli, the driver bought us a cake and for the first time since we left Vienna, it rained. It was a bad thunderstorm and with terrible lightning and this gook who had been so nice to us wanted us to eat with him on the beach and go swimming! He got mad when we refused, and we started getting out of the car to hitch on, then he motioned he could take us on.

Tripoli

When we arrived in Tripoli, he took us through small streets on a long dirt road, and I thought he was getting back at us for not swimming and I said, "This so bad." He thought I said he was bad and he got insulted, and started driving like a maniac, and boy was I scared. Finally, he let us out, and we had to walk and walk for blocks, looking for the American Embassy and a policeman had to show us because too many men were following us. When we got to the Embassy at 10, Jim and our marine friends from Cyprus were there, as we had hoped! They gave us coffee and tried to find a cheap hotel for us and one of the Embassy drivers took us around but they were too expensive at $1. So we went back to the Embassy and they said we could stay at the Marine House, but had to wait until the guard changed so we would know where to go, so we both slept on a couch for three hours. Ed, the marine on duty, woke us up at 1 and then we walked around to the Marine House. They gave us a lovely room, and we took a shower and went to bed.

We woke the next morning (Saturday, August 14) and the whole house was waiting for us to wake up as they had heard that two girls were in there and they saw our packs sitting outside the door. They were floored when they saw how small we were – they were expecting two Amazons! We messed around all day washing clothes and our hair and had charcoaled steaks, and then we were told we were going to the ambassador's cocktail party so at 6.30 pm we were picked up by a chauffeur and off we went.

I went with a boy named Michael and he was a dear. The party was on the beautiful lawn of the ambassador's house and the house itself was gorgeous. Everyone there heard about our adventures, and they were so curious to talk to us – we really felt like queens! The boys we were with said they were really proud of us. After the party we went to the Wheelus American Air Base and had a blast. The boys invited some English people back to the house and they all stayed up until 5 am, but I went to bed. Barb and I woke up the next morning (Sunday, 15) with terrible headaches so we weren't able to leave. We went back to bed, and woke up at 4 pm and dinner was waiting for us. Michael, the marine I liked, had guard duty so I went around to the Embassy and sat with him until 12 and then he took me to Wheelus again and there I had a chocolate milkshake and two hamburgers and gosh, it was good. Then we went back to the house and watched a late night show, and then Barb and I went to bed.

Leaving Tripoli and going to Tunisia

Monday, 16 Got up at 6 am, and got ready then went downstairs and had breakfast. Michael got up at 7.30 am and took us to the main road. There we sat for about 20 minutes and two French boys picked us up and gave us a ride to a small town, and then one man gave us a ride and let us off in the desert again. This was terrible and we sat for about two and a half hours. Finally, a Libyan man picked us up in an old smelly truck, and dropped us off in another small town. We were walking through the village, and an ambulance picked us up and put us in the back with their patient! She was completely veiled, but when the sun hit her, you could see her beautiful face through her veil, and I thought how sad for such loveliness to be hidden. I think she had rickets, as her legs were extremely thin and the bones were showing through her long dress.

The ambulance let us off at the Libyan/Tunisian border, and there we sat for seven and a half hours. The officials were beginning to get smart and the flies were worse than ever. We sat on the side of the customs building in the shade on some cool cement, and the men came and sat there too, so Barb and I put a scarf completely covering our heads and neck, and a towel on our legs, and rolled down the sleeve of our shirts and laid down and went to sleep. I woke up at the sound of a car coming around the corner and lo and behold, it was an American who worked at the American Embassy in Tunis! He told us that the marines had asked him to keep a lookout for us! His Chevrolet was packed with stuff and his little girl of three. It was turning dark and he wouldn't let us stay with the officers so in we crammed.

Tunisian Border then Tunis

We went through two more checks and then we hit the Tunisian border, and there they wouldn't let Barb in cause she didn't have a visa. However, in Libya, the American Embassy had called up for her and they said she didn't need one! Well we just couldn't stay there, and they told her to go back to Tripoli, Libya and get one. Barb really is a hard person to make cry but I told her she had to do it! So, she pretended and it worked but then they said she had to stay overnight, and she pretended to cry again. For an hour Barb tried to talk them into letting her go in French, and finally they did. The American man was so kind. Barb, the little girl and I slept all the way and arrived in Tunis at 2 am on Tuesday 17 and he took us to the American Embassy and called his secretary and he took us to her house and we slept there. She was really an ass. She gave us a ride to the American Embassy and there we were told we had to go to the Algerian Embassy and get visas, so we left our things there and off we went.

Well Barb had to get a visa for Tunisia and then we went to the Moroccan Embassy way over town to make sure we didn't need visas to travel there and had to have three pictures taken and waited until 7.30 pm. We then went back to the American Embassy and asked the marine if he knew of a place we could sit up all night, as we didn't want to cash a check since we would be out of the country tomorrow, and you weren't allowed to change Tunisian money into other currency. He said we could stay at the Marine House, so we waited for some of the marines to come and pick us up to take us there. They took us first to a drinking house (tea house) and people were sitting on rugs on both sides of the stairs, and inside were large square stones covered in rugs, and this is where one sits with shoes off. The peasants smoke hubble-bubble and the tea has grains in it that looks like puffed wheat. It was a pretty little section and all the buildings were white with blue doors and windows, just like all the little villages in Tunisia. (By the way, try not to say anything about us staying at Marine Houses, as it is not allowed, and they can get into a lot of trouble if it is found out.)

They then took us to the Marine House and cooked us corn and spare ribs and milk (powdered) and then we had a shower and went downstairs and talked to them for a while. They then gave us a water jug, five packs of alcohol wipes for cleaning our faces, shampoo, aspirins and matches. In the morning (Wednesday, August 18) one of them, Bob, woke us with a cup of coffee, and he had fixed breakfast for us. Eggs, sausage, tomato juice and coffee, and then another guy drove up to take us to the road. Bob then handed us a basket full of sandwiches! These marines have really spoiled us. They dropped us in a nice spot on the road, and we were picked up by an Algerian who then dropped us off in a small town in Algeria, and he wanted to pay for a taxi for us to Constantine which would have cost a bomb.

Algeria – Constantine

There is no borderline between Tunisia and Algeria, as during the Revolution, lots of Tunisians went over and helped the Algerians, and so they left the border open. Algeria is a beautiful country and quite large, but the people are turning away from Western culture and turning toward Eastern cultures. Ben Bella[8], the president, is changing the language to Arabic, and on all posters they are showing that they are going to be a stronghold in Nasser's Arab world.

The Algerian took us to the police station, where we met two French boys and asked if we could have a ride to Constantine. They said yes so in we climbed into their Citroen, and Barb and I sat on large wooden trunks with our heads hanging out the open top. It started raining and we had to shut the top and lay all squashed up in the back. We slid off

[8] Ahmed Ben Bella, politician and revolutionary who was a crucial in the Algerian War of Independence against France. He was the head of government from September 27, 1962 to September 15, 1963 and then the first President of Algeria from September 15, 1963 to June 19, 1965.

the road and went tearing into a ditch, and I thought that was the end, but we turned back on the road. Algerian roads are dreadful, they're more like paths.

Constantine then Algiers

Arrived in Constantine at 9.30 am and a young man we asked for directions invited the four of us to stay at his house. We ate cheese, bread and jam and then Barb and I went to bed. Woke up (Thursday, 19) at 9 am, and the boys said they would drive us to Algeria, but first they wanted to look around the city, so off we went through the old section, and I almost fainted from the smell of raw meat and wine in the streets! The Algerian boy treated us to dinner, and then we set off for Constantine at 2 pm. We sat with the top opened again, and it was freezing. The countryside was lovely, mountains, no deserts thank goodness! It turned dark and the boys said they didn't want to drive in the dark, so we camped out, and Barb and I slept in a smelly small tent, and they slept outside and I absolutely froze.

Friday, 20 We got up at 6.30 am smelling like the tent, and then were off to Algeria. The wind hit our faces the whole way, and when we reached Algiers at 12.30 pm we both had terrible headaches. We also had a flat tire! Algiers was really a lovely city, but terribly expensive, more expensive than Washington DC, or so the Americans were telling us, and quite clean on the outside. They took us to the American Embassy which was located on one of the hills, and there we left our packs while we went to the Moroccan Embassy. On the way we stopped at the British Embassy, and just sat outside, because we were too hungry and tired to walk down the hill to the Moroccan Embassy We sat there for about an hour, and two Englishmen came up and asked what we wanted. They asked us to come to their house for dinner, until the Embassy reopened at 4 pm, so off we went.

Sorry I didn't get this off on time, but I mailed from the American Embassy in Algeria.

Morocco

Chefchaouen

September 25, 1963

Morocco

Dear Mother and Daddy,

We have traveled without rest and are now in Chefchaouen in Northern Morocco. One can see Spain from here! I really hate to get back to civilization, because this is so exciting. I will be in London in two weeks on October 10 and will speak to you by telephone from there. Mother, I am sending you picture postcards so you can see the places I have been and the types of people I have been associating with. Please keep them safe as I don't have a camera here. I will get one in London. We have the papers to emigrate to Johannesburg and will go before the end of the month. Our passage has been paid and we get to live and work there for a year. I know you will be disappointed, but I won't be coming back to Savannah until I don't know when.

South Africa

Cape Town

November 6, 1963

Cape Town, South Africa

Dear Family,

I have a fabulous job with an advertising firm called Lindsay Smithers and Sons Ltd. It is right in the center of town, in the most modern building in Cape Town. Completely made of glass, called The African Life Building. They are training me, and I really love it because I'm learning so much about advertising, and I run around to people's offices to look up files and so on. I honestly love the South African people.

Barbara works across the street for Caltec Oil Co., and makes 14.00 more a month than I, as she is a professional IBM operator. But in this country, time in a firm has more clout than a new person who has just qualified, thank goodness! I make 98.00 a month before taxes are taken out, but that's average. We asked if we could stay at the hotel until December 1, so I will save this month's salary.

In December we are moving into a room (very large) furnished, with a large bay window that overlooks the sea, and is the most beautiful view. We have to share the bathroom with two people, but never mind, because we only pay 28.00 together a month! It is in one of the places in Cape Town where all the young people live. On the weekends we sit on the beautiful sandy beaches in our bikinis and with a tan I really look pretty good. Barbara is in the bed with shingles, and will probably be there for three more weeks, and her firm doesn't pay for her absence. The doctor comes and gives her an injection every day, and it cost 5.60 for his visit and 3.80 for shot, and she has already paid 14.00 for medicine. Thank goodness it isn't me!

I am sending about seven copies of an article that was in the *Cape Times* about me, along with a picture. Also, I am sending one to *Savannah Morning News*, hoping they will put it in the travel section of the paper. I sure will be made if they do because the stupid pictures and articles they write up about people in Venice etc. are so corny.

By the way I called up Pat Flynn [family friend] and it was the wrong Pat! It was a girl, so now I don't know where to begin in looking for him. Is he married? Give a copy of the article to Jane and maybe they can put it in the Atlanta paper, since I am a Georgian. Hope y'all get to Europe next year, it's worth it! I am having pictures made from Barbara's slides from the Middle East, but most of them didn't come out. Call up *Savannah Morning News* and ask them if they are going to put the article in the paper, but wait until you received yours, because I shall mail them at the same time. Also, when we start traveling again, I shall write them and ask them can I write for them once a week, and pay me for it.

I hope you are keeping all my letters in order and postcards, because postcards I shall use for describing things. I am definitely planning on writing a book or article on it. If you could type each letter you receive it

would be easier for me to correct when I return, if I make it. Also, don't give my stamps to anyone, cause I definitely want them.

Please don't send me cigarettes, because they are cheaper here than in the States. What I would like are some small pictures of my debut pictures from Heriot's studio[9], black and white, some more Helena Rubinstein waterproof mascara like Jane sent me, and four pairs of rubber thong shoes. The ones that look Japanese, or what Jesus wore. Size five. I might still have a pair of yellow ones in my room, but I want new ones, but not white if you can help it. Ask Jane what they are, if you don't understand. Got to go now.

⊸⊷⊶⊷⊶⊷⊷⊶

Cape Town

December 18, 1963

Cape Town

Dear Family,

Sorry for taking so long to write, but Barb and I have been so busy moving into our new place. It really looks good now and Barb made curtains, bedspreads and covered the furniture with lovely material. We are very content here and our view of the ocean is fantastic. The sound of the waves breaking over the gigantic rocks puts us to sleep at night. The other night I was reading in bed and felt something nasty crawling on my neck and brushed it off and it was the most gigantic, black, fuzzy spider with tremendous eyes! I screamed and jumped out of bed and fainted. The neighbors came charging in and revived me and I told them about the spider. When they found it they all laughed and said it was called a baboon spider and it was harmless. It is quite common in the mountains where we are. I'm so afraid another one will crawl in my mouth as I always sleep with my mouth open. Also found a crazy large yellow lizard in my sweater drawer, and it frightened me to death, so now

---

[9] Callan was presented to Savannah society at the 1959 Debutante Cotillion. Her formal portrait shows her in an intricately beaded gown before a massive antique mirror [see overleaf]. Within two years, she was traveling and this traditional southern lifestyle was, for her, gone forever.

we spray our rooms every night with DDT. Apparently, the U.S. is about the only country that has screens on the windows.

Everyone is fascinated by my steam iron; they don't have them here. I have three bikinis now, black, pink and red with white polka dots, and am I so brown! My camera is fabulous, it takes 35mm slides (color) and I get the films wholesale from the firm.

The fruit here is fabulous and cheap. Barb and I bought 60 large oranges for $1.40 and they are so sweet and juicy, also 8 large bananas for 10¢, 20 plums 10¢, 8 large tomatoes 8¢, apricots 30 for 15¢, peaches 8 for 10¢, eggs 30¢ doz. And a whole lobster 60¢! We haven't been getting meat so next month we are going to a restaurant every night to eat. You pay $14 per month and eat as much as you like. I really love Cape Town and have grown very fond of the South Africans but the Afrikaans language which is of Dutch origin is quite strange. In January there will be what is called "Kaapse Klopse"[10] in Afrikaans, when all the locals go wild and wear crazy costumes and dance through the streets, so I hope to take lots of pictures. They work in ¢ now but 5¢ S.A. = 7¢ U.S. 100¢ = 1 Rand which is $1.40 but when I speak of cents I mean U.S. for future reference. They have a 2½¢ piece which is called a Tickey, and it's smaller than our dime. The movies are called bioscopes. There is no TV and by the looks of things it will be years, for political reasons. Some of the locals had planned a revolt, to overtake Cape Town four months ago but were caught two days before; a drunk woman was bragging that she was going to cut off all the white women's heads! (continued next week).

---

[10] The festival is now known as the Cape Town Minstrel Carnival.

CAPE TOWN

December 25, 1963

Cape Town

Dear Family,

Of all the days of the year, I wish I could be with you today. When you open the presents I hope you won't be too disappointed, but the thought is behind the gifts. I lagged the things all across Europe on my back, and when I return home I shall look at them (that is if they haven't fallen apart!). I remember wanting to throw them away but the thought of all of you opening them kept me going. Kiss the four children for me and have a lovely and happy Christmas.

⸺◦⊹⊹◦⸺

1964

Cape Town

Cape Town

Dear Family,

Sorry for the delay in writing you, but honestly each day becomes shorter and shorter with all the things I have to do. Thanks a million for all the presents. Especially the money, and as soon as I can I will write to MaryAnn thanking her for $5.00, Jane for $5.00, Bubba for $10.00. Thanks Daddy for the $50.00 for my birthday, I am saving it to buy presents in Durban which are much cheaper than here. I mean real crazy things like native drums, gigantic spears and fur covers, and some other crazy stuff!

Daddy, I am now 24, not 25, or 26! I must look like a hag in pictures if you think that! Mom, thanks for the money for the camera. Gee it's really great, and I can get my film at a discount from the firm which helps quite a bit, because it is terribly expensive here. The picture of the three children at Page's [Callan's sister Jane's daughter] birthday was adorable, but I felt terrible because I didn't send little Harry [Jane's son] a present, but so many times I have gone in the stores, and everything is so expensive because all toys come from England, Germany and U.S. God the import taxes one has to pay on them, and they're not half as good as you get in the States!

Received a letter from Diala [family friend] and answered her. Today I have to go to the doctor again, because I stepped on a shell on the beach over a week ago, and my whole foot got infected very badly. I've been in bed for five days and didn't get paid for being off work, which kills me, plus doctor's bills! I know a boy who distributes medicine, and he got me my antibiotic pills free, thank goodness. Barbara has been in bed for four days with flu. Honestly, I wonder what will happen next!

On Sunday, Barb and I went all around the peninsular with a German friend of ours, and I really didn't realize how beautiful it was. We saw zebras and Barb got a picture of me running from one that was chasing me. Also got pictures of baboons, which were jumping on the car, and practically tearing it apart. Gosh they were funny. We had a fabulous time. Been to so many parties lately, and have been taken out to dinner almost every night which helps my financial part. A Portuguese (male) friend gave me a gorgeous Mexican blanket for Xmas. I would have had to buy one if he didn't because my duffel coat didn't cover my whole bed. I finally broke down and bought a pillow, because my raincoat in a slip cover was very uncomfortable. We are just adjusting ourselves to where we can save money now.

Honestly, we are so silly, the other day we were measuring a small map of the world with a measuring tape and figured if it was 11 inches to Cape Town from England and $6\frac{1}{2}$ inches from C.T. to India, what would the price be. That's how we do everything. I don't see how we made it this far, because we just say we would like to go somewhere, and we leave not knowing a thing about it or how to get there, but that's half the fun of it all. I bet three years ago you never imagined your youngest mixed-up daughter would be doing things some men are afraid to do. You can write that on my epitaph!

I was supposed to pay $2.80 on my package, but I got through with it for nothing, because I threatened them I would leave South Africa, and when the government subside foreign workers by 1,000, they are not going to let them be dissatisfied over a little article. I still like my job very much, and find it quite easy except for the spelling. I can't spell in American, and English words are spelt different.

We don't know what we are going to do about getting to India, because ships that come to South Africa are not allowed to land in India, and in all the hotels and airports are large signs "No dogs and South Africans allowed". The South Africans have great humor, and just laugh at it, which I respect them for. I guess after Rhodesia we will have to fly to Tanganyika.[11]

On Xmas day I went to the beach and drank a fifth of Champagne and went to a swinging party that night. Barbara's Daddy is reading a book about South Africa and in every letter he gives us South African expressions such as *how's the bull tongue*[12][sic], and crazy things like that which he learned from the book, and we understand! The 2½¢ is called a Tickey! We're even beginning to talk like the locals! *Auch man* is said in every sentence, and even Grannies say to the children, *Auch man, don't do that*. It really is funny. Bought more oranges. About 100 in this lot. We really look funny carrying the sack down the streets.

Daddy, why don't you go to the post office and get a bunch of these Air-mail letters, they only cost 14¢ to South Africa and when one writes small it's amazing how much one can get on them. Saves a lot of money. Better go now because I can't think of anything else to say.

———————— ⋘⋙ ————————

Cape Town

February 26, 1964

Cape Town

Dear Parents,

Honestly the time has just flown by and I really didn't mean to let it go on for so long. I have about 25 letters to answer and I just don't know where I shall find the time. Right now, we are in the midst of moving and I can't find anything as usual. I work three to four times a week and it really wears me out, but I look forward to every working night. I am dating a Jewish lawyer and he is so kind to me. Barbara is coming to Savannah with me in five years' time, and her mother is knitting me a London sweater for when I arrive in Vancouver. I am searching around for Pender mugs for you, Mother, and getting them for $2.80. I've gone

---

[11] Now known as Tanzania.
[12] Barbara's father means "biltong," and not "bull tongue" as it sounds like to the uninitiated.

crazy over these wild-looking African things, so don't be surprised when you receive them all and take very good care of them because I love them so much. Some boys I know will be in Savannah in two months' time. They're English and sailing a yacht all around the world, and they said I could go with them if I paid for my own food. They will look you up when they arrive, so be kind to them, for they have been lovely to me. The American millionaire ship is here, and all the prices have gone up. Mother, you're so formal. The native dress is a blanket wrapped around you when smoking a long pipe. Don't worry lovey, I'll get you gorgeous things in India.

A friend of ours (an Indian girl) from Uganda wants to meet Barb and me in August in Dar es Salaam, Kenya and she will drive us all around Kenya, Uganda and Zanzibar in her car, but I won't be able to save enough money by then with all these crazy things I'm buying. I got some real cute things for Harry (little) and Page, but the other children are too small. I really miss them. Have to rush and pay my bloody doctors' bills. Love and miss both of you. Will send pictures very soon.

⸢◦⊰⊱◦⸣

Cape Town

March 9, 1964

Cape Town

Dear Mother and Daddy,

The heat today is unbearable and I can't sleep for the dampness. Our new place is fabulous. Very homey and clean looking. We don't have the gorgeous views of the sea now and I miss the sound of the waves crashing against the beautiful gray rocks. I feel wonderful, and I am eating very well now thanks to my three nights a week working at the Wooden Shoe, getting gorgeous steaks and Barbara's home cooking. We still drink a quart of milk a day, and she makes me eat vegetables. Also, a glass of guava juice each day.

I shall start printing because I can't read what I have written. The other day I went to a fortune teller and I really got scared at what she told me. It was all good except she said someone in my family was ill. She also said that my mother has made herself sick worrying about me not eating properly and not taking care of myself. She said my Daddy was very intelligent but very stubborn and lazy, and my mother was very introjected and all these crazy things. She also said there was brilliant child in the family, a boy with blondish hair and blue eyes. Also, that I would not be in Cape Town in a year's time and that I would be traveling to the other part of the world within two years. I would meet a business man with dark hair who I will marry, and will adore the ground I walk on, so maybe there's still a chance for me! Couldn't tell me what nationality or religion. She also said twins were in my line, and that when I got home there would be a new baby boy, and that nothing is going to happen to me. She knew so much about y'all. Things I haven't even told Barbara. Gee it's really crazy.

I'm having a ball but I have caught up on my sleeping. Honestly I get worried about y'all, when you worry about me. Honestly, I can take care of myself, and I won't leave here before I get a $1,000. Daddy if you're ill, please go to the doctor. I am enclosing a slide, and you can have a picture made from it if you want.

Thursday I am going to see *Showboat*, and a lady called me and asked me to come and talk to the actors so they could imitate my accent, and I asked her how much she would pay and she said nothing, so I didn't do it! They would have thought I was putting it on anyway, well I guess I would, because I am really beginning to speak with an English accent! Daddy, don't be too shocked by the bikini, if one wears a one-piece suit, it is more conspicuous. Crikey, I just remembered little Harry's birthday is March 17, so will have to rush and get him some crazy native drums and masks and send it airmail.

Jane the big bean never writes, so I never hear about the children, so when you see little Harry next, tell him Auntie Barby thinks of him all the time, and would like to receive a letter from him when he is capable of it. I hate to admit, but I don't know anyone's birthday in the family except mine (naturally because I want presents!!) and Harry's. So how about sending me a list, and who knows maybe I'll get generous and send someone a present. I really would like to knows y'all's.

I just put a gorgeous red coat on Lawley[13], and from my money at night, I'll be able to get it out in no time. I save my day money from Lindsay Smithers, and when I receive my check at the end of the month, I immediately put it into traveller's cheques. So, my darlings I'm doing fine. Our new place is a crazy house, but fabulous, and there is always excitement going on. One doesn't have a chance to get lonely, because so many people are charging in and out. It's a darling room in a house with other young people, and we take turns cooking for everyone – but I'm not allowed to cook, because no one will eat it, so I have to clean up everything which 'yuks' me.

The men here are the most spoiled things in the world, because there are so many more women, and all they're out for is a ring on their left finger, but I won't put up with it. When anyone calls me up and asks me for a date, I say, *Sure, if you take me to dinner.* They're so dumbfounded because a South African girl wouldn't dare say anything like that, that they do it! Since I've been here I've racked up loads: a Mexican blanket, a bottle of perfume, two bouquets of flowers, 10 pairs of Cameo stockings, and cigarettes galore! I tell them my time is valuable and they have to pay for my company, if they don't want to they can bugger off (English expression!). I figure I may as well get what I can out of the stupid nits, instead of them doing it to me. All in all, I have been a very good little girl, because I realize I'm the only one to take care of me.

Aren't the men gorgeous in the picture? They all look like this, that's why it's so easy to wrap them around your little finger. Don't get worried if you don't hear from me for a while at a time, you have nothing to worry about while I'm in Cape Town, it's just that I get so busy with two jobs, that time is very consuming. I must go now before my boss catches me typing this. I love and miss both of you very much. Please take care of yourself, because I also worry about you too.

---

[13] Lawley – possibly some sort of financing company, like a credit card or loan – or could even be a pawn shop.

Cape Town

April 13, 1964

Lindsay Smithers, Cape Town

Dear Mother and Daddy,

Just received your letter with the pictures enclosed, and they are marvellous. Little Harry looks precious. The package for little Harry was his birthday present, and it was a mask. I hope it doesn't scare him because it sure did me! Jim, who flies for the navy, is bringing my blue suitcase home, and I will send the key to you separately. It contains mostly letters and pictures, so go through everything but please keep everything together because I definitely want everything in there. Jim is saving me about R14.00. He's a very nice chap and is bringing a camel for little Harry, and some gifts in a wooden box for you. Also, the other day I bought a gorgeous mask and a statue of a native beating a drum and it should arrive in about three weeks' time. Take care of this because I love it and paid $23.00 for it. There is also a leaflet with the history of all things.

I am still working very hard in the daytime (mostly trying to stay awake!) and at night. The money I make at night I live off and my day money I put in the bank, or at least try to. But there are so many fabulous things I want to buy while I am in this country, that I feel I will always regret it if I don't. Also, I am sending a picture of a zebra chasing me and I had it made from Barbara's slide so take good care of it. I thought maybe it could go in the living room. It is an unusual picture, and I wouldn't be a bit surprised if it could win a prize.

Life is getting very boring with me again, and I'm ready to hit the road, but I don't want to leave here until I have saved $1,000. We have been invited to visit an old man in Salisbury, in southern Rhodesia[14] and he is going to take us everywhere, including the Victoria Falls. We definitely wanted to visit some of our Indian friends in Uganda, Kenya and Tanganyika, but we have given up that idea. I know you are relieved about that. We also might be able to catch a Indian Curry boat, which

---

[14] Now known as Zimbabwe

takes hundreds on board, with no bathrooms and we all sleep in one room! Very cheap and it sounds very exciting.

I bought a zebra handbag the other day, and it is the most gorgeous thing I have ever seen. Only $22. I am also working extra nights to buy a leopard handbag. I have been promoted to secretary to Mrs. Smith, Head of Administration! I know by my typing that you won't understand it, but for some strange reason she likes me because I'm quiet (so she thinks) and try to do my best. The funniest thing is that I have to answer the phone for her a lot, so each morning I have a 'speaking lesson' for 15 minutes and honestly you just wouldn't believe me. I'm not allowed to say y'all, o.k., yeah, thanks, don't mention it, can (may instead) and I have to speak like the English do, because the Afrikaans-speaking people cannot understand me. They think I'm quite shocking the way I address the managing director, and the poor man himself doesn't know how to answer me. I also have a spelling lesson (English way) such as colour etc.

Mother, I bet the new-look rug in the living room really looks bad. God, I hate those things. Jim will probably tell you I need a good spanking for my attitude but he just can't seem to understand that I get so cheesed off with the Afrikaans men. I feel I am wasting my precious time by going out with them. I never have been one for letting men treat me like dirt.

It's turning winter here now – seems funny, doesn't it! Received a letter from Comer [a school friend?] and she said she might go work in a missionary in Nigeria. I wouldn't do that if you paid me. Barbara has really gotten me on to vegetables, about the only thing I don't eat is beats. I am going to the dentist regularly now, and it costs the same as the States – that really cheeses me off! The movies here are called bioscopes, and one sits for 45 minutes watching advertisements before the film comes on. It's such a waste of time. Street stops are called robots (I mean stop lights) – can you believe it?! I'm very lucky because I have some medical reps as friends and they give me all my medicine for free. Our room has been fumigated for flies, but it hasn't done any good. Each night Barb and I have to cover ourselves in repellent to keep the little bastards away from us. I got bitten so badly I had to go to the doctor. This place is infested with them! They are blown in from the sands of the beaches.

There's not much else to say, and it takes me quite a while to say what little I do. So many people have asked us if they could go with us to Japan, but we're afraid they will cramp our style. I'm a naughty girl as the American consular (a bachelor) asked me to have dinner with him, and I never showed up. I bet he won't be to glad to give me information when I want it.

I bet the garden is fantastic. I honestly can't wait to see it. I'm thinking of having my face lifted when I reach Japan, because it is cheap there, and I have aged so quickly in my face from strain. It's what I want though, and I'm content with life when I'm on the road. Please forgive me if I don't remember birthdays, I never have been one for dates. Little Harry's and mine are the only ones I can remember! I've got a crazy mood to go on safari, but they're so expensive.

I know you don't approve of what I'm doing, but it's what I want, and I've never felt so free or happy, and I'm definitely planning on writing a book when I return. Every now and then I think of all that I have done, and you know it's really hard for me to believe it! From Japan we go to Hawaii and then Vancouver to stay with Barbara's parents for a month, then we are hitching to New York and maybe from there we can come to Savannah by train. You don't believe me, but you didn't believe I would get this far. I don't like writing too much because I get very homesick. I would love to come home for about two weeks and just sit around the kitchen table telling you all my wild adventures, but I know if I went home I would chicken out. It would be great though. Never mind, I can hold off three more years.

Received a letter from Mrs. Frame [a family friend] and she said you both look fabulous. I am eventually going to look up the lady she told me about. The only problem is she lives a long way from Cape Town in Rondebosch, the oldest and richest place in South Africa.

Weekend after next, we are going to an old Afrikaans farm for the weekend to visit a New Zealand girl named Claire. She's driving into town to pick us up and I have gotten off my night job for that occasion. Ask Bubba if he wants me to get him some masks. Hope you don't think what I have sent is too ridiculous; if it is tell me, and I'll choose other things. Must go now. Take care.

⊶⊶⊷⊷

Cape Town

May 25, 1964

Cape Town

Dear Mother and Daddy,

Thank you so much for the fabulous letter, but honestly Daddy your writing is atrocious! First of all, if the coat is going to cause that much trouble, forget it. It was bought in Paris (God don't ask me where) and it was stolen in some little crazy town in France where we stopped and bought some bread and wine (some sort of café) and I had it two days. I never mentioned it because I know y'all would know I was freezing.

Barb and I have decided to leave at the end of August, and we are going to stay with a family for a month in Salisbury, near the Falls. From there we really don't know except we are determined to get to Japan. Received a letter from Dez Brown and he thinks I should give it up. I got a lovely letter from one of the boys that saw Barb and I on that trip to Algiers. Terribly kind of him to write. I'm going to try and get more things for the children, but I'm sweating the money part since I haven't been saving too much and we're leaving earlier than planned.

I have been in an utter state of depression from working too hard but I am on pills now to relax my stomach and feel 100% better.

I'm really so sorry to hear about Jane. I must write her a sweet letter sometime.

Remember when Wendy and I were in Majorca, well she's back there again with the American that let us have his villa. Jim will bring the suitcase (God, I forget to mail the key, I still have it!) and a crate with things for the house. Also, the picture of the zebra should arrive, as well as a gigantic beautiful tusk, and the gorgeous statue – what things is Daddy talking about when he says what I have sent are pretty and unique?

I shall have $1000 by the end of August plus $100 to buy souvenirs. We are going to Kruger National Park but it is quite expensive. Got six Pewter mugs, but will send them with my luggage. Bubba's house sounds gorgeous. So sweet of him to write me. I'm so sick of my day work, and I'm sick and tired of my English boss telling me to speak proper English!

Last weekend we went to a lovely Afrikaans farm and was it beautiful. Honestly, this country is gorgeous. Barbara is coming home with me. That's a springbok on the stamp. My doctor bills for the last month have amounted to $25. It's just nerves. I am determined to make it all the way to Savannah on a thousand dollars. I'll make a bet with you I can do it!

Please let me know each thing you receive from me. Barbara works for the Wooden Shoe too, but she never gets to work with me which angers me very much. I'm buying a roll of film each week, and hope to have 30 rolls when I leave. We have heard from Peace Corps[15] people that Kenya is alright to go through by train. Save the stamps on the inside, there should be seven! A girl at the office is knitting me a gorgeous thick sweater and it cost me $10 for wool. Barb's parents just received presents from her but they were mine to y'all!! So watch out and let me know everything you get because they will probably be Barbs! If you get a tall giraffe, that's hers!

Must go now. The weather is gorgeous and Barb and I are just getting ready to go for a walk.

Two masks, two spears and a tall giraffe are Barbara's, not mine. Please draw pictures of masks and color because I am really confused. It looks like my things were sent to her house!

———————————— ◦⋙◦⋘◦ ————————————

[15] The Peace Corps is an American agency that sends volunteers all over the world to provide international development assistance. It was founded by John F Kennedy in March 1961.

Cape Town

June 15, 1964

Cape Town

Dear Mother and Daddy,

Well I don't know where to begin. First, I must say that Barb and I are leaving Cape Town on July 16, because we were fired from the Wooden Shoe so we quit our day job. It's for the best because we are unhappy here now. I just bought 10 rolls of film for $56. I think for my birthday I would like film (35mm). I've changed my mind – Kodachrome and the price of developing is included. Right now, I don't know if I am coming or going. We have accumulated so much that it will cost us a fortune to send home. I am afraid I can't buy anything else because I don't have as much money as planned. Will try and get local things in Rhodesia for Bubba and myself. After July 16, send my mail to c/o American Consulate in Salisbury, S. Rhodesia or American Consulate at Broadway Building, Cape Town.

Just got home from work and received your letter with drawings of mask. Honestly, Mother, you're really kinky at times. First, I have too many worries to add more to my troubles about things that are gone. I have a very nervous stomach so I just can't worry. Don't you either. The only thing that matters is my safety and health and you. My fur coat and other things are being sent home when we leave. The clothes and things we don't want we are selling to locals. The huge mask is mine and not Barbs!

I'm going to Rhodesia and Japan, so you just have to accept it. Will get Bubba $25 worth of things, but will wait till I get to Rhodesia. It's cheaper there. I don't know what kind of paintings you're talking about, but I have some in mind. You must stop worrying about money, everything happens for the best. I also wrote a postcard to the German boy. It's amazing how many nice people I have met like him. Mother – in one part of your letter you say you can't wait for Jim to bring the suitcase, and in another you say you haven't had time to go through it. Did you receive the blue suitcase or not? The ox blood mask is mine.

The rest is Barbara's. Don't know how it got in with her things. We will talk about hitching in the U.S. later. I probably won't.

Mother, every writer in the world hangs out there. Plus, the Spanish don't live there. It is a waste of money! And no, I won't be home before 1½ years. Sorry about that. Just found out where Watusi Tribe[16] is. It's near Kenya and I know what the picture looks like (paintings) and funny enough I was planning on buying some anyway.

Forgot, but we are sending a suitcase to the American Embassy in Japan so we shall have some decent clothes to wear, because we are having a ball. Honestly, I am so glad to be hitting the road. I don't think I will ever get the travel bug out of me. Will send you a surprise in a week. Remember, I love and miss both of you so much, but I know if I went home before I finished my round the world trip, I would never forgive myself. You do understand, don't you?

June 21 We are going to send Barbs' suitcase to American Embassy in Japan with clothes. Two New York Jewish girls are moving in here on the weekend and we are selling them the sheets you sent me in London and pillows, blankets etc. and getting $15 apiece plus all the clothes we sell, so we won't be doing too badly. Also, we get to stay in a boy's flat while he is on Reserve with the Army. When I start sending things home, be extra careful, because I have things everywhere. Even under cotton in small bags, and in wallets. Will write next week.

⬦

---

[16] Watusi is the former name for the Tutsi people.

Cape Town

July 4, 1964

Cape Town

Dear Parents,

Glad to hear that you have a map of the world and use little red pins to follow us as we go along.

We are not going near the Congo! Johannesburg is in the upper part of South Africa called the Transvaal. This is where the Bantu people live and they are under the control of the South African government. I landed in Johannesburg when I arrived in South Africa from London. Look at your map closely. From Johannesburg we go to Kruger National Park and then head for South Rhodesia. From Salisbury on to Bulawayo, South Rhodesia, then we are cutting across east to Mozambique which is Portuguese, South Africa[17] controlled by the Portugal government and is a safe area. From there we go all the way up Portuguese East Africa, until we get to Tanganyika but if it gets dangerous, we shall catch the train, or go by boat to French Somaliland[18] (which is straight across from Arabia on the Red Sea). If things are o.k., we shall continue through Tanganyika to Kenya until we reach Uganda where we have Indian friends.

Mother, I read *Time Magazine* every week and know more about Africa than you can imagine! All the things you read about are in the Congo in a section called Katanga[19] which is about 500 miles away from our route and I have no intention of going near there, Mother! I hear much more about these places than *Time Magazine* tells; we get reports every day, and also there are hundreds of refugees here from the territory.

I'll send the address of a family who have a large farm outside of Johannesburg; we are going to stay there for a week. This lady will take a large suitcase of mine to Japan and leave it c/o American Embassy and I'll pick it up when we finally get there, if we ever make it.

---

[17] Now known as Mozambique
[18] Now known as Djibouti
[19] The Congolese prime minister of the former Belgian Congo was assassinated and led to the Katanga Crisis (also known as the Congo Crisis), which lasted from 1960 to 1965. This is what Callan's mother is worried about.

Must get something for Bubba's baby but whenever I think of it I haven't the money to spare.

⸺⸺∘⧉∘⸺⸺

Bantry Bay (Cape Town), Caledon, and various towns including Oudtshoorn, George and Knysna to Port Elizabeth, East London, then Transkei and on to Durban, South Africa

July 24, 1964

Durban, South Africa

Dear Mother and Daddy,

First of all I have sent to you all my clothes and personal belongings in four medium-sized cardboard boxes and one very small one, so five all together. You are not to spend one thing for customs because they are all my personal things. They will arrive at different times, maybe two months apart. Secondly, I sent my large blue suitcase home via Jim, with my fur coat and seven rings. The gold one with 12 rubies is for Jane, the greenish glass one and the large light brown one I want for myself. Your ruby ring is there, Mother, and you can choose from a green (aqua) dark stone and two chipped diamonds. The kidney-shaped one has a diamond missing, but is lovely when it is shined. The odd-shaped one has a cultured pearly missing from the middle (you can see where it's missing from the cement) and it is gorgeous polished with pearl in it.

Please put my fur coat in fur storage and have it glazed[20] for me. Also, there are things tucked away in every wallet and every other place, so please don't throw anything away. There is an English gold coin tucked away somewhere worth about $55 so look through everything! I think it is under the cotton of a little black box with a red top. The necklace in this box (gold and black) is for Ticky. I got it in Spain. The suitcase was insured for $1000 and I am enclosing the insurance policy. Give it two months to get there and if it doesn't reach home, claim from the New York branch on the policy. Also three handbags, the zebra, leopard and

---

[20] A specific finishing process that offers a barrier from wear and tear.

ostrich. These are definitely mine. Call up Kirschner[21] and ask them how to preserve them. I think the roll of film in the case are of the Carnival, so don't have it developed. The case was sent off two days ago. Also, you should receive a package with a shield (block) and two spears that have been cut for shipping. If you want this to be put up in the house do so, and put a X in back of the shield. To dust it, you stroke a soft brush through it. If you don't want it hanging around the place, put it in moth balls until I get home. Also, in this package is a small drum with little bone spears, which is for Harry. In the insured suitcase there are two necklaces (one with an elephant made of bone, the other a little round bead that is real ivory). You may open these if you wish, but please be careful with them.

Now I am 600 miles away from Cape Town. Finally, we are on the road again! I shall start from the beginning. We gave up our flat at 1 Romney Road on July 15 and three Jewish girls moved in our place and we sold them everything we had. The girl next door to us was called Ann. Her boyfriend went in to the Army for three weeks, so he let us move into his flat with his flatmate in Bantry Bay, the most gorgeous section of Cape Town. It was a lovely modern flat with the gorgeous Twelve Apostles Mountains in the back. We had a fabulous time there with his flatmate; he was very moody, but we got him out of that! I told my firm I was meeting you two in Japan but you didn't know I was going to hitch there. We ate very well while we stayed in Bantry Bay. We got all our medicine and makeup wholesale and thanks a million for the $25. I have spent every cent of it on supplies for nine months.

We were awakened Monday morning at 4.45 am (July 20) by a crash and someone pulling off the covers. It was Kevon, my Russian Jewish friend, and he fixed breakfast while we took a shower. We were on the National Highway at 6 am – it was freezing and dark. We were right next to a location where all the bachelor locals live at 8 am we got our first lift but it was only for a mile! Our feet were numb and the stupid clot let us off in a lonely spot. One of the locals came up to us and asked for food, and we told him to get lost! We walked away and finally a young chap gave us a ride to Caledon, 23 miles from Cape Town. He let us off on a mountain which overlooked the city and we stood there still numb for

[21] Established 1895 in Savannah, Kirschner Furs is the oldest full-service furrier in the southeast USA.

about 20 minutes, when a man drove up from the other side of the road and said very angrily, "Where in the hell are you girls going?"

We were spellbound and told him Port Elizabeth which is 516 miles from Cape Town. He started screaming at us saying we were mad and then he told us he would take us because he couldn't stand the thought of two girls in wilderness! Then we mentioned we were going to the Transkei – 142 miles of nature where the people govern themselves and are supported by the South African government. He got terrified and said he would take us all the way to Durban – 800 miles! So, in we climbed with Nick who has an American accent and embarrassed us because he is loud, and everyone thinks he is a Yankee! He bought me cigs and our meals. We drove all day and whenever we wanted to stop for pictures, he would. We went through the Riviersonderend, Heidelberg, Riversdale, Albertinia, and Mosselbaai. Nothing exceptional about the small towns, except the scenery.

Nick decided he wanted to take us to the largest ostrich farm in the world which is in Oudtshoorn, called Highgate. It was a gigantic valley of 11,000 acres surrounded by gorgeous mountains and Highgate is 6,000 acres. We learned quite a lot about these dangerous birds – they can kill a man with their feet. After the demonstration, Barbara and I sat on one which had a board between its legs so it couldn't kick hard. I lost my balance and fell right on his legs and thank God it didn't kick because I wouldn't be writing you now!

From there we drove to George and all the way we were crossing mountains. In one particular place, there was a monument to the settlers who crossed this place with oxen and cattle. I wouldn't have believed it unless I had seen the monument. It's really fantastic! We spent the night in a place called The Wilderness! We stopped at a motel on a lagoon with no electricity and I froze. God, it was cold. I woke up at 3 am and had to go to the bathroom but couldn't get out of bed for the cold.

July 21 Woke up at 7.30 am and had to take a bath (cold) across a field in a small little room! We were off at 8.30 am and Nick paid the bill. We drove over mountains again until we came to the town of Knysna (pronounced Nysna) where the largest elephants in the world live (naturally, we didn't see any!!). Also, it has the largest stinkwood trees. After Knysna, it began getting more lush and jungle. Monkey, apes, banana trees, the whole works – Tarzan style! Then we finally reached Port Elizabeth.

Gee, it is a disgrace to South Africa. It was so dirty! But before we hit Port Elizabeth we passed a place called Storms River (which the South Africans think is wonderful, but just looked like a bridge to us!). Finally, we got to East London just before dark. We stayed at a cheap hotel and had a nice meal and went to bed at 7.30 pm – boy, we're tired!

July 22 Got up at 6.15 am, had breakfast and were on the road at 8.30 am. East London was a lovely clean city, but rather dead. We started approaching mud huts, so we knew we were coming to the Transkei. It is just about the richest land in South Africa but it was so primitive it was hard to believe. Each tribe wears different clothes (if any!). We took about 15 pictures and one time we stopped at a round hut with a family sitting around in a circle. The mother had white paint all over her face and beads all over and anklets almost up to her knees, and gigantic bosoms hanging with no top. We took pictures of all of them and gave them candy, but they wanted more and started getting stroppy when we had no more. We ended up by running to the car with them chasing us, and when we reached the car they started beating on it with their sticks. I can honestly say I have never been so scared in my whole life! I was quite shaken up over it but didn't say anything.

We kept driving and I honestly can't describe the different tribal dress. We couldn't take pictures of some, as some tribes are very proud and they think it is an insult. We saw boys in the nude – Daddy, don't you throw my pictures away when you see these things! All they do is sit around, and then carry sticks on their heads. It's very dangerous to travel in this territory at night. We also took pictures of three boys who were being initiated into manhood. Their whole body is painted white and they have to stay by themselves for two months. At the end of this period, the men in the tribe search for them and when they find them, they beat them with sticks until they find water to wash themselves off and then their body is painted with red clay and they receive a red blanket to wear – then they are men.

The women either wear red or white clay on their face to protect their skin from the sun. They never take baths and the skin under their anklets is cut dreadful since they never take them off. They used to take the wire from the fences and telephone poles until the government got fed up and started fining anyone caught. Most of the women wear blankets of beautiful, bright colors, called Bantu blankets. Bantu is a particular tribe and they smoke long pipes. Getting closer to Durban, we saw a different tribe – here the women wore little beads around their bottom and were bare-busted. They put long beads in their hair with mud and clay and it gives an 'Egyptian effect'. They carried many sticks on their heads that were about 10ft. long. I haven't ever seen anything like this before. Oh, and their ears are pierced with long pieces of wood.

Nearing Durban we started running across the Zulu tribe where the women wear long dresses but their shoulders are exposed – they also do their hair with beads and clay, except it is red instead of black. Zulus are respected by the white people. They wear the brightest colors of all and the most gorgeous bead work. On a hill in the Transkei one can see nothing but thousands of round mud huts with grass roofs. Really breathtaking. This section of South Africa is very hilly and fertile and they grow wheat and corn and some of them are quite rich.

We finally reached Durban about 6.30 pm and we came to stay with a Jewish family by the name of Adderley (Barb roomed with Mrs. Adderley on the ship). They were giving a dinner party so we said goodbye to Nick and ran upstairs, had a bath and dressed in heels and dresses and went downstairs after all the guests arrived. Had a lovely meal which was served by a Zulu boy. All the white people here speak Zulu because the Zulu people refuse to speak English. We sat and talked until 11 pm and then went to bed in our gigantic lavender and blue room. I woke up in the middle of the night with terrible stomach trouble, throwing up and chills. God, I was ill. If this happens again I think I shall have to come home. I think it was the strain and fear of the journey. By the way there is a great distinction between each tribe here – they never marry outside their tribe.

July 23 In bed all day with fever and chills. Didn't eat one thing. It hurt so much. Barb went out with Mrs. Adderley and saw Durban which is subtropical. Thousands of Indians here are hated by everyone.

July 24 Woke up feeling terribly weak but much better. Went out to see the town and went to the Indian market. God, was that a place. All the Indians in their saris and I bought a tom-tom drum 3ft high for Bubba for $6.30. Couldn't find one cheaper. Have to carry it to Johannesburg with me because I don't have time to ship it here since we are leaving on Monday. In 1949 the Zulu tribe attacked the Indians in Durban and hundreds were killed.[22]

Durban is really a lovely clean town with sophisticated people. Maureen, a girl who lived at 1 Romney Rd. with us in Cape Town, is here in Durban and we are going out with her on Sunday. We are going to stay with her parents on a farm outside of Johannesburg for a week and then we go to another farm 100 miles away from Kruger National Park on August 6 and will be in Kruger for a week. Will be in Salisbury on August 23 so write to me c/o Mr. W.B. White, 19 New Africa House, Union Avenue, Salisbury, Southern Rhodesia. I don't think we will go through Kenya or Tanganyika. My stomach just can't take it.

———— ∞§∞ ————

Durban, Orange Free State, Krugersdorp, Johannesburg, South Africa

July 29, 1964

Krugersdorp, South Africa

Dear Parents,

I am now 25 miles from Johannesburg on a gorgeous farm, July 25 in Durban.

Went to the Indian market and had my handbag pickpocketed! Fortunately I looked down and saw a hand in my purse! I went crazy and chased him through the crowd, and when I caught up with him I grabbed him and started shaking him, screaming, "Give me back what you took!" Lo and behold, my wallet dropped and we were completely surrounded and he started running and that was that.

---

[22] The Durban riots were an anti-Indian riot that took place between January 13-15, 1949, primarily by Black South Africans targeting South African Indians. It was the second deadliest massacre during apartheid.

That afternoon we met Maureen (whose family we are staying with at present) and sat and talked for hours. That night we went to a party and boy, did we have a blast. We met some fabulous people and I wasn't too well, but borrowed a suit from Maureen and looked very nice.

July 26   Got up and had breakfast and went to meet Maureen again. Was picked up by Jeffery Adderley and taken home for lunch and then went back to Maureen. The rickshaw driver kept chasing Barbara and she was really terrified. We also went to the aquarium and saw sharks. Started getting dark (oh we met an actor who plays in the movie *Zulu* and he was a very nice chap) so we went home, packed and went to bed.

Monday, July 27   Got up at 7.30 am and were on the road at 10. No word from Nick so we gave up. We stood on the highway with our two packs, one large, a large medicine bag, one library (a bag), two bags with seven months' supply of soaps etc. and that damn 3 ft. drum for Bubba! Five cars stopped but couldn't take us because we had so much stuff. 20 minutes later two boys picked us up and said they would take us halfway 200 miles so in we got, drum and all.

It was a lovely drive but not as lovely as the Garden Route. Honestly, this country is just gorgeous, it is winter and the trees look dead and the South Africans say it is not pretty and in summer it is gorgeous, but Barb and I think it is beautiful! When we arrived in the Orange Free State it started getting flatter. We were let off in a small place called Hammersmith across the highway from a garage and a boy saw us and said he would take us to Johannesburg. He was a gigantic rugby player and he was shocked at two girls hitching through "Kaffer" [sic] territory. We shocked him on purpose because he was shy! He treated us to tea, and at 7 pm he let us off in a small town about 20 miles from Johannesburg. We bought tickets for Krugersdorp (where the farm is) and the man asked if we were under 16 and I said yes, so we got children's tickets. How about that at 24, I get a child's ticket. Pretty good aye!

While we were waiting for the train, the rugby player called the Terre'Blanches[23] to inform them that two straggly girls were arriving at 8.30 pm. When we arrived, they were waiting for us – boy, was it cold!

---

[23] Eugène Terre'Blanche (January 1941-April 2010) was an Afrikaner Nationalist who founded the AWB (the Afrikaner Resistance Movement) in 1973, meaning Callan's encounters with them were 10 years' prior to this. He was a major figure in the right-wing backlash against the collapse of apartheid whose beliefs and philosophy continue to be influential amongst white supremacists in South Africa and across the world today.

We drove and drove through the bush and finally entered the gate of their land. Drove and drove and finally the car lights revealed the most gorgeous thatched roof house. We went into the kitchen for a snack and it is larger than our living room. We were given a gigantic, gorgeous bedroom. Took a hot bath and went to sleep.

Tuesday, July 28 Got up at 7.30 and had breakfast with Mr. and Mrs. Terry and Granny and we piled into their 1964 Ford and were off to Johannesburg. I bought a handbag that can't be pocketed and it killed me to spend my money. We were looking around the stores and met Mr. Terre'Blanche. I had a runny tummy all day (as usual). We arrived home at 4.30 and had tea and just sat around and talked until dinner. It was Mrs. Terry's birthday (Terre'Blanche is too long to say!) and Barb and I gave her two pairs of stockings and we had Champagne for dinner. Went to bed at 9.30.

July 29 We were so tired, we got up at 11.30! Meanwhile I had been up all night with my runny tummy. I honestly don't know what I'm going to do about it, because I'm always in pain. We had brunch and then just sat out in the sun 'til dinner. After dinner we four females went on a walking tour of the farm's 332 acres. Today was the first day in about six months that I have felt so wonderful. We drove four miles in a new truck on a dirt road to the post office. We came back and had tea in the sun and I wrote until dark. It is so lovely and peaceful and I am slowly regaining my strength.

The Terrys are rich as hell and they are so natural and lovely. We just adore them. They are going to Japan by boat at the end of September and they are taking a suitcase for us that weighs 35 lbs. so we will look respectable there! They have three servant girls, one male cook that makes their butter and cooks fabulously, a man to clean the house and seven boys just to clean the farm and area. Actually, they don't farm, it's just more recreation than a living. They have a gorgeous swimming pool, tennis courts and they have their own electricity plant next to the kitchen. They have two reservoirs which hold the water pumped from a river and then it goes through the land through pipes. It really is lovely. Went to bed at 10.

July 30 Woke up at 8.30 feeling really refreshed. Had breakfast and now we are sitting in the sun. Hot enough now to go swimming. They have two guest houses that are copies of the master house and are as large as our house. We drink cream and milk straight from the cows. All the floors in the whole house are slate stone, which is shiny and rather dark, and cool. Also, we play golf on their five-course golf green. Did we ever have a ball?! Barb and I were really comical. Everything (grass, trees, etc.) is dead from the frost. Shame because the pictures would have been gorgeous. I am going to pack Bubba's drum tomorrow and will address it c/o y'all. The people are fabulous.

Shame it isn't summer or spring. We are sitting in the round living room floor by the fire and Mr. Terry just came from a rugby team and said there were road blocks everywhere trying to find the saboteurs who set off a bomb in Johannesburg train station and 13 children and adults were seriously injured and one died. The whole country is livid including all the locals – involving innocent people has just gone too far. Before I forget I wish you would send me the date of everyone's birthday so I can at least send them cards. (The little mask with the shield is for Bubba's little girl.) Please don't laugh but you said "just a little something".

This house is fantastic and beautiful. The living room from floor to ceiling is about 25 ft. says Mr. Terry. The art in these thatched roofs is brilliant. This house is indescribably. So many rooms. The thatch on the inside is a lovely straw color supported by lovely beams (wood) which are dark. 15 cross bars and 23 beams pointing upwards. The actual thatch itself is about 1 ft. thick.

It is now evening and we are sitting in the lovely round living room in front of the fire again. I am leaning against the chair Mrs. Terry is sitting in and Mother, she is stroking my hair exactly like you used to! We were so tired we took a bath and went to bed.

July 31 We were awakened by Mrs. Terry at 8 to go to Johannesburg. We just looked around and Barb and I bought a Bantu blanket. I really shouldn't have, but I know I would have regretted not buying it when I got home. Got home about 4, played golf again and had tea and just talked in the gorgeous sun. Went to bed early. About 2.30 in the morning, we were awakened by the dogs barking up a storm. All of a sudden there was a figure at the window – and it was Maureen! The whole family was up in no time making coffee for the two boys that bought her from Durban. We were all so excited we couldn't go back to sleep so we just tossed and turned in bed.

August 1 Got up at 9.30 and had breakfast. Maureen, Barb and I walked about three miles for cigs and on the way, we visited the locals in their huts. They were so friendly and just love Maureen. When we got back Nan, Mr. and Mrs. Terry and us three played golf again and was it funny. As usual Barb and I came in last. We all walked around the farm and picked out the turkey we wanted for Sunday's dinner and saw a 12-hour old calf. Gee, it was sweet. Maureen has a terrible cold and I hope I don't get it. We had drinks as usual in front of the fire before supper and George, their cook, who claims he is of royal stock of the Swahili tribe in Northern Rhodesia, cooked a gorgeous meal. Mr. and Mrs. Terry have to go to a party given by the family on the adjoining farm so the four of us sat around the fire until 9.15 pm and we were so tired, we went to bed. Barb and I have such difficulty in breathing here because we are so far up. I feel like a new person now and even look it.

Love Barbara

Krugersdorp, Johannesburg, Pretoria, Middelburg and Transvaal, South Africa

August 12, 1964

Transvaal, South Africa

Dear Mother and Daddy

Now we are at the other Terre'Blanches, about a hundred miles away from where we were last week. It is the highest of the Transvaal provinces, strictly nothing but farming. This farm is 2,000 acres and milk and potatoes are their biggest crops. They also have a gorgeous swimming pool which is almost finished, and tennis courts.

Let me begin from when I last wrote you. Monday through Friday, we did just about the same thing. Took me two hours to wrap Bubba's drum, and when I took it to the post office they said it was too large so back to the farm and another two hours wrapping it again. I left it with Mrs. Terry to mail and gave her the money. I just pray they will accept it because I had my boots, a Bantu blanket, film to be developed, pamphlets, and some lovely native beads. The drum is just for Bubba.

On Friday we drove to get their son Chris at his boarding school (a Catholic one) and he spent the weekend at the farm with us. Gee, he was a lovely smart boy. One day we hitched to Pretoria to get Barbara's passport renewed. It is the capital of South Africa and only ½ hour away from Krugersdorp.

On Monday, August 10 Mrs. Terry put us on the road to Pretoria and a Jewish man took us to Pretoria, and it wouldn't have taken him five minutes to drive us out of the city's limits, but the so-and-so let us out right in the middle of the city, and boy, did we ever get stares. You just couldn't imagine all our stuff! Our packs which were so jammed we could hardly close them, we had to carry our coats, one medicine bag which is really heavy, an airlines bag with books and the iron, our two large Egyptian bags, cameras and our water canteen. I thought my heart was going to give way! It was too much to carry so we got right out in the middle of the main street and started thumbing. The Dutch Reformist locals couldn't believe their eyes. Hardly anyone spoke English. In time a man pulled over and gave us a lift half way to Middelburg, and then we got a ride with a man who bought us a milkshake and a box of candy. Then we got a ride with a young chap who let us off at the Commercial Hotel in Middelburg and they had been expecting us since August 6!

They called up the other Terre'Blanches and the mother who we had met in Cape Town picked us up in a 1964 Mercedes. The first day we just talked and took it easy, and that night we sat around the fire, and the son who has taken over the business of the farm asked us if we would speak at a Rotary Club meeting. We said yes, and in return, the Rotary Club all over the world will assist us if we need accommodation or anything else! They have a black crow that they tamed and it is about 13 inches high and it walks all around the yard – really crazy-looking!

The locals are from the bush. The unmarried girls wear colored things around their necks (sort of what a ploughing mule wears) with beaks all over it, and they never are allowed to take it off until they get married and then they get a larger one! Also, they wear the brass and copper anklets up to their knees, and they can hardly walk they are so heavy. When one of them is sick, the Terre'Blanches tell them that part of their machine needs fixing, so they think they are like the innings of a tractor. They are not allowed to be treated by a doctor (their witch doctor's orders) and so the Terrys often have to tell a little white lie for their own safety and health.

Ron is showing us so many things about farming and it is very interesting. He takes us around to all the different lands and explains the functions of the machines they use. This morning he took us to a coal mine and we were underground for an hour. There were lights and thousands of locals working there – Gee, I was so afraid it was going to cave in. We walked right to the end of it where we watched them blast. We were standing around a corner and when it went off I was so scared I grabbed a miner standing next to me! There is nothing but coal under the land and the superintendent of the mines said there was enough coal in this region to keep the whole world going for 200 years! It was really interesting, but I was very glad to see the light. We were so dirty we had to scrub and scrub and wash all our clothes when we came home.

Tonight, we are going to some of their neighbors' houses to see slides of the game reserve and different scenes of South Africa. Tomorrow a Jewish doctor is going to take us to one of the hospitals for the locals. Ron said the whole town couldn't believe what Barb and I have done and everyone has asked us to different things, so our social life is quite fun and different. Some of their friends are "proper Boers[24]" but still nice. Next Wednesday eight of us are going to the game reserve for eight days. I am so excited, I can hardly wait! I hate to think how much it is going to cost us. Oh well, we will never get a chance like this in a life time.

These people have been so nice to us and one of the things I like about South Africa is they have such crazy names! I will give this address

[24] The word Boer is Dutch for "husbandman," or "farmer". The Boers were South African of Dutch, German or Huguenot heritage, especially the early settlers of the Transvaal and Orange Free State. Today, descendants of the Boers are commonly referred to as Afrikaners.

as a return because we go to the reserve on August 19 and will be back here on August 27, and then go to Salisbury in South Rhodesia, so if you want to write me right away, send it here and I will just get it, and if I don't they will forward it to Salisbury.

Barbara's mother sent us to gorgeous sweaters she knitted herself and they are exactly alike. Also, Barbara's mother has gone a little weird, so don't pay any attention to her, she keeps telling Barb she has a booking for her to come home. She just won't get it out of her head that we aren't going home until we have seen Japan. In Salisbury we are going to try and get odd jobs for about two months because we are in the Southern Hemisphere winter and we are going into the Northern Hemisphere winter, which doesn't make sense, especially me hating the cold weather so much!

Please give my love to Jane and Harry and the children, and Bubba and Ticky. I can just imagine how boring Savannah is, but you must let me know how conditions are in the South since the Civil Rights Bill[25] has been passed. People ask me all the time and I never know what to say to them. I hope the family is going to pay for our expenses on the game reserve as it is very expensive but Barb and I feel it is only right to offer. I pray every night they will say no! I just don't know what to do about East Africa, it would hardly cost us anything to hitch to French Somaliland, but on the other hand I'm not exactly in the mood to lose my life. Also, Kenya is supposed to be the most gorgeous country in the whole of Africa, so would really hate to miss it. Everything will work out for the best as usual.

Please write soon. I love and miss you.

---

[25] The Civil Rights Act of 1964 was a landmark civil rights law that outlawed any form of discrimination based on race, color, religion, sex or origin. This includes prohibiting racial segregations in schools and other institutions. The act "remains one of the most significant legislative achievements in American history".

Kruger National Park, South Africa

August 20, 1964

Kruger National Park, South Africa

Dear Mother and Daddy,

We are now in Kruger National Park and do I have some interesting things to tell. First from my last letter, the whole week was spent in getting prepared for the trip here, and Barb and I spent a lot of time helping the locals put tiles on the floors of the swimming pool they are building. They have a river next to their house but it contains bilharzia[26] which is a terrible disease only a human can get and it comes from snails and it makes one crazy. Almost all the rivers in north South Africa have it. Our speech (to the Rotary Club) has been called off until September 8 but I really can't say if we will still be there. We are definitely going to spend a week there when we leave here and will probably leave on September 2.

Wednesday, August 19 were awakened by the local girls at 4.30 am with coffee and were on our way at 5 am. Still dark and cold, we were on our way in the 1964 Mercedes with Ron, Berrell and the two children in the other car. We went through the middle, high, and then the low veldt. It was really a gorgeous drive especially through the citrus section, but almost everything was destroyed by a heavy frost.

At 9 am we entered the park and the first thing we saw were impala (small bucks) and elephants – I just couldn't believe it. The park is exactly the same size as Israel – 50 miles by 250 miles. In the northern part it is closed in summer because of malaria and the tsetse fly. We traveled on and saw kudu [a type of antelope] which are 58" to 60" in height, weigh 650 lbs. and live 11 yrs. Gestation period is eight months. The record length of horns 21 1/2" which twist. Impala are height 34" to 38" weight 130 to 160 lb. and birth period six months. Looks something like deer. We drove up to a water hole and looked down and saw zebra and impala drinking. Gee, it was gorgeous. Everything here is dry because the rainy season hasn't arrived, but all in all we saw quite a lot on our first day.

---

[26] Bilharzia is caused by parasitic flatworms. Those who have been infected may experience liver and kidney damage as well as infertility. The disease is spread by contact with fresh water contaminated with the parasites, which are released from infected freshwater snails.

We reached our camp (Lower Sabie) about 2 pm and unpacked, ate and went out again. This time we came upon six lions who were sleeping in the sun. Apparently, they had just made a kill because a giraffe walked right by them and they weren't interested! Also saw vervet monkeys, chacma baboons and banana birds. They are small and all colors and their beaks look just like a banana. Also, we saw warthogs which are very short and dreadful-looking and a lot of different bucks and plenty of elephants. Gates close at 6 pm so we came home.

Our little modern hut faces the Sabie River and it is gorgeous and plenty of game. We take a bath at 6.30 in a commercial place, and sit and have drinks and listen to the native drums and the hippos playing in the Sabie River. There are thousands of gorgeous birds that make a lovely noise! This is the time I really wish y'all could be here. It is truly what I imagined Africa to look like. Went to bed at 7.30.

Thursday, August 20 We were awakened at 5.30 am by Mrs. Terry's sister Ginny calling us for coffee. At 5.45 we left, looking for leopards and lions. Early in the morning and late at night are the best times for them. Saw many elephants, a hippo crossing the road (which is very unusual!), crocodiles, lizards, storks, African buffalo and blue wildebeest. We got back at 11 and had breakfast and we were so tired we slept until 3 pm. Mrs Terry, Ginny, and Barb and I went to a water hole and saw six giraffes drinking (they put their legs wide apart to drink) along with baboons, impalas and warthogs. Ron went to a place right down the river from where we are in camp and went off road and watched a mother lion with three cubs. She made a kill and he saw it all. If the authorities caught him, he would be fined because you're not supposed to go off road. He is going to take us there Saturday! Also, I sit on the door of the car and take pictures while the car is moving – gee, if I fell! Tomorrow we are going on an all-day safari, and if I don't calm down I won't have any film left. In two days, I have taken 12 rolls of film, 36 slides. It is exactly as you would see in the movies. In a week's time it will be raining and all the water holes will be full and everything will green.

Friday, August 21 Saw three giraffe drinking and a gorgeous toucan with a gigantic red and black beak in the marsh. A herd of about 40 zebras were just coming down to drink when we left. We kept driving and didn't see much more and at 3 pm we reached a camp called

Skukuza and had tea and sandwiches and were on the road again back to our original camp. We then saw crocodiles, a hippo, and when we were turning a corner we ran into some wild dogs – five babies and the daddy. They were playing with each other and Daddy was very nervous because it was getting dark and the mother hadn't returned from her kill.

August 22 We got up at 7.00 am and cooked breakfast on a grill and were ready to leave at 8 am. It was a dreary day and at first I thought we were never going to see any game, but as we drove on at 15 mph, we finally ran into an elephant knocking over a tree to eat the roots. I got some fabulous pictures of it. We kept driving on not seeing one bloody thing except the usual giraffe, kudu, impala. We stopped at a little shack for tea and it was built around a gigantic tree called a sausage tree because it has fat, long grayish things hanging from what looks like string so looks exactly like a sausage – it really looks as if someone hung them up there! After that we went to an enormous natural water hole with swamps and I had just changed my film and took pictures. Now I don't know what all these numbers mean, but I would like the same film in Kodachrome instead of Ektachrome and the numbers will be different on the Kodachrome. I think it will be Kodachrome X, 36 exposures, color. So, could you please send me some for Xmas since I can't buy them in other countries. Really all I want is film. I will let you know in a little while where we will be at Xmas.

August 23 We were up at 5.30 with just coffee and were off at 6 am. We drove and saw three rhinos (white) but are really gray and were they fabulous. It's very rare to see them because there are only 77 in the whole reserve! Kept on driving looking for leopard and cheetah because they can run so fast and they don't kill the animal before they attack. They just tear meat off their prey and wait for it to bleed to death. Also, it is one of the rarest things to see in the park and people who have been coming here for years have never seen them. After that we didn't see too much so we came straight to the camp. We did about 160 miles in the day and when we got back I realized that my light reading was wrong so all the pictures I took at the water hole (which was 15) and after will not come out. I just cried when I realized it!

Went back to camp and had tea and went looking for cheetah and warthogs but were unsuccessful. On the way back to camp we decided to drive by the river again and lo and behold, in the bush was a gigantic Daddy lion. Was it every magnificent, I really couldn't believe my eyes! Everyone in the camp knows about it, and everyone will be packed on the road tomorrow waiting for it. About a year ago a hyena got into the camp and was roaming all around. The camp is only blocked off by a small wire and anything could come in here. A hyena bites anything it sees. I have found so many bugs in the bed, now I sleep with a scarf around me in early morning and in the evening. Didn't see too much more, but we went to a river where the hippos stay and were they funny to watch, shooting water in the air and splashing and making the craziest sounds. We then came back to the camp and had breakfast and went to watch Ron's secret place on the river where the mother lioness was with her three cubs. They had moved, but we could see bloodstains and fresh bones and horns of impala. We were sick, because we know if it was still their home, buzzards would have been in trees, since they always follow the lions. We left and went looking for crocodiles and just missed a lion making a kill!

⚬⊰●⊱⚬

Kruger National Park, South Africa

August 23, 1964

Kruger National Park, South Africa

Dear Mother and Daddy,

Today we awoke at 7 am to learn that a night adder (a very, very poisonous snake) was killed outside the ladies' room! It kind of shook me up. We saw buffalo and hippos in the Lower Sabie River and it was gorgeous. We went to a resting place called Tshokwane and had tea and watched the crazy banana birds eat. Then we went to the Orpen Dam and was it a fabulous view and so green. It was on a high plateau overlooking a valley. We say two crocs and one elephant. We didn't want to wait so we continued and came to another big drinking pool and there were zebra, warthogs – the clowns of the pack! Giraffe, gorgeous birds and impala all drinking. Gosh, it was beautiful. We kept driving, hoping for leopards, lions and cheetahs. We didn't see any but when we drove back to a water hole we were at before, a man said a lion had just passed by the water and we sat there awhile looking for it, and when we were turning a corner as we were looking at two elephants, a man just told us that his wife had just seen the lion springing for an impala and we just missed it! Gee, I felt sick. Anyway, the elephants were getting nervous and started flapping their ears so we beat it because when they do that it means they will charge and they have crushed many cars in the camp! Also, they knock down all the trees to eat the roots.

We drove on and lo and behold, in an opening we saw eight lions walking in single file. Gosh, was it fabulous. Also saw an ostrich, and herds of zebra and wildebeest and just at 5.20 we drove by the wire where the lions once were and we saw a gorgeous male lion on the rocks. This is the first male we have seen with a mane and we watched him for 10 minutes looking as if he was ruling over the land! He was magnificent. Went to camp and went to bed pretty early because we are going to another camp up north.

August 24 Got up at 5 am and had coffee and were on the road at 6. We saw seven lions 10 minutes after we had been on the road. Went to a gorgeous resting place and two locals said all the animals were going to the river to drink. The locals were making gorgeous spears out of the trees the elephants had knocked down, and were selling them for 35¢, but I will chance my luck in Rhodesia with them. We could see baboons charging across the gorgeous green valley and a slight wind was blowing and I never wanted to leave this spot. We drove on and on and things became greener and there was much more game. All in all, we drove 78 miles to Satara – a new camp – and I spotted four lions. Then suddenly, the zebras in the bush were charging and we could hardly keep up with them in the Mercedes and all of a sudden the wildebeest were charging and one went crazy and leaped right in front of the car and Mrs. Terry just missed it! Gee, was it exciting. Got to the camp and it was full of the thatched round huts like the locals live in. It is lovely and very clean. (Forgot to tell you, but at Lower Sabie I was taking a bath and heard this strange noise, and all of a sudden I felt boiling water on my back and the tank at the top was overfilled, and was being flooded and scorched and I ran out in the nude. Thank God no one was there!!)

The land up here is green because they have had rain up here. We had tea and then went on another run but the wind started blowing like mad and it became very dark and all the animals were in the shelters or wherever they stay in the bush, and so many of the natural water holes were dry. We decided to come back to camp. I had a migraine so I went to bed in Barb's and my hut. There is an umbrella tree here that is so large and they have tables and chairs underneath it. Will try and get a picture of it. Tomorrow we leave the reserve at noon and I am so sad because I love it, and know I shall never see it again. Right now Barb and I are in a tent and none of the damn sides meet and there are plenty of snakes and spiders around here for it is very hot. Also, the hyenas are known to get in this camp and we are next to the fence and there are two out there howling! God I'm so scared because they have the strongest jaws and can take a human limb off in a blink. I'm so nervous – I have a runny tummy and an old hair band is around my chin to keep my mouth shut from spiders!

Middelburg, South Africa

August 28, 1964

Middleburg, South Africa

Dear Mother and Daddy,

Received your letter when we came home from the game reserve. You are right when you say we really are lucky with the people we meet. Honestly, you just wouldn't believe how kind the Terrys have been to us. All together we have been living with them for three weeks, and they won't let us buy a thing. Not even candy for the children! They bought Barb and I lovely wallets made of impala fur in the reserve. Plus, they paid for our accommodation and everything else. Also, I went to the doctor here in Middleburg before the reserve about my stomach and Barb and I got free tetanus shots through Mrs. Terry. Barb and I went to town yesterday and bought each of them a present; it was the smallest thing we could have done for all their kindness. I would hate to think how much money they have spent on not one but two of us. So, will you do them a great favor? They cannot buy magazines like *House & Home*, *American Homes, McCall's, Ladies' Home Journal, Holiday,* etc. because they cost about $1.50 for one, so can y'all send them any of the magazines y'all get about a month after you get it and send it as old printed material and leave the ends unwrapped because it is cheaper when the ends are open. They love gardening and they are building a new house and want a lot of American ideas. Honestly this would mean so much to them.

Ron is giving us a letter from the Rotary Club since he is Secretary and if we ever need anything we just go to Rotarians in any country and they will look after us. Beryl, Ron's wife, likes *McCall's* best. By the way, our speech at the Rotary luncheon was called off because they had someone else before us, and it is planned for September 8, and Barb and I are leaving on Mon 7, so we won't be able to give it. They have given us the names of some swinging people in Salisbury, who they are sure will give Barb and I a job for three months!

Another favor to ask of you! Mrs. Terre'Blanche and Beryl have written a child's story about a little local boy and all his animal friends. I typed four copies of it for them to send to agents and it is adorable. Any child would just love it. Now the thing is they don't have any ideas how to get in touch with U.S. publishers, so if you have any ideas, please write them and also look in the front of some children's book and get the name of some publishers, and send it to them. Mrs. Terry is going to drive us 100 miles to Pretoria so we can get a decent ride to Salisbury. They are lovely people.

Tuesday, August 25 Was this ever our lucky day! The weather was beautiful and we saw three majestic-looking lionesses and one lion on a kill, a leopard on the kill, and just missed another kill but saw the blood in the river. We think it was a crocodile that got a waterbuck. A herd of about 400 buffalo, tsessebe [another type of antelope], and a jackal with two cubs. That was the most wonderful day we have ever had!

That night we heard the hyenas howling next to the fence and we on the other side of the fence, and God was I scared. Didn't sleep all night and had to go to the bathroom but was too afraid to get out of bed for fear of stepping on a snake. Our tent had a large hole in one of the flaps so Barb and I put a table and four benches in front of it and filled a pot with water to throw on a hyena if one got in. We had heard last year the gates had been open and a hyena walked in and dragged a little boy out of his tent and ate his leg. Also, we knew they have the strongest bite of any animal; one bite and the limb is off.

Everyone but me heard a lion roar that night. At the lion kill, the jackals kept trying to steal the meat and the lions kept shoving them away, and there were thousands of vultures around the place. Barb, the fool, got out of our car and ran to Beryl's car to get the binoculars! The lion got up and she ran back to our car – my heart was pumping! Ron was standing on the door looking over the top of the car and the lion had just had enough and started growling. Later, Beryl stopped at a dry river bank and went in to the bushes, and brought out a large piece of wood from the tamboti tree which smells gorgeous when it is burning. We couldn't believe it when we looked back and saw her doing that, because we were right in the middle of leopard country and she didn't even think of looking in the trees! Later we learnt that the leopard had made its kill close to where she had picked up the log.

Wednesday, August 26 Were up at 5 and packed and on the road at 6 am. We drove in the park until 12, and we were all kooky from exhaustion. I really hated to leave, but was exhausted from riding and looking every minute. The ride back to Middelburg was through the mountains and was it gorgeous. The tallest, Mount Anderson, is 60,050ft. above sea level, and on a clear day one can see Portuguese East Africa. The trees were not green but looked like a gold and rusty velvet. In certain places there were man-made forests, and the highway was fabulous. Arrived home just at dark and the pool was almost finished. We were so exhausted we went to bed without a bath.

Thursday, August 27 Were all up late and just relaxed around the house and washed everything. Our hair was so dirty, that brown clay clogged up the sink.

Friday, August 28 Got up at 7 and went to town with Mrs. Terry, and bought them gift and got our shots as mentioned. Came home and read the rest of the day about North Rhodesia[27] in the olden days. Went to bed at 8.

---

[27] North Rhodesia gained independence and became Zambia in 1964.

Saturday, August 29 The pool is being filled today but I'm afraid it won't be finished by Monday because it takes 3,500 gallons and is being filled by two garden hoses! Took pictures of the locals doing their washing, I know you just won't believe it – rituals handed down over the generations. We were fussed at for buying them presents. All in all, we saw 33 lions. Will write again from Salisbury. Keep writing me and please don't send any more money. It makes me feel terrible. Tell me the things you would like and I will get them. Also, for my birthday please send me by sea mail Kodachrome X, color, 36 exposures. Will let you know later where to send them. When you receive my slides please put glass frames on them like the cardboard, because this will protect them from the light and heat of the viewer, and they will last much longer. Also, I don't want any of them bent so be very careful and don't touch them with your fingers because it ruins them.

South Africa/Rhodesia

Pretoria, South Africa, then Messina, then Limpopo River, then Salisbury, Rhodesia

September 4, 1964

Salisbury[28], Rhodesia

Dear Family,

When we left the Terrys on Monday we got a ride to Pretoria and from there we got a lift to a small town. The man treated us to dinner and then we met Rommel's[29] personal chief! We also saw a 'family of trees' (apparently the only ones in the world) – it starts with one and when the larger branches touch the ground they start new trees – about 10 of them! Then we got a ride with a Boer and he gave us a ride to a small town and it was an hour from dark when he dropped us. Got a ride with another man who he let us off nine miles from the Rhodesian border in

---

[28] Salisbury was the capital of Rhodesia. When Rhodesia became Zimbabwe, the city was renamed Harare.
[29] Erwin Rommel, known as the Desert Fox, was a German Field Marshall and Tank Commander who commanded the 7th Panzer Division in World War II.

a town called Messina and we spent the night on the floor in one of the cells as there were no beds. I didn't sleep a wink because we killed two gigantic spiders and there were mosquitos and this is a malaria area. It was the worst night I have ever had and my back really suffered.

September 1 Got up at 6 and took a shower and went to thank the police who told us the inspector's wife had made two beds up for us in their house but when they came to get us, we were asleep! She had prepared a breakfast for us so we went. God, was she ever a religious fanatic and when we left she gave us all the religious jazz to read and said a prayer for us that lasted 10 minutes. I've never been so glad to get out of one place.

The Transvaal was so dry for all the way up and they have started cutting the water supply down because they haven't had rain for five years! Had to walk about three blocks to the highway and people couldn't believe us. It's pretty bad when even the locals stare! No traffic at all and what little there was were filled. After about ½ hour of sitting, an old man stopped and took us to the border and we went straight through because he goes across the border every day. We crossed the large river called the Limpopo which is the border line of the two countries, and it was completely dry. It's getting serious, all the rivers have dried up.

At the Rhodesia border, a large British flag was flying and we had to declare how much money we had. I said $900 and he didn't believe me because we were hitching. He made me show him and since they were at the bottom of my pack I had to take everything out. I was really embarrassed because the place was packed. But thank God, he didn't count it because I lied! Finally got through and sat for an hour next to the customs house. Then a South African boy picked us up – he was a proper Boer and his English was dreadful. Had to put up with his silliness all the way to Salisbury. The roads in Rhodesia are terrible and, in some spots, they look like country roads – we saw a giraffe and there were road signs warning about elephants crossing. The trees and flowers are coming out for summer and they are the colors of autumn. I thought they had been burnt in the heat and lack of water, but not. It was 450 miles from the border to Salisbury and we only went through two country towns. Arrived here about 4 pm.

Barb called up Mr. and Mrs. Welch, people she met in Cape Town, and they came and picked us up. We have been staying with them and they terribly sweet and kind to us. They live six miles out of town and they drive us everywhere we want to go. The father has only one leg and the mother has to work, but they have two cars and two men servants. They love us being there and were very disappointed when we told them we were moving into a flat on Monday.

Mr. Welch dropped us off at one of the tobacco auctions and we were the only females there and Barb couldn't believe how fast they talked. I have never seen so many good-looking men, and rich too! The largest things here in South Rhodesia are tobacco, diamonds, gold and emeralds. 50 cigarettes cost 40¢. There is a shortage of women here, thank goodness. We were getting embarrassed at all the men staring at us so we left and stayed in the road and hitched to town. Two men picked us up and took us to their firm for coffee and then took us to the American Consulate. There were several letters for me and a parcel of dried meat and fruit from Cape Town. Also, a letter from the German boy who wrote y'all and he said he received a lovely letter from you and to thank you for him. We were interviewed for the TV the second night we were here and I was so nervous that I got a twitch in my jaw and couldn't speak and so Barb did all the talking.

We are looking for jobs – the pay is very good. I am being interviewed today for a job that will take me to Northern Rhodesia twice a week, so I will get to see the country with expenses paid. Gosh, I hope I get it. The government sponsor a sweepstake – one ticket cost $1.40 and the prize is $60,000 so if I win I'll send the two of you on a world tour, first class! Bubba's drum has been sent. Received a letter from you mother which Mr. White was holding. Glad my things are arriving. All together you should receive seven parcels plus Bubba's drum which has film in it, and blanket for me. The mugs you received were pewter. The locals here have rights and make the same salary and Southern Rhodesia is fed up and are is trying to get their independence from England. However, England won't allow it unless Southern put in a black government which Southern Rhodesia refuses to do[30]. By the way please don't send me any film because if I work here I won't need it and I still have 14 rolls left.

---

[30] Southern Rhodesia, in contrast to Northern Rhodesia, wanted a white government, and most of its white population was strongly opposed to the introduction of black majority rule.

This city is gorgeous and one of the cleanest cities I've ever been in. Think we will like it but one can never tell at once. I'm so excited about Daddy's invention [Callan's father, Eustace, had his own construction engineering business so perhaps the invention was something to do with the business?]. Hope everything works out alright. I'm having a ball, so don't worry. Things are cheaper here than South Africa. I really like this place.

⊸⦿⊷

Rhodesia

Salisbury

September 16, 1964

Salisbury, Rhodesia

Dear Mother and Daddy

Well I finally got a job with a timber company as secretary for the Sales Manager for Rhodesia. Pretty good, ah? My salary is £50 per month ($140). My boss is English, but went to school in Vancouver, and is more efficient than most English! He wanted someone with shorthand, but since I'm too daft, he writes out each letter for me putting in commas, and all I have to do is copy. I guess he felt sorry for me so I got the job. Plus, it is quite an experience. The only thing is I have to order wood, and I don't know if 1/8 is larger or smaller than 3/16, and everything deals in these figures. I started working last Monday, and as usual I didn't report to the government telling them that I wanted to work here, and did I ever get into trouble! For five hours I tried to straighten it out, and finally I was sent to the Head of Immigration and he got in touch with the Minister of Labor, and they gave me a temporary permit to work until my case is brought up before some board which is tomorrow. Gee, I'm really scared they will get nasty about it. Thank God I'm not English, because they're not the most popular people here at the moment.

Barbara is working for the government, but she won't get in trouble like I did, because they need her. I think I am meant to have a police certificate for the last five years, but they will also bring that up at the meeting. Since I have been away from the States for two and a half years, I might not have to have it. So, if you receive a letter from the government asking for one, immediately get in touch with the police and ask them for one, and send it immediately to the return address they give.

Our flat is really cute. Nice bathroom (first time since home that I've had my own bathroom!). Boy, is it ever nice. Small kitchen with small fridge, stove and cupboard space, bedroom the size of Daddy's den and it is furnished and serviced every day, so we don't have to do anything except cook and wash the dishes. We pay $18 apiece per month. That also includes four sheets, two pillow cases, blankets (not that we need them), four large blue towels, bathmat and two dish towels. Barb and I have four dresses between us, but they have to do, because clothes are more expensive than Cape Town, and they are terrible looking.

I have been going out every night since we moved into the flat, but I must stop it, because I'm dead at work. Have met some really fabulous people, and the men are gorgeous and kind. We were taken to the agricultural show last Saturday at 12, and saw high-jumping on horseback. Gee, it was really fabulous with their hunting jackets on. After that we went into a crazy pub and met up with some girls we met when we first arrived, and they introduced us to a lot of men. Stayed till 12 pm. One of them, Lee, was a U.S. college student who is working for the government and he is checking up on bilharzia in all the lakes and rivers – that's the germ that is carried by snails, like I mentioned when we were in South Africa. All the water here has it and people go swimming, but it is dangerous. The only way they can get rid of it, is if people don't use the water for three months, but that's impossible, because most of the locals wash their clothes in it so I won't go near it. I'm dating a medical rep and he's always buying me presents, taking me out to dinner etc. He's really sweet, but I'm not interested in him. He looks like Prince Philip and has an Australian accent.

I'm afraid to tell you my bad news. A week ago I was eating some biltong and it was so dry I had to really pull at it and my left front capped tooth came out. I cried for an hour. Went to the dentist the next morning and he put the same cap back on with a long, thick solid gold spike, and you just won't believe where South Rhodesia gets their gold – the States! So I paid only $11 but it looks like hell. It was put back the wrong way and is really obvious. Look like I need braces again. Glad I wasn't in some crazy country where they don't have a clue about teeth. This Australian chap is going to the Congo on Sunday, so I will get him to get the rest of Bubba's things.

Honestly Mom, I just don't know what to do about Xmas presents. I feel so badly but I just can't buy for five children. The only things I can see that are really cheap in this country are emeralds. Was thinking of getting you some pierced earrings, but they don't sell them. For God sake, don't send me any film. I'm trying to get rid of what I have because they have to be developed before May 1965, and I have two more rolls left. And since we are going to stay here six months, I could never use them up.

Salisbury is really pretty, but terribly small, about half the size as Savannah. All in all, you should receive parcels from me, including an insured suitcase. Hope you like the pewter mugs. Hang them in the kitchen, and when I get home, if ever, we can put the country and date of each Xmas I was in. The money I make here will get me home. Will save $75 a month. The locals here are really cheeky. They sit on the sidewalks and make nasty signs and sounds as you walk by. They call themselves "African Gentlemen".

In South Africa, if a local even made a pass at a white girl, he would be imprisoned. The funny thing is the South African locals have more respect than the locals here. Mr. Smith[31] the Prime Minister (I think) has just come back from London trying to get independence, but with no luck. Everyone here is really bitter about the whole situation and I really can't blame them. England only gives independence to black controlled countries. Apparently, in Nyasaland[32] the people have to bow with their heads touching the street when the new black president drives by. In North Rhodesia, all cars have to stop when theirs drives past. Southern Rhodesia will take her independence, but if she does, no Commonwealth country is allowed to trade with her, so the only country who will be willing to help her is South Africa. The locals put up blockades and then

[31] Ian Smith was a white Rhodesian who was Prime Minister 1964-1979.
[32] Now known as Malawi

stone cars every night on different roads and highways. Several people have been killed. Also, a lot of bombs have gone off. I keep forgetting about all this and often walk in the dark, but won't from now on. You never see someone like me walking at night time and if a police car sees you, they pick you up and give you hell. Some of the locals hold quite important positions and get the same salary as their white colleagues. Barb's boss is a "kaffir" and he represents South Rhodesia at all the Afro-Asian meetings because he is black. She knows so much about what is going on, and was sworn not to tell. If she does and gets caught, it is 10 years in jail, even though she is a Canadian citizen! If she makes a mistake on paper, it goes through a machine that completely destroys the paper. I would have got a job there, but I got this one first.

Give my love to all, and let me know what you would like for Xmas. Remember it takes longer for anything to reach here because South Rhodesia is inland. Let me hear from you soon. Love and miss you.

——— ∞ε⅜ε∞ ———

Salisbury and the Sinoia Caves[33], Rhodesia

September 21, 1964

Salisbury, South Rhodesia

Dear Mother and Daddy,

Just received the letter of August 20 which was returned for more postage. Glad all my boxes have arrived. All together there should be seven, including the one mailed from Johannesburg with a brown and white blanket in it with the drum, which you shall be receiving any day now. The striped blanket is a Mexican one, and smells like hell. Glad to hear Savannah didn't get much of the hurricane, I was very worried about it. The straw hat is a Transkei hat. Crazy, ah! Yes, there are two blankets. Mother, I can't remember sending any silver bracelet so please give me a clue as to what it looks like. The only one I can remember is a copper one with a black design that should have been in one of the boxes. Did you ever receive the six pewter mugs?

[33] Now known as the Chinhoyi Caves.

Mother, it was very kind of you to ask Iris Terry if they would like the mags. I'm sure they would but it was Sandy Terry and the family who really wanted them. By the way the two families hate each other, so in writing them try not to mention the other! I don't think a can opener would do although it would be quite unusual, but the current is different than the States, and the plugs. They couldn't use it. Nice thought though. I'm sure the magazines are all they want, because both families are rich as the devil. I know they will love Bennie Candy and cookies. You must write on it "Cookies" because they call them biscuits. Sorry my letters are so messy, but you are supposed to open the letters straight down the middle with a knife! I will write to Mrs. Frame next week. She really was good to me.

Stop worrying, I had my film (the one I thought was ruined of Kruger) and they are fabulous! What a lovely letter Mrs. Terry (Iris) sent you. They really were good to us, and they did like our company. We could cut cheese in front of them, which we do all the time. For God sake, don't send any film as I'm trying to get rid of the 12 rolls I have left. I have got some Watusi prints done by hand for you, and will get more. I know the Gullings [family friends] will love the *Reader's Digest*. I am also sending them a present. I don't think they take it. Hope not anyway. If you don't write so large, you can write quite a lot on the airgrams. Please again no film but will let you know if I need any about a month before we travel again.

My job is really difficult. You know I never was good in math, well this all deals with fractions! Gosh I don't know if I am coming or going. Hope I don't get fired. Barb took a typing test for the government on Saturday and she had to type 40 words a minute, and she would get £50, but she only typed 38, and now she is getting £12 less a month, so I am making $33.60 more than she a month. Shame, but for the first time I am making more than she is. Right now, Barb is cooking liver, peas, carrots for supper, and I wash up. We eat darn good and still drink a lot of milk. I have to be at work at 8 and get up at 6 and walk to work at 7.30, and I make it. We're quite content here in our little flat. We have two portable radios (wireless) as they call it.

I have met a chap of 32 who works for a Swiss Medical firm. His name is Tony and he is Australian, tall 6'4", blonde hair, dark blue eyes, and a gorgeous smile. Honestly, he is so good to both of us. Every morning he picks me up at 7.30 and takes me to breakfast and then to work, and then picks me up for work at 4.30. I have gone out with him every night to eat and he is ever a dear to me. He buys me anything I want, plus we get all our medicines free, and make-up. He has gone to the Congo and Northern Rhodesia for six weeks and he is getting me all the things for Bubba, and I know he isn't going to make me pay him back! I know 32 seems quite old, but don't forget I'm not a little girl anymore. 25 is getting pretty old, you know. From what I can see everyone seems to have the greatest respect for him including doctors. It has been a long time since I have been able to talk to a man sensibly, instead of "micky-mousing" around with all the bloody juveniles.

On Sunday, he drove Barb and me to a place 77 miles out of Salisbury called the Sinoia Caves. It was marvellous. We walked into a gigantic hole in the ground and it looked like something you would see in the movie of *Aladdin and the Lamp*. We walked down winding stairs made out of rock and stalactites were hanging from the ceiling, and in the distance as you went deeper was the most gorgeous reflection of blue from water. All of a sudden we came to a clearing with the sky for a roof, and inky blue water that was perfectly still. Man has not touched this place, except to put steps in it. They can't figure why the water hasn't evaporated. Many animals have fallen in it as it is a gigantic hole in the ground. It has straight stone walls and lovely birds live in this cave – I must take some pictures of it.

Mr. White is a lawyer of about 60 who I met in Cape Town. We are planning on staying here six months since this is the last place we can make money, so we are taking advantage of it. Want to save enough to get to Hawaii and home, and can do it. The other night, Tony took Barb and me to a Chinese restaurant and when he brought us back home, there was a gigantic black spider on the wall. It was the largest and blackest we have seen yet! Barb and I started screaming – this was 2 am! – and the landlady came tearing up stairs to find out who was attacking us, and we told her it was a spider. Tony killed it and it landed on Barb's pillow! We had nightmares about it, thinking its mate was around.

We have just been told that all clothes, especially underclothes, must be ironed, because there are bugs that live off of them, and they lay eggs in the clothes, and if they get on your skin, you can get worms. Also, Barb and I have a dreadful rash on both of our feet from going barefoot. The locals have it, and you can pick it up even if you wear sandals. Honestly, one has to be so alert – the spiders and snakes in the place are shocking! In about two weeks, we have to start taking anti-malaria pills all through the summer, and Barb and I are going to get anti-snake bite kit and learn how to give injections. All the trees are coming out in their gorgeous purple blossoms and it is as ever gorgeous. Clothes are terribly expensive here and it is junk.

Will write again next week to let you know if I have won the sweepstakes. Lots of luck. Y'all can have 15 thousand if I do, or more. Let me know about the children. You never talk about them and since my sister and brother aren't great with corresponding I have given up! I don't even know Jane's last baby's name!

Daddy, why don't you say hello sometime? It doesn't take much effort.

Salisbury, Rhodesia

September 29, 1964

Salisbury, South Rhodesia

Dear Mother,

Just received your letter of September 25, and honestly I just about had kittens over it and the previous one! Mother, both Terre'Blanche families have more money than our whole family could ever spend. I just about hit the roof when you said you spent 24 dollars on mags. Christ, you could have bought something for the house! In the first place I said they had to be a month old so that when customs open them up (which they will do) they will be classified as "used reading material". Now they will have to pay customs on them which will be the exact price they pay for them in S. Africa. I don't care what the Americans say about them not having to pay customs, because they will. Remember I have lived here, not the people you enquired from.

Secondly, I was just mentioning the magazines they liked the best, because I knew you subscribed to some of them, and if you didn't, one of those magazines would do. I mentioned one year's subscription to one would have been enough. That is really all they need. Can't you cancel the order? I know your heart was in the right place, but as far as Iris Terry is concerned, just send her some old mags too. Mother, they have to pay taxes on everything that comes into South Africa, although they wouldn't have the heart to tell you. For God's sake, don't send the books – 8 bucks for one book is absurd.

Have you written to publishing companies for Sandy Terre'Blanche? They really will appreciate it. When we left we bought 20 dollars' worth of nice presents for them, in return for them taking us to the game reserve. Please Mother don't send anything other than old magazines. Take back the powder. I'm just sick at the money you're spending. We have repaid all of them back. The only reason I ever mentioned anything was they asked if you could send old magazines because each one cost 1.00 apiece, and they liked them. I just can't say it enough, please don't send them anything else such as cigs. They would have to pay a bomb to customs, and they are cheaper and better in South Africa. The powder they will have to pay customs for. It is rubbish that the bloody post office doesn't know what they're talking about!

I had to pay taxes on some of my clothes when I emigrated to South Africa and they were my personal things which I needed. How in the hell can they know all this? Remember the cigarettes you sent me in England? The post office said I wouldn't have to pay customs, and yet when they arrived, customs wanted 23 dollars! What you haven't yet sent, take back to the shop and get your money back. Please don't send me any cigs either. I also would have to pay a bomb. Cigs here are 15 cents for 20, and I hate U.S. cigs now.

I'm sure the Gullings will love *Readers' Digest*. Now that was a good gift, and I thank you for it. Also, no food is allowed into these countries. They have very strict rules. So Mother, once again, everything you have bought and haven't sent, take back. Cancel the subscription on the magazines. Find out if they were sent a letter telling them that they have a year's sub. If they have, I guess you can't cancel it. Mother, this is why I love you so much because you have such a good heart, but please do as I ask. We have repaid them. Remember the post office doesn't have a clue about customs in other countries. Sorry to have upset you, but I just wanted to throw up when I thought of all the money you had spent.

Now to more pleasant things. I have written Jane a long letter and one to Bubba. Tony will be back October 10 with Bubba's things. I can't wait to send them to him. I am really fond of Tony, and is he ever so sweet to me. I guess he felt so sorry for me the way I dress (I have two dresses!) that he bought me a gorgeous skirt for 12 dollars. He is in the Congo now, and he called me long-distance Saturday to wish me happy birthday. Gee, it made me feel great. Barb bought me a cute nightgown, because I was sleeping in my slip. Still trying to get an emerald out of him!!

Thanks a million for looking after the children for Xmas for me. Now what would you like for Xmas? Copper is cheap here, and if you would like some copper mugs like the pewter except different shapes, let me know, or would you like pewter again? Did you like the ones I sent? Please find out from Jane what they would like, and if Bubba would like some more African things or mugs. Please let me know very soon because it will take longer from here for parcels to arrive there than South Africa. I have already started shopping, so let me know soon.

Glad you liked the statue. Did it have the history of the statue with it? If you don't know what to do with all the African jazz, I will lend it to Bubba if he wants to borrow it for his room. The drum should be arriving any day now, so look carefully inside it because it contains film etc. How many boxes from South Africa have arrived? I've lost count. There should be seven in all. I am dying to read *Uhuru*[34], but I'm afraid it will put me off. Do you know what that word means? "Freedom". It is pronounced *Ouhooroo* with a roll on the R. Tell Roz Frame I really appreciate it, and I shall be writing her soon. I'm very tired so I shall close. Give my love to Daddy.

---

[34] *Uhuru* by Robert Ruark, published in 1962. Ruark was an American journalist who took a year out in Africa. Uhuru was a bestseller.

Salisbury, Rhodesia

October 13, 1964

Salisbury, South Rhodesia

Dear Mother and Daddy,

Thanks ever for the birthday card. I really did laugh over it. Mother, a can opener to screw on the wall would be fine, but if you do send it, send it to Sandy Terre'Blanche (Mrs.). Bubba and you shall get plenty of Watusi prints, although they are quite commercialized now. God no they don't have unusual material in Salisbury. All comes from England and the States, and costs a bomb. This talk does not drive me batty, it makes me feel good that y'all are interested. I didn't win the sweepstakes but they have them every month. Hate to ask this, but what is the name of Jane's last child? I'm having a hell of a problem with my teeth, but this is one thing I'm not going to save on. I don't care how much it cost, they're all going to be filled. Honestly, Bubba really makes me laugh. His letter was so funny, and the remark you made about him not writing on the back of paper really made me laugh.

Now here goes to answer Bubba's letter. I wrote him that Tony was going to Elizabethville in the Congo to get him everything he needed for his room, but the poor thing was stoned by some dreadful locals 15 miles from the Northern Rhodesian border, and was really shook up. The only thing that saved him was a Land Rover police car patrolling the area, and the tribe ran when they saw it coming. He immediately turned around, and swore never to go to that country again. I am ashamed that I laughed when he told me this – he was almost killed! So I have to do the looking and buying myself, which makes it difficult, but I can manage if I take my time.

Right now, I have about five local boys looking out for me, but of course they want a commission for it, but will still be half the price as the stores. One of the boys, called Good Luck, just came in with some things he made by hand. A lamp 10" high and 6" wide (across the bottom) with a mother elephant and baby made out of gorgeous pine, and they both have real ivory tusks. I went wild when I saw it. The only problem is that the plug doesn't fit U.S. plugs, but Bubba can figure that one out. I suggest a tall thin, white lampshade. It would look gorgeous. The price was $3.15.

Good Luck also bought a boat 11" long with two locals in it, all of wood, price $1.40, and a lovely bowl with a handle 70¢. He is coming back next week with more things and I can't wait. All is made by hand, and the work is five times prettier than the large statue I sent. By the way you keep saying "circumcision", but if I'm not mistaken, the man is supposed to have a drum between his legs and he is playing it. Hope they haven't sent the wrong statue!

Will get Bubba everything he wants, also I got him artefacts that have a cork on them to fit on top of whiskey bottles. Also, a copper bottle opener with a woman's head on it. That would be really super for a bar. Will go to the expense of having my film developed, because I have heard reports that they have a habit of bending film or prints out of shape in the States, but here there is less of a chance because there it all looks normal to the locals. I will make Tony pay for them. I had one roll of Kruger developed, and was it ever fabulous.

Mother, I felt like crying when I received the check from Bubba. By the way thank you very much for yours, but you mustn't, I feel very guilty, especially when y'all go without things. When y'all get loaded then you can send the odd little check. Does Bubba live in Ridgewood? God, I hope not. Tell Bubba I shall do more than my best about getting him things, and the 25 he gave to me I shall save and buy him things when I am in another country. The things that I would want to buy him if I had the money! Can't believe Daddy has finally broken down and going to buy a new car. Hurry and get rich, because I want a brand-new car to pick me up from the airport when I return from my world trip. Gee, one would think I was going first class.

I've been thinking it over, and Daddy, I think you should take up golf. You would look super in your Bermuda shorts, swinging those clubs. Why don't you think about it? Would do you the world of good. Sitting here thinking I have been halfway round the world, and this being our last working place, I am getting kind of excited about arriving home. What I was thinking about, is if Jane and Harry still live in Atlanta, we could go there and y'all could drive up there and bring us to Savannah, or we will fly in – probably hitch to Charlotte N.C. and fly from there to

Savannah, but I want the Pinkney clan waiting on me at the airport and I mean all the children too.

Mother, Mrs. Brimacombe (Barbara's mother) is driving her up the wall. Each letter she receives her mother has booked her on a ship! She just can't seem to understand that we don't want to come home yet. Shame, she said they are so tired of writing letters, and want their little girl home. Now Mother, don't start conspiring with her cause it will just provoke me too, now see. I am still hoping for the sweepstakes, and boy if I win, y'all will go to Europe, and then fly out to deep Africa to see me. This I promise, so here's hoping. I'm getting pretty good at writing, don't you think?

Oh, by the way clothes are so expensive here, that I as a result have had to learn to sew. Barb is trying to teach me, and loses her temper about four times a night! She can't understand how someone could sew the top and bottom of one side together instead of the front and back together. Tony bought me a pair of Italian sandals, they're super. Is Bubba happy and why is he working for Hugh Armstrong[35]?

If Bubba would like another drum completely different from his current one I will get it, but I don't know if he would like two. Mother, I hope you are keeping all my things together. Somewhere in my blue suitcase there is a small, and I mean really small, bead. It looks like a bean, and is brownish red with a tiny white cap. It is so small that one could easily miss it. If you take off the tiny white cap, there is an ivory elephant inside, but you have to turn it upside down and the elephant will fall out. I hope you have found this, because this is my most prized possession. Did you find all seven rings? Isn't the large brown and green one gorgeous?! The greenish blue stone is called spinel – just for kicks take them to Desbullions[36] and ask them how much they cost, if they were bought in Savannah. Mother, please let me know what you would like for Xmas and Jane and Harry. Time is running out. Must go now, my boss thought I was typing a letter for him and was cheesed off when he found out I wasn't!

⸺⊶⧉⊷⸺

[35] PIER Commercial Real Estate Brokerage, LLC, a commercial real estate firm based in Savannah, was formed in September 2013. Originally founded in 1954 as Hugh Armstrong Real Estate Company by Hugh Armstrong Sr, the company constructed many properties in Savannah.
[36] An old Savannah family jewelry store.

Salisbury, Rhodesia

November 4, 1964

Salisbury, South Rhodesia

Dear Mother and Daddy,

Thanks ever so much for the long letter from everyone. Honestly Mother, you are a great one for getting things mixed up. Was quite nice hearing from Daddy, although it was quite sarcastic. Now Mother, don't cause any embarrassment on Terry's part. Just write and ask if they have had to pay any import tax, and if they have, cancel their order, and send them your mags. One month old, see. And from now on, don't listen to the post office concerning other countries.

You haven't said anything about my gorgeous handbags. Spent almost $100 on them! Don't undermine Daddy. Bought $30 worth of things for Ruby, and I'm going to the bloody post office at lunch to see how much they will allow me to send. Will be quite expensive because they are railed to Mozambique. Please Mother, tell me how many films you had developed – slides, I mean. I had pictures of local "in the raw" in the drum that I sent Bubba. Let me know. I don't know if I can get a carving of a berry with an elephant inside. Different tribes do different things, and the people who made this are in the Cape, not Rhodesia. Paid 35 cents for it. Pure ivory! I will try though. The necklace in the box where the bean was is for Ticky. Black and gold, from Spain, please give it to her.

I am getting along very well with sewing, on my second dress now. Can't believe y'all are getting a new car. How old is the other one – 10 years old? Mrs. Brimacombe is nutty, don't pay any attention to her. The absentee ballot came too late, so I couldn't vote. Just sick Goldwater[37] didn't win. It is not called Southern Rhodesia anymore, just Rhodesia, since North Rhodesia became Zambia. I received a $50 cheque from Bubba in your last letter, so all-together I have $125 of his. Bubba –if they didn't cut spears in half, they would have to be sent through a shipping company which the minimum is $28. They are too long to be

---

[37] Barry Goldwater (1909-1998) was an American politician who served as a U.S. senator and was the Republican Party's nominee for president in the 1964 U.S. election. He had a large conservative constituency but was beaten in the election by the incumbent Democratic president Lyndon B. Johnson by a landslide.

sent through post office! Sorry about that, but glue them together and put them back on shield, crossed. What is Bubba talking about when he says send him some small fur shields like I sent you, Mother? I can't remember. There is no such thing as "African" furniture. The locals sit on the ground in their huts. They use straw mats, which I could send you. The blankets came from South Africa, but when the Terrys get back from Japan, I could ask her to get you two and send them to you and I shall send her the money. Have several Watusi pictures for you, and many other things. Thanks for the additional $10 – $125 is more than enough. Maybe I can get you some local material, but most of the stores get their things from England. The only problem is everything I am buying for Bubba I also want!

Daddy, you're being very cheeky with me these days. Thanks very much for the $50. Just to make you not worry, I shall use it for buses through the rest of Africa. Daddy, I am not doing this to impress anyone! One cannot learn and see a country through a hotel window, or on a boat. I hate staying in places for a long time. The happiest time of my life are when I'm on the road in a foreign country not knowing if I shall eat or sleep that night. I know it is very hard to understand, but I always have been different, and at least I think I know my own mind now. Believe me, I wouldn't change it for anything in the world. I didn't win the sweepstakes, but will bet on it each month I am here. The only thing is I don't like to tell you everything because I know you will worry, but God protects the fools! So glad you sold the Sylvan Terrace house, I always wondered about that. What does 31405 mean on all y'all's letters? [Zip codes were introduced to the U.S. postal system on July 1, 1963.]

Your airgraph letter just arrived. Rhodesia is really up in arms with England. I don't know if y'all have been getting the news, but the Communists have really been telling some lies, and Zambia is printing the most dreadful lies too. I can tell you haven't been getting the right information. There were 800 chiefs at Domboshawa[38] which is 25 miles from Salisbury. No one was allowed to join, not even the Prime Minister. They have always represented their people, and what they say

[38] The UK government told Prime Minister Ian Smith that a positive result at national *indaba* (tibal conference) would not be recognized by Britain as representative of the people, but Smith pressed on, telling parliament that he would ask the tribal chiefs and headmen "to consult their people in the traditional manner". On October 22, 1964, 800 chiefs and headmen from across the country gathered at Domboshawa. Smith hoped that Britain, having taken part in such indabas in the past, might send a delegation at the last minute, but none arrived, much to his annoyance.

goes, and they voted for independence under the constitution of a white government, but England wouldn't even listen. I think Rhodesia will declare its independence, but none of the Commonwealth countries will have anything to do with her. England has said that all Rhodesians will lose their British citizenship (all countries belonging to the Commonwealth are English citizens) – well, the answer here is, "So, who wants to be a citizen of a third-rate country?"

The U.S. has been keeping all eyes open here, and the people are now anti-American because America is backing England, and the people want to know who in the hell do we think we are! No Mother, they don't have harems. Harem is an Arab word, and only used in Muslim countries. *Something of Value*[39] will scare the life out of you, Mother. It's about the Mau Mau[40]. I read it six years ago. Just asked Bengie, one of the local boys who works here, how many locals are in Rhodesia and he said four million. I think there are around 160,000 whites.

Just went to a Curio shop and ordered $60 worth of things for Ruby. They had a chair made out of hide that has three legs (sort of like a golf chair) but I didn't know if he wanted me to pay $14 for it, about 3ft. high. They have some crazy things, and I'm hoping the man will give me a discount. Bengie is going to teach me "Shona" which is a Bantu language, when the boss goes away. It is one of four main native languages spoken in South Rhodesia. Let me know if Bubba wants the chair. It's lovely. Must go now, my boss is coming back in a minute. Write soon and maybe I shall be home for next Xmas, I don't think so though.

P.S. Went to a cricket game last Sunday. Rhodesia v England, and did I ever have a blast. First time in over a year that I've had too much to drink. Can you believe I'm 25 now!

---

[39] *Something of Value* is a novel based on events that took place in Kenya during the violent Mau Mau insurrection of the 1950s, an uprising that was confined almost exclusively to members of the Kikuyu tribe.
[40] The Mau Mau rebellion (1952-1960), or Mau Mau Uprising was a war in the British Kenya between the Kenya Land and Freedom Army (KLFA) (also known as the Mau Mau) and the British authorities.

Salisbury, Banket, Jamaica Inn, then back to Salisbury, Rhodesia

November 23, 1964

Salisbury, Rhodesia

Dear Mother and Daddy,

I bought you a lovely present for Xmas, but it won't arrive there in time. Gee, I hope you won't think I'm a meany! As for Jane and Harry I'm really cheesed off because I have never heard from them, and I must send them something – but what? We have been having a fabulous time. Gee, I love, love this place. On November 14, we went to visit Henry, the chap that I went to the cricket match with that Sunday. He lives about 100 miles from Salisbury and he met us at a small town called Banket. It took us four rides to get there. From there we traveled 40 miles on a dirt road, way in the bush.

Henry is the manager of a tobacco farm, and lives in a big house with a thatched roof. We drove his Jeep, and a tractor while we were drinking beer (one cannot drink water from the tap), since it is the only thing that quenches your thirst in the sun, and did we ever get looped – I almost ran into a tree. There aren't many roads, so we were having to find our own paths. The locals were also drunk since it was Saturday, and we went to a local beer dance. Gosh it was fun to start with! Their beer almost made us sick, and we were dancing with them. But then a few drunks got nasty, so we left. We were going about 60 through the bush and Barb almost turned us over! That night we drove to a small town to the local pub where all the farmers hang out, and had a super time.

They were so nice and friendly and some of them had Cambridge and Oxford degrees. About 12 pm we started singing local warrior songs, and people were jumping off the bar and having a hell of a time. Henry and I couldn't even attempt to drive so Barb did 40 miles over dirt road. Got to his place at 3 in the morning and the servants helped us in, and put Barb and I in a small room and the next morning all our clothes were laid out on a chair, washed and ironed. The servants are grouped into their various tribes as they can't live together. Each servant we went to say thank you to bowed and said something in Shona which meant "Praise you, white boss." Honestly, I just can't describe the feeling it gave us – we were so uncomfortable. Something like one would see in the movies.

On Sunday, we went crocodile shooting in a gorgeous river with ferns and elephant ears growing over the side of the flowing, peaceful river, but couldn't find any. I saw a little boy hidden under the elephant leaves in a small boat made out of a tree, fishing with a long spear. He scared the hell out of me at first when I first saw the hidden boat, but I really appreciated him trying to help us. We couldn't find any crocs, so we left after Henry had ripped up a fishing net which someone had put across the river to catch fish which is strictly against the law, because the government is trying to save what little is left. It was such a beautiful place but I kept looking over my shoulder just in case a crocodile was looking and waiting for a nibble!

From there we went to a small river about five miles away from the previous one, and had to walk in the bush on the banks for about a half mile to reach Henry's boat. My heart was thumping, I was so scared of snakes, spiders and sleeping crocs. I made it but was afraid to go in the boat, because it had a big hole in it, but I was too afraid to go back to the Jeep by myself. Well, was that river ever filthy, and the banks were really smelly. I had to wade to the boat, and I had the delightful job of bailing out water, as the bottom was corroded. I just know we got bilharzia – sometimes it doesn't show up for 10 years after you touch the water, and it slowly eats the liver. It's much worse than malaria. Just my luck to get it, and that was the ideal spot for it.

Rowed down about a mile, and on the banks of the river were locals sitting on large high stones, just in case a croc was hidden close by. Henry's six large dogs swam, and when they saw a croc on the edge of the bank, boy did they ever get pulled into the boat! We got soaking and I was terrified they were going to topple the boat! Didn't get any crocs, but it was an experience which I don't think will happen again.

At noon we went back to the pub from the night before and had a rip-roaring time again with the same people! I really love the bush, and would adore living in it for about two months. Such a change from the cities, and so natural! Got a ride back with one of the families that was at the pub in a Jaguar and when we got back to Salisbury I went around to Tony's (he lives around the corner) and we went to the drive-in and then for chicken, and he took me home.

Mother, could you send me two Merle Norman brown eyeshadow, and two Elizabeth Arden black waterproof mascara – not roll-on type as they are no good but the type with the brush, that comes in a white plastic container, nothing else but Elizabeth Arden. Also you know those little travel toothbrushes and toothpaste that come in a plastic container (all colors) for a $1 in any chemist, sorry drug store? Well could you send me one of these with maybe two extra tubes of toothpaste. Send them surface, not airmail. What size shoes do you and Daddy wear?

The rest of the week I just went to work and went out to dinner every night with Tony, who dropped me off around 10. On Friday night he and a friend took Barb and I to a fabulous Chinese restaurant and we had Champagne with our meal. Had a lovely time and after that we went to a hotel called Jamaica Inn, 30 miles outside Salisbury, and was it ever swinging. Lot of jamming policemen – the police in this country are quite the thing, not hicks like in the States. Most of their fathers have English titles, and are they ever tuff. The lady that owns the place is called Ruby and was she ever a honey. Everyone adores her, and they say she can handle anyone and everyone!

You have most probably heard of Joshua Nkomo, the man the English want to make head of this country? He went to Jamaica Inn one night with 20 locals at 2 in the morning when she was closing up and demanded to be served. She was the only one there and told him to "voetsek" which is only used for a dog. He leaned over the bar to grab her, and she pulled a long hippo hide which could kill one if hit hard enough, and lashed him across the face. The others were so scared they ran and with blood running down the side of his face, Nkomo apparently threatened to torture her when he became prime minister. I didn't believe it, but a lot of the police chaps said it was true and Nkomo threatened her when he was in prison. These people that live in the bush are really tuff, they have to be. By the way one part of the hotel was burnt down the following week after Ruby whipped Nkomo.

My sewing is improving and Tony is going to buy me some gorgeous material for a cocktail dress.

⋯⋯⋯⋯⋯⋯

Salisbury, Umtali and Inyangombe Falls, Rhodesia

November 24, 1964

Salisbury, Rhodesia

Received your letter yesterday just after I had mailed mine. My boss is in Zambia for a week and I have nothing to do but play checkers with bottle tops with the boy. Kind of embarrassing because he keeps beating me!

Now to answer your letter. Mrs. Terry has already written to Walt Disney regarding the book, and the other Mrs. Terry (Iris) is probably still in Japan. Daddy, you must get it out of your head that I am going to tour like the typical stiff-neck Yankee, that's too common for me, now no more mentioning about fares and boats. Now Mother, I just about died when you mentioned about the film, and I am sure there was a film in it, but I went through the film that I have not developed, and found the film of the Transkei with the local boys. The film that was supposed to be in there was of the ostrich farm and the Garden Route from Cape Town to East London. Boy I'm really angry about it, because I remember taking it out of my camera and putting it into the drum. It cost me $2.10 to have a roll of film developed here, but I guess I better not take any chances. I shall write to Gam Avery about the shields, and ask them what happened to the other part. The blanket covered with animals cost $4.20. Will have to wait until Iris Terry comes back because they are only in South Africa. The stripe is a Mexican blanket. Skins are very expensive, but Tony is looking around for a zebra. Will cost about $20 though. There are no naked people in Salisbury, Mother – this is a civilized city, and all the locals wear western clothes. You may find some bush locals are naked, if you are lucky. Honestly, I am so sick of African things, I just can't think straight, so I will hold on to Bubba's $50 for a while. Bubba can borrow any of my things, but must give them back when I get home. I still haven't packed the things I bought for Bubba, but I'm trying to make three dresses before Xmas, and that takes up my time.

Last weekend Tony came back and we were going out of town for the weekend, but I had to work on Saturday morning, so he came to pick me up at 10 and my boss kept me for an hour longer, and didn't even thank me – ruddy cheek! We went to Umtali which is 161 miles from Salisbury and is known as the Eastern Highlands, and it looks very much like Scotland. The weather was lousy, raining all the time and foggy. We then went to the Vumba which is part of the Eastern Highlands, clothed in forest and lush vegetation, and gorgeous mountains. Gee it was gorgeous, and from the top of some mountains, one can see Mozambique! It is quite different from the rest of Rhodesia. We stayed at the Leopard Rock Hotel, which was a castle at one time, and the Queen Mother and Princess Margaret stayed there on one of their visits to Rhodesia. Tony drove me everywhere, and I took quite a few pictures. Tried to take one of him, but he won't have his picture taken – says he doesn't want to be remembered!

We went to the Inyangombe Falls on Sunday, and it was cold and rainy and it took us 15 minutes to climb down the cliffs to see it. Took pictures of me with his shoes on, and a local's raincoat. Then we went to the highest point in Rhodesia called World's View, and darn it, it was too cloudy to really see far. Saturday night we went into Portuguese East Africa and went to a fabulous place called Freitas and had prawns (extremely large shrimp), four beers, a bottle of wine, gorgeous chicken, and a salad for $3! I was getting jealous because all the Portuguese women were going up to Tony and rubbing their fingers through his lovely blonde hair, and kept saying he was beautiful! He laughed it off and thought they were disgusting! We sat there all night singing with the Portuguese, and some chaps that Tony hadn't seen in years came in, and we had a ball. The flying ants are out and they were in our food, hair, everywhere. Thousands of them on the bar, but you get used to it, and don't pay attention to them.

Started back for Salisbury about 4, and managed to smuggle some wine across the border! But the fan belt broke, and we were pushed to a gas station, and it took Tony two hours to fix that and something else while three local boys held a light for him. Gee they were giving me funny looks, but when he had finished, Tony gave them all the wine he had bought for me. Bought me $12 worth of things. He's so sweet, he just tells me to pick out what I want. Got a pair of bed slippers made in Kenya out of sheepskin, a belt the native women wear around their privacy, made of all different colored beads, and a cup with designs on it.

I didn't tell y'all, but Tony has about five months to live. He has cancer and I have to clear out of here before it happens, because it would tear me up. When I look at him I just can't believe it, he's so young and energetic – why to such a kind and good person. We never talk about it and when we were driving back from Umtali he was telling me about how they did post-mortems on people they found dead in the bush, and I accidentally asked him how long did it take for a body to rot after it is buried. He then asked if I had read any interesting books lately, and stupid me, I said "Answer my question – I want to know?" and then I saw his eyes were watering and he had a lump in his throat. Imagine how he felt, thinking of what he may be like soon. But he forgave me and in a half an hour we were joking. He's going to the Zambezi for Xmas and I am trying to talk him into letting me go with him, but he says he wants to be by himself, but I know he just doesn't want me to miss the parties over the holidays.

I don't know what's happened to the weather, but this is supposed to be the hottest month of the year, and I'm sitting in the office with the heater on and a sweater. Tomorrow it is supposed to be 97, but don't see how. I will draw a picture of the chairs for Bubba and if he still wants them I will send them. They're only about 3ft. high, and just enough room for your bum. I don't think Barbs' mother realizes that below the equator the seasons are different. She can't understand why we wear cotton dresses in November. Continuation to follow.

1965

Salisbury, Kariba Dam on the Zambezi River, Rhodesia

January 5, 1965

Salisbury, Rhodesia

Sorry I haven't written for so long, but being with Tony on vacation I just haven't had time to do anything. Thank you very much for the Xmas card and money. Will write Angele [Callan's step-grandmother] and Granddaddy and thank them for $30. Received the parcel with mascara etc. and they wanted me to pay $4.27 because you valued it at $12. Fought with them for two hours and had to go see the head of customs and told him I was rather cheesed off with the officials. Boy was I mad and really gave them something to talk about. Finally got by with only paying $1.40. Everything that comes into this country is taxed 25%, unless it is marked personal belongings. Poor Barbara received a parcel from her parents with clothes in it, and the delivery boy was caught selling the things in it, so now she has to go to court. Barb was really thrilled to receive a Xmas card from you, Mother.

For Xmas holidays Tony took me to Kariba Dam which divides Zambia from Rhodesia on the Zambezi River. There is a gorgeous lake and we spent three days there. Tony is mad on big fishing, so he rented a boat and we went out fishing all day. I caught a fish about two inches long – big deal! It was my first one and was I embarrassed because Tony was catching tigerfish which are 20 pounds (that is baby ones!). The next day Tony and an old police force friend of his rented a yacht, and the man's wife and two children went with us. I think without a doubt it was the best day of my life! This was the place where they had to move all the game because the dam was going to flood the islands. Tony and the other chap fished for tigerfish with their large hooks flowing behind the boat. We came to some islands and saw elephants on the banks. Went in as close as we could, and was it gorgeous. We kept to the bank and went very slow and saw impalas, sable, zebras, kudu (which is on a 3d Rhodesian stamp) and buffalo which is on a 1d stamp. For lunch we tied the boat to a tree in the water and sat watching the elephants play in the water about 300 yards away from us. They were blowing water on the babies and also trumpeting.

After that we saw a carcass and Tony walked to shore with the local and it was a large sable. I asked Tony to ask the man if he would hold it up so I could take a picture of it. Tony spoke to him in Shona and he called back to me saying it is a superstition of theirs if a picture is taken of them with a dead animal, the spirits will haunt him! Tony wanted me to see it so he came back to the boat and carried me to shore, because I was afraid of the bilharzia and crocs. Boy, could smell the lions and there must have been a terrible fight because lions' footprints were everywhere. They had eaten everything – even the eyeballs – and there were hundreds of vultures and flies on the carcass. I took a picture and Tony asked me for my camera so he could walk up the bank and take a picture of some gorgeous birds about 5ft. high.

When he and the man were halfway there, they stopped and didn't move for a minute. Gee, I knew something was wrong. I just froze because I knew the kill had just been made about two hours before, and lions always sleep by the carcass because their bellies are too full to wander far. They both turned around together and walked fairly fast but steadily towards me. Tony leaned over to pick me up and whispered that there were lions about 40 yards from me and not to say a word. God, my heart was in my stomach. He waited back to the boat with the local behind him. When the man got on board, he looked as if he had seen a ghost. The poor thing was shuddering.

After that we went to another spot close to shore, and Tony was helping the children and the little girl dropped his fishing rod into the water! Tony was quite annoyed but didn't show it and he dove into the water. It was about 20 feet deep and he just couldn't get enough wind to

go that far. Was very much like the Savannah River, couldn't see a thing, and twigs from the trees all under water. Tony kept going down and I saw the boy anxiously looking all around in the water. I asked him what was he looking for and he said, "Crocodiles, Madame." Well that was just about it for me! I couldn't watch anymore, because if one had attacked him he didn't even have his knife. I must have lost two pounds! He finally got the rod and his lungs really suffered for it. We got back to the hotel about 7, had dinner and listened to Tony and the other chap talk about their times in the police force. I was really impressed since Tony never talks about himself. I heard the other day that Tony was in the 1948 Olympics in England! When he was in the police force, Rhodesia was still raw. I could sit for hours listening to those type of stories.

On the third day we went out again in a small boat but I wanted to go watch the game again. We went into Zambia and you just wouldn't have believed it – everyone we saw was drunk, and some of them had passed out on the highway! I was really repulsed at the sight of men and women doing their business in the streets. It was very degrading. Tony asked direction to a friend's house from a drunk that was walking down a dirt road. The man was wearing a big fur hat which is a sign of freedom, but wouldn't tell Tony and was rude. Tony was furious, screaming at him in some native language which I have never heard before. I was terrified because if the Zambian officials had seen us, we could have been put in jail for insulting an African gentleman!

The dam itself is beautiful, and was built by 2,000 Italians during the period of the Federation which included Rhodesia, Northern Rhodesia (now Zambia), and Nyasaland. Naturally Southern Rhodesia paid for it all, but now Zambia owns half of it. Tony let me drive home and we had to go through a tsetse fly control stop, and they sprayed our car inside and out to kill them if they were in the car, and to prevent them from entering the car. That's one thing I don't need now is sleeping sickness!

We drove a different way back and it was very mountainous and extremely beautiful. We went to the escarpment (which is its proper name now) which is the Zambezi Valley, mountains on the Zambia and Rhodesia side and a valley of 40 miles, with the Zambezi flowing in the middle. It is full of wild game and Tony patrolled 375 miles in six months on foot with a local constable when he was a policeman. He had to check on malaria (catching it three times himself!), keeping account on where the elephants, leopards and lions were roaming, and seeing that the locals had enough food and medical supplies. During this time (I was told by a chap who was in the force at the same time) Tony shot two elephants, hundreds of mambas, black and green, and several other types of snakes, lions, leopards and crocodiles. I just can't understand how anyone who is used to luxury could stick something like that for six months. The flies and mosquitos and heat are unbearable. Tony finally let me take a picture of him next to a sign, and when I looked through the viewer, the words were double. Gee, I hope they can fix it. Barbara's camera has had it, and she has to buy another one. Will cost her about $70 for one like mine which I paid $45 for in Cape Town.

I was offered a job with Shell Central Africa but have to turn it down since we are planning on leaving in April. Would have made $30 more a month with Shell.

The pictures of Jane and the children on the beach are lovely, but when were they taken? The picture of the children with Page on the chair was precious and little Harry looks adorable as he did when I left. I really miss them. Mother, is that woman leaning over the chair in a blue and white stripe dress you? If so, you look very young, but what's with the light hair? And as usual your powder is too light for your face. Please get a darker shade. I can just imagine Daddy griping like hell every time you receive a letter from me!

Received a postcard from Siegfried Chemenski [family friend]. God, what nationality is he? He seems quite nice but signed the card "Your Servant" and when I saw that I thought a local had written me! He mentioned that he will be in New Delhi in January, how about finding out where he will be other times? Maybe we will run into each other.

Please find out from Bubba how much money I have of his. I've lost the paper with the information on it. I'm not going to buy anything else until I know if he liked the things I sent.

I'm rather glad I have a mean streak, because no one has ever taken advantage of me. That's another reason why I'm glad I have and still doing what I am. I've become completely independent. The one problem left is not to let my emotions get the best of me – my stomach just can't take it.

Hope everyone had a lovely Xmas. I can imagine the house looking gorgeous as usual.

Had all my pictures developed, and the ones of the Transkei are with them. Thank God for that. Tony bought me a viewer so I could really see them well. I'm labelling them and when I finish I will send them on.

Salisbury

January 20, 1965

Salisbury, Rhodesia

Dear Mother and Daddy,

I can't begin to tell you how thrilled I was with the pictures. They are absolutely gorgeous. Jane looked like a little girl, and you and Daddy look so aristocratic and reserved. The painting of Jane and children is super. What ever happened to the picture of me wearing the black dress? My friends are really impressed, and so am I. Bubba's little Lauren is beautiful! The things that fascinate me with all the children are the eyebrows.

I work for Timberit Rhodesia Limited, P.O. Box 3118, or 2nd floor, Sarum House, Monica Road. I have had all my pictures developed and did it ever cost me a bomb. $3 for just one reel to be developed, and they have confiscated a picture of a nude Transkei native woman with slits in her nose and all the jewellery covering her neck, legs, head and arms. Tony is going to try and sue them for me! I am putting them in order and have written down what each picture is in a notebook. I'm not going to send them yet because I want more pictures of game and I want to compare them with my previous ones. Although I have a marvellous camera, pictures look further away than they really are. The ones of Kruger Park are not as good as I thought because all the animals blend in with the bush, and I haven't been able to identify the animals in some of them. Tony is going to rent a projector and then we will be able to tell on the big screen. Mother, let Bubba use some of my African things for his bar instead of letting them sit in my room, but if you do please mark them so I can tell which are mine, because I will have forgotten by the time I get back. Sorry about the musical instrument. I won't buy anymore for Bubba until I know exactly how much money I have for him. Another parcel should be arriving soon.

The other day I answered the phone and this strange Southern voice asked if I was Miss Barbara Pinckney. He then asked if my father was E.B. I asked him how he knew this and he said he had just received a telegram and then he started stuttering. I dropped the phone in shock and Bengie picked it up. I thought the man was going to say Daddy had died! When I finally got my breath back, he told me what the telegram said; Daddy was just checking my address! But now the authorities have been giving me hell for not registering with them.

I forgot to mention in my last letter that I was sick for two weeks. They thought I had malaria at first but then realized it was a bug. Had a temperature of 103 for a few days which scared them. I lost over 10 pounds and haven't gained it back. Tony and Barbara say I look dreadful, so thin, and with Xmas coming on I just didn't have time.

Mother, it is not unusual for arms to be smuggled into Rhodesia, but they always catch the smugglers. Don't you worry – these police are well prepared! I'm rather annoyed with Barbara and so is Tony. Clothes are the same here as in the States, so she makes everything. I have given up on sewing, I just mess everything up and am wasting material. Barb has about 20 dresses now whereas I have one that I can wear out at night! But she won't even help me and starts shouting at me when I ask her what to do next. She asked Tony for some pills which cost $7 for 20 and he said he would get them for her plus a camera at 33, a third off. So, when I told Tony that she wouldn't make me a dress until she had finished all her hitching things, he blew up. He said if she was that stingy it worked both ways. So, when I went home that night she asked me where were the pills and when I told her what had happened, she started calling him names so we really had it out with all sorts of things, including the milk – I pay for half of it, and never get any!

Next day I came home from work and she was very upset. I asked her what the problem was and she said her sister's four-month baby had died. Vancouver has 4ft. of snow and her sister was having a party so she put the baby on the terrace from 11 in the morning to 6 at night, and only went out once to give it a bottle and put another blanket on it. At 6 pm when the last guest had left, she went to bring it in, and it was dead! The doctor said it was overexposure to cold that killed it. Her sister might have to go to court!

The ring I got for Jane is solid gold with rubies and I bought it in Barcelona, Spain. Will write a letter to Roz Frame when I get time. Mother, all these books you are reading mostly deal with Mau Maus who are in Kenya and I am a long way from there, although we will catch a train through Kenya to Uganda. I wrote Jane a letter in Atlanta. Please tell Bubba to write and let me know if he wants a zebra skin. They are rather large, and I don't think I can get one for under $24 but it would really be unique.

Tony and I have been playing a lot of bridge lately, and is he ever so good. We go to different people's houses all the time. I love this city so much and hate the thought of leaving, but with Tony I just can't be here when it happens. I almost wish I had never met him. For Xmas he gave me a 14c gold broach with a topaz in it. Boy, it must have cost him a bomb. Boy I'm going to be like Louise Lane[41]. Wish I could have gone to her wedding. I bet it was a blast! Seig didn't give a return address on his Xmas card, but wouldn't it be super if we did meet in some crazy place. You must ask him when he returns if he has any friends in the Middle or Far East. We're looking for every possible clean place to stay. I often think of the day I shall return too, God willing. I'll probably look like an old woman from my nerves. I will check up on emeralds for you. Wouldn't be but half the price as the States.

Must sign off now. Write soon.

Love Barbara

⸻⸻⸺⸻⸻

[41] Louise Lane was the wife of Remer Y. Lane, a member of one of the most distinguished banking families in Georgia and South Carolina.

Salisbury

February 9, 1965

Salisbury, Rhodesia

Dear Mother and Daddy,

Was so sorry to hear about Granddaddy. I hope he pulls through. He's lived longer than most people though.

Have received two postcards and a letter from Seig and I have written a long letter to him in Frankfurt, Germany. I loved Frankfurt, but there were too many Americans there to suit me. I also gave him my telephone number just in case he gets here.

I did the most stupid thing. When I sent Bubba's parcel, I forgot to put 'Via Cape Town' so now it has gone to Beira – those that work for the government are known to be crooks, so I have a feeling it will never reach Savannah – if it doesn't, that's $30 down the drain! Please let me know the minute you receive it. I'm not going to buy anything else for Bubba unless he writes me personally and tells me how much I have left of his money, and if he wants a large zebra skin for $60, and anything else. It's very hard for me to do this, so I wish he would cooperate.

The rainy season is driving me up the wall. It never seems to stop, except during office hours. I have lost Barbara's umbrella, so have to buy her a new one which is absolutely killing me. Every weekend seems to start out lovely and then that rain comes. My hair is so kinky from it. I have bought a nice pair of evening shoes and a dress, and Tony pays for my hair to be done every week! Wear my hair up all the time (it's very long now) with little bows at the back. Tony just couldn't believe the difference. He said there was no "in-between" with me. Either I looked like a princess, or a street urchin! Every foreigner I met wants to know where I got my frightfully English accent. Even the American Embassy made me show my passport to prove I was a Southerner! Speaking of passports, this is very important. I must know the date of birth and place of birth of both of you before I can have my passport renewed. So, let me know very soon.

I will find out about emeralds soon but I'm wondering how I'm going to get them out of the country. I'll find a way somehow!

Tony has been away since January 25 and I get so bored when he's away. Tried renting a bicycle, but they want $5.60 a month plus $30 deposit. I really did want one, but I guess that's out of the question. I really need the exercise. My legs have become so skinny. I never have gained back the weight I lost when I was sick before Xmas. I don't think I mentioned it, but I had a temperature of 103 for four days. I think the doctors were scared, but wouldn't say anything. I was in bed almost two weeks. I thought I had malaria, but I didn't.

Tony is taking me to Victoria Falls and Hwange Game Reserve over Easter – can't wait! Every time I think of leaving, I get chills. I'm so afraid I will never get to see Rhodesia again. I love this country so much. Lee, the American chap that is working for the U.N. on bilharzia, is going to test Barb and me. If we have it, we are sunk because it cost about $90 for the treatment. You go through absolute hell for two months from the fluid they pump into you. Several people have died from it and I don't think I have ever met anyone here who does not have it. Also do you remember me telling you that we had to iron everything before we put it on? I didn't know how bad these maggot flies were until I saw a girl whose legs are scarred for life from their bites. She put on a pair of slacks, without ironing them. Also, with the rainy season a lot of people have had tick fever, and two children have died from it. God, I'd never even heard of such a thing. The tick gets inside you and enters the blood stream and gives you terrible fever. Everyone overseas seems to think malaria is terrible, but everyone around here would rather have that than bilharzia!

Friday night I went to Bretts (one of the nicest bars in town) with a friend of Tony's from Bulawayo. I was so bored with him, but at least I got a lovely Chinese meal from him and 60 cigs.

I'm sending Little Harry a book for his birthday. I don't think it will be too deep if Jane reads it to him. As far as the other children are concerned, I feel pretty guilty, but there are just too many, and I just don't have a clue when anyone's birthday is except mine, which is typical of me! I'm sweating getting fired. The other day I got so cheesed off with my boss and told him to stop being so childish. I don't think he appreciated it. Oh well, that's the least of my problems right now.

Tony will be back on February 22 and I am just dying to go out into the bush. Maybe I can get him to take me. Winter will be here in two months' time and I'm not looking forward to it although it doesn't get that cold.

Here's a list of things I need for traveling, and when you send them, just mark on the package "own personal belongings", and then write a little note inside saying you found these things in my room and thought I would want them, and make the containers looked used. Also write on the parcel "no commercial value".

Helene Curtis Suave (hair cream in tube)
Helen Rubinstein black mascara with brush
Merle Norman brown eyeshadow
Lady or Miss Clairol black hair dye
Eyelash curler rubbers (not the eyelash curler)

Cottage Shop has a sale once a year on Mary Chess[42] products – see if you can get me a plastic jar of the yellow cream that smells like perfume if it is on sale. I think it is $3 off sale and $1 on sale. It's a tall bottle. The hair cream is what I want to put on my hair after I wash it to put grease back into it. They just don't have things like that here, and my hair is so dry. Write soon,

Love Barbara.

⸺⸺⸺⸻❦⸻⸺⸺⸺

[42] Mary Chess started making perfumes in New York in 1932 after she was disappointed by a bottle of eau de toilette. She created all her perfumes herself, using natural ingredients. Her most famous perfume was Tapestry.

Salisbury

March 4, 1965

Salisbury, Rhodesia

Dear Mother and Daddy,

Again, I'm sorry for not writing for a long time, but quite a lot has happened since I've last written. First of all I had my blood tested for bilharzia (that terrible disease) and it came out double positive. I was so frightened I couldn't sleep for a week until the next test which was a skin graft, and thank God that came out negative, and also one specimen. Have to take a certain pill tomorrow and if I react to it they will have to clip my intestines. Keep your fingers crossed, because some people actually die from the treatment, and if I have the treatment over a period of two months, which is the safest, it will cost almost $100 and I will go through utter hell.

Secondly, Barbara has decided it doesn't suit her to leave until December – not giving a damn about the condition I will be in when Tony goes. If I had known that I would have taken that job with Shell with more pay. I've talked it all out with Tony and he says I am a bloody fool to travel with that selfish pig, but what choice do I have? I want to go to the Far East but I'm not brave enough to do it alone, and Barb knows this and is taking full advantage of it, and I can't stick this lonely job out for 10 months, so I'm packing up here the end of April and Tony is going to take me all around Rhodesia in May and beginning of June. He's such a darling and trying to keep me from worrying, and said the best thing for me to do is to go home, because at the rate I'm going (living on my nerves) my face will drop more and I will look like an old woman. He said if I definitely can't get it out of my head to go to the Far East that he will scrape up the money to send me to Japan by freighter. I just can't accept his offer though, because he has quite a lot of bills and wants them settled before he goes. I definitely have to go someplace and try and get a job to give me time to think what I'm going to do. He also has bought two tents, a baby boat and motor because I said I would like to do a lot of camping out, and he bought me a lovely sleeping bag!

I decided to give in my notice at the flat because I couldn't afford it if I am going to look for another job, and have been staying with different people which is getting me even more down.

Last weekend I didn't go to the flat at all and Monday morning Barb's boyfriend called me up and said Barb had been taken to the Welches – the family we stayed with when we first arrived in Salisbury – on Saturday with a fever of 105! They asked her where I was and she said she didn't know because she hadn't seen me for two days – knowing all along I was staying with three girls. She has an acute infection of the kidney and I had it too except I kept a hot water bottle on, even at work. Tony called me up from Zambia and gave me the name of some pills to take and it cleared me straight up.

I informed Barb the other day that I was giving up the flat and last night I went out to see her at the Welches and one could have cut the air – the reception was so icy. From what I can understand, Barb has blamed the whole thing on me and told them she just doesn't know what she will do because she can't afford to keep the flat on her own. Her boyfriend even went so far as to say I did a dirty thing! I figure since she doesn't give a damn about anyone but herself, that I would have to make plans to suit myself. They feel so sorry for her that they have invited her to live with them and only pay $14 a month, meals, washing etc. included. Luck just always seems to go her way. Oh well, I shall work everything out.

The other day Tony and I were at Lake McIlwaine and we had to walk through a lot of bush to get to a large rock on the water. I walked back to the car to get my cigarettes and I just missed stepping on a green mamba. Thank God it was going in the same direction as me or it would have definitely have bitten me because I let out a blood curdling scream. Tony said I turned completely white! This weekend we are going out on Lake McIlwaine in his boat. I am going to wear rubber gloves and boots in case I have to put my hand in the water to pull up the anchor so as to protect myself from bilharzia. Tony goes into hysterics every time we come near water – I act like there are 50 crocs in the water! We are going to camp on the Zambezi River for three weeks (this is really wild territory), but Tony is afraid of the hippos and elephants coming to our camp. I think it sounds quite exciting.

I still haven't heard from Bubba and I would like to know how much money I have left, and what else he wants, because after June I could easily get into a crazy mode and catch a plane to India or somewhere. I then won't ever get the opportunity to get him the things he wants, so if I don't hear from him soon I'm going to forget it because I've got too much on my mind.

I still love this country. It's so funny about this continent, but once you live here, it seems to grip you, and one is always wanting to return. I don't know why I tell y'all all these things, it just makes you worry, but I really don't have anyone to pour out my troubles to. I don't know what I will do about my mail after this month. Will let you know as soon as I have figured something out. You must let me know about both of your dates of birth and place. I don't think I shall be coming back to Salisbury after May and this is the only place in Central Africa I can get my passport renewed, so please hurry and send the information.

Hope all is well with everyone. I'm sending a parcel with the rest of Bubba's things and some of mine. Sorry, two packages. Boy, did the chiefs give Bottomley and Lord Gardiner[43] a hard time. Some of the newspaper clippings are in the boxes. Read all of the papers.

Must go now,

Love Barbara

⋯⟡⋯

---

[43] Arthur Bottomley (1907-1995) was a British Labour politician, Member of Parliament and minister. In Harold Wilson's government, he was the Secretary of State for Commonwealth Relations (1964-66) and had to deal with the crisis of Rhodesia's Unilateral Declaration of Independence. Gerald Austin Gardiner, (Baron Gardiner (1900-1990), was a British Labour politician who was Lord High Chancellor of Britain at the time.

Salisbury

March 13, 1965

Salisbury, Rhodesia

Dear Mother and Daddy,

As you can see by the address, I have moved out of the flat, but my landlady is going to forward any mail to me that arrives to 24, Norbridge. I am going to hand in my notice next week and quit work at the end of April so Tony can take me all around Rhodesia in May. As I think I mentioned, he had bought a small boat so we can go camping on the Zambezi River. He is also going to take me to a missionary somewhere up the Zambezi towards Zambia in his little boat. He's picking me up from work at 10.30 and we are going on Lake McIlwaine again this weekend. It's so much fun. We stop on different islands and cook chicken, although I'm not allowed to cook anymore because last weekend we couldn't eat it!

Thanks for sending the information about your births. Went yesterday and had my passport renewed. Can you send that parcel to the American Consulate General, Central Bank Building, 76 Jameson Avenue? As I do need these things, and appreciate you getting them for me and as I really don't have the foggiest idea where I shall be when they arrive, the American Consulate will forward it to me. Please mark on the parcel, "No commercial value, personal belongings".

It's now March 16 and we had a marvellous time on the lake, except Tony and I really got into a fight because he wanted me to pull in the anchor that was caught on a rock at one of the islands and I refused because I didn't want to get bilharzia from the wet rope. No one here understands – they say *So what? Everyone in Rhodesia has it*, but the clinic in Salisbury is the best in the world to be cured. If I arrived in the States with it, they wouldn't have a clue how to treat it and it would cost a bomb. Lee, the American chap working for the U.N. on bilharzia, gave me a pill and 48 hours after taking it, I was supposed to take my specimen to the clinic to be tested. They were closed, so now I guess I have to go through two more days of being ill. I was so sick from this pill. Vomited about six times, and was dizzy all the time, along with having chills. If the next one comes out positive, I will have to start treatment right away. Thanks for the list of birthdays. Is Farrell a girl or boy? Honestly, I just can't keep up with all of them.

I have a fabulous New Zealand friend Claire (the girl I wrote about in Cape Town) who is living in Italy, and at one stage I thought of going there for six months but would never be able to get a job, so I guess that's out of the question. I still have my mind set on Japan, and will not come home until I reach my destination. I'm trying to talk Wendy into emigrating to South Africa, and then going to the Far East, but she could never scrape up the money. I really don't want to travel with Barbara after the dirty trick she played on me, but I guess I have no other choice.

The chiefs gave old Bottomley hell when he was out here. Everyone has respect for the chiefs, including the white people. One of them saved Tony's life from a crocodile about 10 years ago, and Tony always stays with him when he is in his area. Someone wrote a letter to Bottomley and took it around to the British High Commissioner to send to London, saying that since the Labour government needed every vote they could get and the Black Nationalist want the vote, why doesn't England take one million of them since both would benefit? Something I didn't realize is that there are 263 major African languages and who knows how many dialects.

Shame tomorrow is Little Harry's birthday, and I still haven't sent the book. Oh well, better late than never. Will also send Page a sweet little book about flowers. Glad to hear Granddaddy didn't have to be operated on. Boy, he has a strong constitution. Daddy, why don't you start smoking with a tar guard[44]? I started about a month ago and I feel great for it. It's fantastic the tar that collects in the guard. I think it stops 80% from going into one's lungs.

Must go now, just wanted to give you my new address. Got my passport all right as well.

⸻ ◦◦⟨⟩◦◦ ⸻

---

[44] A tar guard is a disposable cigarette filter that removes tar and nicotine.

Salisbury, Zambezi River, Karoi, then Salisbury, Rhodesia

March 23, 1965

Salisbury, Rhodesia

Dear Mother and Daddy,

Well here I am with the shakes after this weekend. Tony came home from Malawi on Friday night and informed me we were going to the Zambezi River (remember the valley I told you about in the Escarpment with the Zambezi running through the valley where he patrolled for six months) the next day! I didn't know if I was coming or going because I had to work Saturday morning, so he picked me up from work with everything we needed with the boat on the top of the car and we were off. Got there around 5.30 after having to drive 50 miles in the bush, and boy, was it rough. Had to stop about every five minutes and move parts of trees that elephants had torn up, and the little narrow dirt road was so bad that the boat almost came off from all the bouncing. Tony has four big dents on the top of the car from pressure on the roof rack. Gee, I never thought we would make it. Each bend we turned we kept our fingers crossed that there wouldn't be an elephant, because we could have never got away from one in reverse. We were very lucky though.

Finally made it to a camp where the local rangers who patrol the valley stay when they are in that particular district. Tony walked all over and said there were just too many snakes. We could look through the bushes and trees and see that famous river flowing across the sandbanks, and there were hippo tracks and some baboons playing on the banks. If they had stood up, they would have been taller than me. God, they were big. I'm really terrified of those things!

Anyway, Tony remembered another camp about five miles upstream and so we headed for that instead. We came to a fabulous place and there were two men already camping there. They helped Tony get the boat down the high cliff to the water and we set up camp. The camp had some wooded frames so that when the locals on patrol live there for a month or so, they can put bush grass all around the frames. Tony put our tents in the middle of these frames on the cement floor. There was a shower and a ladies' room which was very unique – you will go into hysterics when you see the picture of it! A big barrel holds the water above your head which is drawn from the river, and the toilet has a lid and a seat, but I wouldn't dare go in there for fear of snakes. I just went into the bush with Tony close by, wearing rubber boots. Tony fixed scoff (Afrikaans for food!) and we sat there with the two men drinking hot beer next to the fire listening to the bloody baboons in the trees and the hippos in the water. It was lovely! The sounds the birds made were so peaceful and authentic – just like one would see in the movies! We were absolutely clapped and after Tony had finished putting up our tents, we went to bed. It's such a lovely feeling to go to sleep with the crazy blowing noises the hippos make.

But before we went to sleep, Tony took me on the banks. I was so scared and walked behind him, holding onto the waist of his shorts hoping the crocs would get him instead of me! I was literally shaking and was too afraid to run back to the camp by myself. I think he was really shocked at me shaking. He can't understand an outsider being scared over such things – everyone is so used to it that they just take it for granted. We saw two crocs in the middle of the river. They have red eyes at night and do they ever glow!

I lay in my tent for an hour scared some stupid big baboon would fall on top of my tent and rip it, until I couldn't take it any longer and got up with my mosquito net and gorgeous sleeping bag Tony bought for me and went to his tent and asked him if I could sleep in there because I was scared. So, I slept in his tent and I think he was rather cheesed off since he had paid about $60 for my tent and I won't use it. Kept waking up on and off by the dreadful noise the baboons were making, but that's part of the game, and the mosquitos were just dreadful. We took our malaria pills. The whole valley was infested with tsetse fly, which gives one sleeping sickness. The darn things were biting me all over and they hurt five times worse than a horsefly bite and they look like them, except longer and thinner. I kept saying to myself, *I can take the hurt from these horseflies just so long as a tsetse fly doesn't bite me*, as I hadn't realized they were tsetse! It was only when we left the camp and many were all in our car and Tony said he wished the bloody tsetse flies would fly out of the car – well, I just about died.

Up early the next morning (5 o'clock). We had coffee and grapefruit and took everything out of the tent and rolled the sides up so snakes wouldn't get in, and we were off in the boat with the two men Tony had invited to go with us. Our camp was on a high bank and to look through the trees and bush across the river to the sandy banks of Zambia really gave me a thrill. The birds were really going to town with the singing and the hippos were having so much fun in the water. We headed up the river against the tide with a 5½ h.p. and the boat was hardly moving. Tony went close to the hippos so I could take pictures and they kept going under, because they are very shy. They love to play and have a terrible habit of coming up under a boat and turning it over! Many people have been eaten by crocs this way. Tony went too close because they all went under and boy, can they really move under water. Got some fabulous pictures but was saying the Act of Contrition the whole time. The water was so clear we could see about 15 ft. below and several times we went over crocs. It really gave me the willies, I was a nervous wreck.

The men were trawling for tigerfish and Tony caught a dilly but it was so big, it took his hook and swam away! We went up and up stream until we came to local villages on the banks of the Zambian side with all their anchored tree boats. We could see all of them peeking over the side of the bushes watching us – the women were washing clothes in the river and the children were standing there hitting the water with clothes to keep the crocs from coming to close. An old man rowed out to us and Tony said to him, "Old One, why do you come out so far in the river with your small boat?"

The man replied, "Master, I am used to the waters and the dead family (meaning his relatives) is keeping watch over me to see harm not come my way." We then went up into the gorge towards Portuguese East. We finally turned back towards the camp and did we ever tear down the river! It was so shallow (3ft.) going through the rapids, that all of us had to watch to see if we were heading into tree stumps which were laying on the bottom. We tried to anchor there but the anchor just wouldn't hold, and we were drifting into some hippos.

We went back to the camp at 1 o'clock and the men left. I was really sorry to see them leave because I was scared with just the two of us there. Salisbury is about 300 miles from where we were, and we had to go 50 miles into the valley, plus we were 150 miles from civilization. I was so exhausted from the strain of the river ride, I fell asleep in the car for an hour and a ½ while Tony pottered around the boat. I just can't tell you how hot it was. If Tony didn't have a canopy for his boat, we would have never been able to go on the water, and this month is supposed to be the coolest on the Zambezi!

When Tony woke me up, I was completely soaked from sweating. We got in the boat and went downstream this time and I was steering while he was trolling[45], and it became so shallow that he took over and I was laying on the front of the boat looking over to see if we were going to hit something, and we did. We were stuck right in the middle of the sandbank, and I hadn't seen it with the reflection of the clouds and sun.

Boy, did I ever get it! He threw every name in the book at me. I just burst out crying and that made him even more angry and he told me to watch the front for crocs while he jumped in and pulled us out of it. I was crying so much, that I couldn't have even seen an elephant walk in front of us, much less a croc. He was like a maniac in the water. When he got back in, I moved and dropped my sunglasses in. Well, that did it. He literally went crazy and, not meaning to, slapped me and I went flying across the boat landing on my hand – I really thought I had broken it. In he went again to get the sunglasses because he thought I had paid $15 for them. I had also got my line caught in his and he had to cut both the lines, plus I broke the top of the best rod he had, and I think from the sun and all, he had just had it with me.

I was so hurt I cried all the way down the river. I was supposed to be looking for hippos but I couldn't even think of them at the time. We just missed going over one and he gave it to me again calling me a *stupid typical American*. When we finally went back to camp, he asked me to steer and I refused and he started apologizing and so did I and he caught a 11 lb. tiger fish. He got so excited, he asked me to open his net and I didn't know how to and burst out crying again. I remember hitting him when we were on the sandbank. The locals on the Zambezi bank must have thought we were mad!

---

[45] Trolling is a fishing technique where you drag a hooked bait through the water from a moving boat.

Finally, we got back and it had been raining. Tony cooked supper and I just sat there on a precious little folding chair he bought for me and cried for about an hour. I had the binoculars on and he went to take them off and hit me on the forehead! I fell to the ground and really don't know what happened, but then I got up and was so dizzy. Boy, do I ever have a bump on my forehead! Tony told me he was so sorry, and that he hated to admit that he was terrified when he had to jump in, because crocs love sandbanks. He was almost taken two times by crocs and he knew his luck was running out. To think because of my stupidity, he could have been taken!

After that he was so kind to me. I really think he feels like a heel for doing that. We both were mentally and physically exhausted that we didn't even wash the dishes. Went to sleep at 7.30 and woke up the next morning at 5.30 again. He was so anxious to get out on the river that I didn't even have time to comb my hair. We washed the dishes in the river and left them on the shore, and went upstream again through the rapids. We found a small creek and the boat just made it in. We saw turtles and hundreds of black bream, but we didn't have any worms so they just wouldn't take, not even the tigerfish that he had cut up. There were monkeys in the trees on the edge of the creek and they looked so funny just sitting there, watching us.

We had run out of water and I was so dehydrated. Tony drank the river water. We kept delaying going back to the camp to pack and I kept wondering if my boss had called up from Lusaka and found I wasn't at work. Went back at 1 o'clock and some men had pitched camp and Tony knew one of them so they helped him bring up the boat and they gave us some ice water. We fixed something to eat, and I sat in the little chair resting while he went over and talked to them. I couldn't believe the things that crawl around in the bush. I even saw some things that looked like Walt Disney would have drawn up for creatures on other planets. Finally, we packed the tent and were off. As we drove along I stood next to the boat on the front of the bonnet looking for elephants, and I couldn't see one even though there must have been herds with at least 100 in each herd. Boy, was I mad. All four men said they saw hundreds of them and the first two men were chased by one!

It took us about four hours to go 50 miles in the bush, and when we got to the main highway (if one could call it that) it was dark and the bloody flies were biting like mad. When we entered Karoi it was about 8 and the tsetse fly control was closed, so there we were, both tired as hell, tearing towards Salisbury with the bloody tsetse flies in the car. Four times Tony had to stop to sleep and one time he slept for two hours. I got in the back in my sleeping bag and went right to sleep. When I woke up, we were in front of his flat. No telling how long he had been asleep. Woke him up (this was at 3) and helped him take all the things upstairs. Washed all the dishes while he took a bath and then he took me to the flat where I am staying temporarily. He was supposed to pick me up at 7.30 this morning for work but never came. I think he's gone to Umtali so I am going around to do the washing and fix a good meal.

Had lunch with Barbara today and she really makes me mad. Now she says if I don't get a job in May we will leave at the end of August, and if I do, then the end of October. I should have just told her I was leaving by boat at the end of May and hope that she would decide to leave too, but I know Barb so well. When her mind is made up, it's made up, no matter who she hurts. I guess I was just afraid she would say that I better make other plans. Will talk it over with Tony when he comes back from Malawi.

Tell Bubba I'm bloody angry I haven't heard from him. It's disgusting, and I'm really getting fed up with all the worrying I have plus worrying about what to get him. Must go now.

Love B

Portuguese East Africa (Mozambique) / Rhodesia

Beira, Portuguese East Africa (Mozambique), Salisbury, Rhodesia

April 22, 1965

Salisbury, Rhodesia

Dear Mother and Daddy,

For the Easter holidays, Tony took me to Beira in Portuguese East Africa (Mozambique) which is on the sea and we camped right on the ocean in a caravan camp. I don't think I have ever enjoyed the ocean so much. The waves were so high and Tony and I were just like little children playing in them. It was hot as the devil but I loved the heat on my body since I'm always so cold in our office. We ate prawns for every meal since seafood in Rhodesia is so expensive.

It's a six-hour drive from Salisbury so we left at 4.30 Thursday and slept on and off. I got in my sleeping bag and slept almost all the way in the back seat. Poor Tony had just driven six hours from Bulawayo before he picked me up, and I'm sure he would have liked some company, but old lazy me! What a dirty place Beira is. The beach and water are just like Tybee[46] except no houses. The first two days we had a ball and I was allowed £1.00 a day spending money. Honestly, Tony treats me like his daughter. We drank a different wine with every meal, something one just doesn't do in the States.

But on the third night I woke up in convulsions with spasms in the intestines like when they put me in the hospital in Cyprus. Tony was fast asleep but a man heard me and came into my tent – I honestly thought he was going to cry when he saw the condition I was in. He had been through the same thing in the Second World War. He finally got it out of me where Tony was and woke him up. The poor thing thought I had had it. He stayed with me all night and the next morning he put me on the floor of the bathroom (which everyone used) since the tent was too hot. Thank God he always carries his medicine around.

---

[46] Tybee Island is a city and barrier island in Chatham Country, Georgia, 18 miles east of Savannah and was once a quiet beach getaway.

It was from those bloody prawns! We were supposed to go back Monday, but I was just too ill. Most of the time we spent walking on the beach and digging for clams. We also went to the harbor to see a gigantic Swedish ship come in and although the people were very curious about it, they didn't exactly give it a warm reception, The country itself is partly swampy and nothing has been done with the rest of the land. Very deserted looking, and even in the small villages there's hardly any life because of that bloody siesta!

We came back on Tuesday leaving Beira about 12 noon and I slept all the way to the border. Finally made it to Salisbury about 8 and I immediately went to bed. Tony picked me up the next morning and drove me to work. Although I was terribly brown, I looked sick as a dog. I walked in the office and told my boss I was leaving the end of May, and he told me I better go home to bed so off I went. I've laid it down with Barb on my terms and I told her I was leaving end of June and if she wanted to come she could because I wasn't going to hang around this place. Now it seems she's eating out of my hand. So, we are back to the original plan, except we are cutting out Tanzania and going through Zambia to Uganda, where we have some Indian friends and will catch a bus through Kenya. I talked to two Rhodesian girls who hitched through Kenya and they said we would be perfectly safe if we caught buses and stayed in hotels. Tony gets livid with me every time I mentioned hitching through Africa. He even threatened to write y'all a letter concerning this matter, but I guess he realizes it won't do any good. Anyway, I am still going to travel around Rhodesia in June with Tony and then we're off.

I have mailed three parcels with mine and Bubba's things in them so he will have to split the cost with me. I still haven't heard from him and I'm bloody annoyed. There is a present for Page's birthday and book for Little Harry for his birthday. There are a pair of slippers for Daddy, size 10 but I forgot that Rhodesian men are larger and they go by different sizes. Anyway, they will be lovely and warm to watch TV. There is also a book which I treasure to y'all which cost over $16 so take good care of it and put a cover on it. There are really some valuable things in these parcels so I hope they reach there o.k. As for the bugs coming out of the wood, I don't think they are termites, but little things that live in the wood for years, and then start to come out. That's why none of the children should put them around their mouths because they are all

handmade by the locals and are not cured. The man sitting on the throne is supposed to be Bubba's. I guess there is a big mix up over what are whose.

I'm kinda itching to get on the road towards home now. I think I have been away too long and starting to push my luck as they say.

Mother, I hope you don't have to go to that hospital in Kentucky. I really do worry about you. I know what has caused it but won't say anything. Each month I put $1.40 on the sweepstake, but I don't think I shall ever be that lucky. Just imagine $60,000.00 – quite a lot.

I wrote Seig in Hamburg but don't know if he ever received my letter. Wendy is going to the States in May and wanted me to meet her, but I'm still dying to see Japan. I told her if she wanted to stay in the States and wait for me that she should go to Savannah and get a job until I arrive.

Must go now. Take care of yourselves.

Love Barbara

Rhodesia

Salisbury

May 5, 1965

Salisbury, Rhodesia

Dear Mother and Daddy,

Thanks very much for the letter. Daddy, your writing is shocking! It took me about six reads to figure out what you had written. In your next letter, please print Dr. Sarthou's name very carefully and thanks very much for the useful information about him. Boy, will I ever look him up.

As of now, I really can't say what is going to happen as far as getting out of Africa. We are leaving Rhodesia on July 1 and Tony is trying his best to get us a lift as far as Lake Tanganyika and then we can catch a ferry across the lake. We will then catch a boat to Lake Victoria (which borders Uganda) and stay there for about two weeks, then catch a train to Nairobi (the capital of Kenya) and try and get as many visas there as possible. From Nairobi, we will take a train to Mombasa to catch a ship to Aden in Arabia or anywhere – just so long as we get out of Africa. Or if that doesn't materialize we will have to go back to Beira and try to catch an Indian ship to Kuwait which will be quite expensive.

Don't worry about me financially, because I will have approximately $1,500 when I leave here. Hope to have some left when I get home to have my ears clipped and my face lifted. I am sending all my slides home so y'all can have a field day with them. Tony took Barb and I to see two German chaps who live in Nairobi and they have given us quite a lot of information. They are also getting in touch with the shipping agencies in Mombasa to see if they can get us fake tickets on a boat because if one doesn't have a ticket out of Kenya, one has to pay $600 at the border and sometimes one doesn't get it back!

I just don't know what to say in a letter to Mrs. Cay [family friend – Bonnie is her daughter]. What if I send a letter saying I know Bonnie will pull through and by the time she receives it Bonnie has died, which will surely happen. It will be a miracle if she pulls through. Received a lovely letter from Linda Smith and Seig the other day. I didn't win anything on the sweepstake, but I did win a booby prize, which was a free ticket for next month. Better than nothing, I guess!

I'm really annoyed with Bubba. I just don't know if I have $100 or $50 of his money and time is running out. Remember I am leaving Salisbury at the end of May. Anyway I will get him a large zebra skin which will cost $67. Please ask Bubba how much money he sent me altogether including the $25 he sent me in South Africa. It is either $175 or $225. I just can't seem to explain that I am most concerned because I want to do the right thing by him, and I can't concentrate on any of the things I have to do from trying to figure out how much money he has left. Also, I sent a parcel from here in December which I can't remember if y'all received. It contained a large light wood mask, 13 table mats, elephant lamp, Kudu lamp, knife, fork and spoon salad set, small boat (wooden) with two men in it, two whiskey bottle tops, small wood (light) mask, curved fruit bowl with handle, one large fruit bowl, four long Watusi paintings, four square Watusi paintings and a small Mau Mau warrior statue with white feathers on his head. Please ask Bubba if he received them. Also, I have sent three parcels in April with my things mixed in with his, so please undo every piece of newspaper. Why I have gotten so mixed up is because I have bought most of the things with my money and then deducted it from Bubba's.

Now I hope I will be on my way home when I leave here. You don't have to remind me I'm not getting any younger. All I have to do is look in the mirror to reach that conclusion. Barb and I are getting along fine now since we aren't living with each other! I might go visit both Terre'Blanches again in South Africa in June, but I haven't written to ask them yet.

Since I've been going out with Tony, I have never had it so good. He pays for me to go to the hairdressers twice a week and I have some lovely clothes now. I eat very well and he really looks after my health. I've never been so content, but that will all be over in two months' time so I must start preparing for it. Mother, you don't have to look stupid when people ask you what I'm doing! Just say I'm learning for myself how other nations live, which is more than those narrow-minded people have done in Savannah! Linda Smith says Caro and Emory [family friends] are getting a divorce, but don't say anything. I will write Caro instead of her parents.

Tony is picking me up in a few minutes for lunch so must go. I forgot to mention that last weekend he took me to Mtoko which is about 100 miles from Salisbury. We saw bushmen's paintings in caves which were up high on different kopjes (hills). We had a guide and was he ever funny! He carried a hatchet in the form of a caveman's stick. He cut me a limb from a tree so I could use it to walk up the rocks and stones. I took many pictures of the paintings and just hope they come out.

Tomorrow is the election[47] and I really hope Smith gets it. He has to get 22 out of 28 seats which is quite a lot for any man to get.

The other night Tony and I met two men friends at the Cock-a-dor (very nice restaurant and bar) and I hadn't had anything to eat all day and got drunk on four beers. Can't remember much but he told me I acted

---

[47] The results of the election was a victory for the ruling Rhodesian Front, led by Ian Smith, which won 50 of the 65 seats in the Legislative Assembly of Rhodesia. Later that year, the government made a unilateral declaration of independence (UDI).

like a perfect lady and no one saw them carry me out. He and the other men apparently were quite intrigued because I speak with a frightfully English accent now, and I went back to my Southern accent without even knowing it! Tony thought it was the cutest thing he had ever heard. Every day he keeps saying, "Let's go drink beer" because he wants to hear me speak like that again. He said it fitted me to a tee because I am the slowest person he has ever met and never before has he heard someone say so many times, "I'll do it tomorrow"!

It's lunch time and I have a hairdresser appointment so I must go.

Love Barbara

Salisbury

May 25, 1965

Salisbury, Rhodesia

Dear Mother and Daddy,

I'm afraid this will be the last letter you will receive from me until we reach Uganda on July 20.

I'm sitting here on Tony's floor typing away at 3 am with a baboon spider across the room from me and my nerves are just shot. Tony is picking me up on May 29 (he's in Malawi) and we are going all over Rhodesia and I'm going to visit both Terrys families when he is in Johannesburg. Will be back in Salisbury on the 15th for a few days, but won't have time to write and will be expecting a letter from y'all and that naughty brother of mine telling me what to get him. I don't have time at work to write because I'm training a new girl and that takes up my time. I'm trying to get organized with shots, packing, sewing, and trying to get everything I need for the journey. Thanks very much for the parcel, except you didn't send the right mascara. I wanted the one with the brush and it comes in a white plastic container. I have just done my hair with the dye you sent, and it is the first time in three years it has been done properly. Gee, I look much better. Do you think you can send three Helena Rubinstein waterproof mascara in plastic tube container with brush to the American Embassy in Kuwait, Iraq? You can get the address from the library. I think when I leave Rhodesia I will be so upset.

Barb came around today (it's a holiday, Commonwealth Day) and I just don't think I shall go all the way with her. What a conniving, shrewd bitch she is! I still will pick up my mail at 19 Wellington House. I will send about 10 rolls of film and just pray they get there. I'm being tested for bilharzia again and just hope I don't have it. Lee – the U.S. student – really has the hots for me and is giving me a gorgeous impala skin which fits on a double bed. You know I have led so many lives in the last years, but I think my life in Rhodesia with Tony is the most tragic and memorable. It will take me a long time to get over him.

Love B.

—⟢∞⟣—

Salisbury

May 26, 1965

Salisbury, Rhodesia

To Jane,

Leaving May 28 to travel all around Rhodesia and going back to both families in Transvaal – going to Hwange Game Reserve, Victoria Falls – back in Salisbury June 15 for three days then off again – come back June 31 to pick up Barbara – Tony will drive us to Ndola in Zambia – another chap will take us to bottom of Lake Tanganyika – we will catch a ferry that goes across once a month to top of lake – will stay in Uganda with Indian friends then cross east to Kenya heading for Mombasa. Can't go up north in Kenya because they are fighting Somalia and it's a restricted area. From Mombasa we will try to work on a boat to Kuwait or if worse comes to worse, we will have to go to Aden. When we get to Kuwait we will go all around Iraq – Iran, Afghanistan, Pakistan, then the border and all around India.

Don't know how we will get into East Pakistan – understand there is no road! In Burma we are allowed 48 hours to get through the country but somehow don't think we will make it. Then to Thailand – Cambodia, maybe Malaya Laos, South Vietnam and then try to catch a fishing boat to Hong Kong, and another to Japan. Don't know how I'll get across the Pacific.

If you write, send it to American Embassy, Kuwait. Will be in Nairobi, Kenya around end of July.

Love Barbara

———————— ⚬⛧⚬ ————————

Bulawayo, Hwange Game Reserve

May 30, 1965

Bulawayo, Rhodesia

Dear Mother and Daddy,

Tony and I are now on the way to Hwange Game Reserve and Victoria Falls. We spent the night at some friends of Tony's in Bulawayo. It's 300 miles southwest of Salisbury and the country all the way down was plain and barren but the gorgeous orange yellowish, gold bush grass just absolutely enthralled me. I thought the whole landscape was beautiful. We passed several little provincial towns such as Que Que (pronounced Kweck Quee), Gwelo and Gatooma. Between Gwelo and Bulawayo there is a large river called Shangani. The river is named after a once very powerful tribe in Central Africa who were wiped out in what is now Rhodesia by the Matabele tribe led by Chief Lobenzula who left the Zulu tribe in Natal in South Africa. The British South African company sent a patrol to the area in 1893 and they were slaughtered by the Matabele tribe.

Outside Bulawayo we saw a large plateau of 180ft. high, 1½ mile long, 600 yds wide where the Matabele drove all the Shonas (the name for all the tribes combined in Central Africa) over the top of the plateau, mostly women and children, and took complete control of Southern Rhodesia. The history of this country is so interesting if one knows a little about the different tribes. The Africans in Southern Rhodesia are so different from the ones in Salisbury and its surroundings. They say it's because the Matabele, coming from the Zulu tribe, are very proud warriors, whereas the Ma Shonas are very different.

Bulawayo is the second largest town in Rhodesia (smaller than Savannah), the people are very friendly and the city is modern, but no skyscrapers like Salisbury.

May 31 Entered Hwange Game Reserve at 2 and didn't see any unusual game. It was packed but since Tony's best friend is a ranger at another camp in Hwange, they gave us a room. Got up first thing and entered the park at 8 am which is late because everyone goes in at 6.30 as this is the best time to see lions and leopards. We were driving along at 40 mph and I kept saying to Tony, "If we see elephants, let's tease them!" and lo and behold, a male elephant ran directly in front of us. If we had been a second earlier, he would have crashed into my side of the car. He turned around and flapped his ears and trumped and started charging us and Tony was reversing with a diesel motor and not a fast pick-up! I was completely paralyzed and couldn't even click my camera for pictures of this thing charging like a bat out of hell!

Tony was really shook up too but didn't let me know. Before that we went to a water hole and Tony told me to get out and take a close picture. My knees were shaking as I was so scared. The elephants started flapping their ears and one burped and I flung around so fast and ran with all my might to the car. Before I could even shut the door, Tony was driving like hell and I turned around to see the gigantic creatures that had chased me and I didn't even know it. I never mentioned teasing them again and every time I saw one my stomach got all shaky. It was mating time which is why they were so jumpy.

Just as we were on our way out of the camp, we turned a corner and there was a herd of about 50 adults drinking with babies. The commotion that went on! Mothers with their young dashed off into the bush with a few males for their protection and all the other males went in different directions. Two were standing in front of us on the road and we didn't know if there were any around the corner. All of a sudden, they had completely surrounded us! Some were only 6ft. away from the car! I had just had it and was almost in convulsions. We sat there for an hour, not even daring to hit mosquitoes. They just stood there eating and watching us. Finally, they edged far enough from the road and we tore past them.

⋯⋯⋯⋯⋯⋯⋯⋯⋯

Victoria Falls

June 1, 1965

Victoria Falls, Rhodesia.

Arrived here 7.30 at night after driving through really wild country from Hwange. We are staying at a camp (naturally on the Rhodesian side) and when I went to bed, I just lay there listening to the mumbling of the majestic Falls only 150 yards away from my window. I soon fell asleep from the exhaustion of driving over such rough country.

June 1 Tony bangs on my door at 6 am to take me all over the Falls while the sun was rising. I didn't realize it would be such a cold, long walk and I didn't prepare myself for it. We first went to the section where Livingstone[48] (I can't go into him so read up on his life) first saw the Falls. There is a statue of him standing looking at the smallest part, but I can imagine he just about fainted when he saw it after tracking through the bush for months with hardly any water to drink.

The Falls has three different sections. We walked all around different parts but sometimes we just couldn't see the water flowing for all the spray. Went through the rainforest and my feet were numb from the spray. We ended up on the train track that goes across one of the gorges after it flows from the main gorge and walked a mile back down the highway to Tony's car. We then drove all along the Rhodesia side of the river and there are large signs on baobab trees warning of crocodiles and elephants. It is so gorgeous, I just don't see how anyone could do it justice in a poem. We then went through the game reserve that borders

---

[48] David Livingstone (1813-1873) was a Scottish physician, Christian missionary and explorer. He was the first European to make a trans-African passage and named many natural features, such as waterfalls and rivers.

the Zambezi and Tony and I kept pulling up to the banks looking for lions and crocs on foot. A little (actually quite large!) warthog was about to charge us, but Tony took care of him. We saw a lot of different bucks and a few elephants. The scenery was real bushy and gorgeous.

In the afternoon we went on a cruise down the Zambezi (on top of the Falls) and saw snakes, crocs, lots of hippos and bucks drinking. We then went to a small island called Palm Island and had tea and the monkeys were really funny. After that we cruised up the Zambia side and circled several islands that were stacked with elephants. It's mating season and two elephants were doing just that and although no one said anything, everyone was rather embarrassed! We docked when the sun was just going down and was it ever green and gorgeous. There is an old saying here, "Once one drinks water from the Zambezi, one can never forget the Zambezi River". We had a barbecue that night on an open fire and a local washed up for us.

Wednesday, June 2 Got up at 7 am and Tony had breakfast waiting for me. He had an appointment at the hospital in Livingston on the Zambian side. After that we took pictures of kraals (locals' villages) and then had tea at a restaurant in a garden right on the banks of the Zambezi. After that we walked all around the Zambia side of the Falls and then Tony took me to see some of the gorges. About 2 pm, we went back to the Rhodesian side and Tony tried to book me on a plane over the Falls but they were booked out. So, we got our raincoats and went through the rainforest again. God, I just went crazy with clicking and took two rolls of film. Without a doubt, it is the most beautiful thing I have ever seen.

We went back to camp at 5, and took a bath, had a barbecue outside on open fire and went to bed at 7 pm. Someone banged on my door at 2.30 am to tell me the 'master' wanted me to be ready at 3 am. Arrived back in Bulawayo at 9 am, had a lovely breakfast and Tony gave me money for the hairdressers (where I am now) and lunch. We will be here for two days and then we are going to South Africa. Winter has come and it is snowing in Johannesburg and freezing here.

⸺⸺⸺❦⸺⸺⸺

Zambia

Kafue, Lusaka, Ndola, Mpulungu

July 2, 1965

Ndola, Zambia

Dear Mother and Daddy,

Tony rented a caravan to bring Barb and me up to Ndola. It took two days. We had a good time but the thought of Tony leaving me just made me sick. Hit the Zambian border at Chirundu and spent an hour and a half on the Zambian side. God, they were so unorganized – the man in charge helped us and was he ever a bastard! Spent the night at a hotel (in the caravan) in Kafue next to the Kafue River.

We entered Lusaka, the capital of Zambia, the next morning. After Lusaka, we passed Chisamba, Broken Hill, Kapiri Mposhi, and then finally reached Ndola. There is absolutely nothing between the cities, and the cities themselves are filthy. We are now five miles from the Congo border. We are staying in a lovely flat (a friend of Tony's) and we were meant to be picked up at 4.45 am tomorrow by Clive, the chap who is taking us to Mpulungu where we catch the boat. However, the boat broke down and we were told we would have to wait at Mpulungu a week and then they didn't know if it could be repaired. Boy, I was really sweating it. Tony will be back in about an hour to hitch up his caravan to drive to Bulawayo which will take three days. This is where we will say goodbye. I'm so upset I just took two tranquillizers to calm my nerves down. It feels like my arms and legs have been cut off.

I don't know how long I will travel with Barb, but honestly, we just don't get along. There are very few white people left in Zambia. Those that are left are making as much money as they can and then getting out. Pay is double here to try and keep people here! You will receive this letter after I have been there so I may as well tell you we're going through the Congo. Only for 65 miles and we will have a Congo guard on the truck to shoot rebels if they attack us. Last time this chap went through, the Congo guard slipped and shot the chap right through the leg. He had to drive 50 miles to a missionary station to have it removed and then they didn't have any antiseptic! Boy, we are really in Africa now. We are 40 miles from where Dag Hammarskjold's[49] plane crashed. You can start marking the map again because I'm on the road. Tony will mail you two parcels. Each of them has semi-precious stones in them so please be careful when you open. Also, a copper bottle opener for Bubba. One is a SAA airlines bag. I will write from Uganda.

Love Barbara

⊷⦿⊶

Zambia/Congo

Kitwe, Katanga Province, Zambia; then Mufulira, The Congo; then Pontoon, Fort Rosebery, Kasama, Abercorn, Mpulungu, Lake Tanganyika, Zambia

July 4, 1965

Mpulungu, Zambia

Dear Mother and Daddy,

Wednesday, June 30 We got up at 4.30, but didn't sleep all night in fear of not waking up. Clive was supposed to pick us up at 5 but didn't come until 8.30. Gosh I was really sweating getting out on the road. He came charging up in a gigantic diesel truck, and off we went to Kitwe to pick up some food for the men who work for Irvin & Johnson[50]. Went through Mufulira and there were loud speakers broadcasting something about the city of Kasanga. It's the largest copper place in the copper belt. We went 30 on up and hit the Congo. Boy, I was fascinated by the way the women dressed and wore their hair. There were about 20 soldiers (Tshombe's[51] men) but they wouldn't let us take a picture.

---

[49] Dag Hammarskjold (1905-1961) was a Swedish economist and diplomat who served as the second Secretary-General of the United Nations from April 1953 until his death in a plane crash in Ndola in September 1961.
[50] One of South Africa's largest fishing companies, based in Cape Town.
[51] Moise Tshombe (1919-1969) was a Congolese businessman and politician. He served as the president of the secessionist state of Katanga from 1960 to 1963 and then as prime minister of the Democratic republic of Congo from 1964 to 1965.

It then took us 2½ hours to go 42 miles as the road was so bad. This was the Southern Katanga Province and three weeks before, many had been killed by the rebels. God I've never seen so much bush. I just don't see how people can escape through it. I kept hoping the Congolese soldiers would jump out of the bush and search the car, but they didn't.

We entered the Congo at Mufulira, 109 miles from Elizabethville, and crossed the Luapula River which divides Zambia from the Congo. We then had to wait for an hour for a ferry to go back into Zambia at Pontoon and headed for Fort Rosebery. I drove 30 miles and my whole body was shaking as the roads were so terrible, that it felt as if my head was going to fall off! We had a beer at the hotel at Fort Rosebery but it was very dirty. Barb drove 100 miles in the dark over the worst of the corrugated road. It got so cold and I felt sorry for the little African boy who hitched on the back. The blankets we had wrapped around us smelt so bad, we could hardly breathe. They belong to the men that ride with Clive when he carries fish. I was so afraid of catching lice or TB! At one time, I was so cold I hid and slept under the dashboard.

We reached Kasama at 12.30 and were so exhausted we slept until 3.30. We didn't see any lions which are always seen in this area. Honestly, Clive knows everyone and always gives them presents so he can get through customs easily! All the Congo officials know him and boy the smuggling that goes on through the Congo is crazy! Apparently, a lot of the stuff for the Congolese people is sold on the black market and smuggled to other countries! A 3¼ lb. ten of chicken cost 28¢ in Zambia and the dollars are just flooding the country.

From Kasama we went to Abercorn and then 23 miles to Mpulungu, arriving at 6 am. The whole trip took 22 hours in all on the truck – 432 miles of dirt road (if one could even call it a road!) and that dreadful smell. I can honestly say it was the worst ride we've ever had, as far as strain and dirt.

We are staying in a large house right on Lake Tanganyika and it is beautiful here. Keith and Tom (who work for Irvin & Johnson) live in the house and they have been waiting for weeks for us to come! The house is so unorganized and the two servants are in a flap because they never have females here. Keith is South African and Tom is Scottish – both around 50 and are they a riot and so sweet. They are running around trying to make us comfortable – and what a sense of humour. Two other Scottish men who flew down from the copper belt to repair the freezers for the fresh fish are staying here plus Clive, so seven of us all together in the house.

Keith gave us his room and he is sleeping on the stoop (porch) under a mosquito net. We have to sleep under one too, and the water has to be filtered after it comes out of the tap. We had a gorgeous breakfast and sat until 2.30 talking. We washed all our clothes in disinfectant and had to scrub our body with a brush. We all took a nap at 2.30 and I woke up at 8.30 to someone talking on the phone very loud in Greek! Went into the living room and two Greeks came for a visit and all of them are getting very jolly with the whiskey which is usual procedure every night because they never see people and they would probably go mad if they didn't drink! They think they have 18 months left before all the Europeans are kicked out of Zambia. The Liemba boat has just come in and we leave tomorrow night. The chaps are sad to see us go because maybe it will be another six months before they see anyone, except Clive. We have to rotate meals because they only have pottery and silver for five, and poor Keith had to eat out of the dog's bowl! Honestly, they were such good sports and funny as hell. We've done nothing but laugh since we've been here. Tony gave us 10 boxes of prunes and I have been going to the bathroom every day and sometimes twice, terrific while it lasts! There are leaches in the lake, snakes and crocs. Went to bed at 11.30 and was so tired I just couldn't sleep.

Love B.

Zambia/Tanzania

Lake Tanganyika, Magiobos, Kigoma, Zambia; then Mwanza, Ujiji, Kigoma, Tanzania

July 6, 1965

Lake Tanganyika, Zambia

Dear Mother and Daddy,

July 5 Clive and Tom took us to the Liemba (the ferry) at 11 am and we had to catch a small boat with hundreds of people. When we reached a certain point, our boat crashed into all the small handmade boats filled with locals and we had to go back to the shore. We started out again and this time made it and people were trying to get on our boat and people from our boat were trying to get on the Liemba. People were being pushed right and left. One would have thought the Liemba was on fire! I have never seen such inorganization in my life!

We finally made our way through all the crowds and went up top and met the Captain, Henry the engineer, and the navigator. They're Scottish and were funny as the devil. They stay drunk all the time because they would go mad if they didn't. We drank for a while and then got back on the small boat and Tom took us to get our things since the Liemba was leaving at 3. Before that we were sat in the dining room and they didn't have any food – damn cheek because we were 10 minutes late! Before we left, Clive gave us $15 for food and he also told Barb that Tony had told him to "do something with that girl because she drove me insane on the way to Nobla." Well, when the boat started, Barb and I had it out and she said the only reason I stayed with Tony is because of all the things he gave me and that I bummed from him. She is so jealous because her boyfriend (first time a chap has taken interest in her!) made her pay for half the petrol when they went on a trip. So, I don't think we will be too long together. I felt ill from the Tanzanian beer and had a terrible headache the rest of the day. Sat on deck (were 1st class, $10) with all the crew and had a drink and then went to bed.

July 7 Woke up at 8.30 and Dennis (Thanos), a Greek passenger who is a friend of Clive's, knocked on our door and wanted to know if we wanted breakfast. We said no and ate steak from a tin from some of the food Tony had given us. We stopped at every port and I wanted to go ashore with Dennis and accidentally walked to 3rd class where all the locals were – I swear there must have been 200 of them all cramped in a small space. Children were doing their business on the floor, women were cooking next to it. All the women's bosoms were bare, there was garbage all over the floor and the smell was unbearable. I got out of there as quick as possible and found Dennis on the other side of the boat.

We stood there for 15 minutes being pushed between the ones trying to get on the boat and the ones trying to get off. People were bringing on pots which they cook their meals in, which got stuck on the edges. Finally, after everyone had moved out of the way, we clambered out and got on the small boat. There were about 40 locals. When we reached the village, we had to stay in the boat and more people got in. There wasn't even enough room for the passengers of the Liemba but somehow, they got in! Went back to the Liemba and saw Barb sitting with the 3rd engineer Some of the women have many tribal marks on their faces and their ears have many large holes. Went to lunch but didn't have much appetite from the stress of the morning. Dennis paid for our meal, and won't let us pay for any of them. The food is excellent and for a change, I am eating very well.

After lunch we just sat on 1st class deck and chatted and then the navigator came to fix my pack. He sewed canvas on the strap with sailing thread and I only hope it stays. I went to take a bath but someone was already there! Henry ordered drinks for us and we stood while an "African gentleman" sat at the bar. The Captain has no control over the third class passengers and one just couldn't believe the utter chaos. Many drink and sit around all day. If there aren't any more chairs left, we have to stand even though we've paid for it! They sleep under and in the cargo boats and cook there as well.

We then went into dinner after watching the shows and two Africans sat across from us. One was really fat and took in everything said. I felt like he's one that would report you. The other was trying to act civilized and he asked if he could borrow my map on East Africa and I had to say yes. He just wanted an excuse to come to our cabin! We can't take any pictures because they have been told that people with cameras are spies and enemies. The fat one eats like a pig and he let out a gigantic burp. It was all I could do to keep from laughing. Dennis paid for it again as usual.

After that Dennis (Thanos) came to our cabin to go over the map with us and then Henry came in to see if we wanted to play bridge with the Captain and himself but Barb didn't feel like it so that was that. All four of us went over the map. From Kigoma to Masaka in Uganda, it's 365 miles and Barb is terrified to even catch a bus! For two years I have been trying to tell her how foolish and dangerous it would be through these pro-Communist countries but no, she knew it all and wouldn't listen to anyone. And now we are right in the middle of it she's terrified and refuses to go the way we planned, but I'm going on. If she wants to come, she'll have to behave herself and stop thinking she's the boss. Went to bed at 10 and slept like a log.

July 8 Woke up by a hell of a noise. They were scrubbing the deck above our cabin, and also in front of it. It annoyed me but was glad to see the crew were working for a change. I was starving so hurried and dressed and went into breakfast. They were scrubbing the boat with sand for soap and a half of coconut for the brush! After breakfast we sat looking at the lovely mountains on the Tanzanian side. At 12.30 we stopped at a small village called Magiabos. Thanos went to shave and Barb and I went upstairs with Henry and took pictures of the loading-unloading. I was shaking that someone would see us but I don't think they did. The crew were buying fish and bananas because on the way back to Mpulungu, the boat doesn't stop anywhere. The bananas were approximately a foot long and I couldn't even put my hand around them as they were so fat! The fish and all the other food are sitting below our windows and boy, does it smell. We had a gorgeous lunch and then we tried to sleep but just couldn't for all the racket the children were making outside our door. Hell, I almost screamed out but something told me I shouldn't.

Left Magiabos at 6.30. We stayed there such a long time because the Liemba docks at 4 am and everyone make a hell of a noise jumping from the boats and customs doesn't come on until 9 so they don't want to get into Kigoma too early. The Liemba was built in Germany in 1913 for the

East African Railways for $60,000 and it cost another $45,000 to ship it to Dar es Salaam and then to the Lake and have it put back together. It is still running on the same engine.

Henry dropped us on the main street of Kigoma and we went to every shop (Indians own all the shops) to try and find a little beany and African shirt. The market place and main street looked like something in the movies, big trenches and large green trees in the shape of an apple lined each side. We walked to the supposedly first class hotel and waited for Henry to come. The Captain came first and then the bank manager, two Belgians, one Italian, Henry and the engineer from the Liemba. Everyone knew we were coming for over a month. We stayed for about an hour and then Barb and I went back to the house for a bath. We looked for the train crossing that night for Tabia and understood the Belgians were getting in touch with someone to see if they were going to Bukoba but no luck.

Just before we had to catch the train, we decided to go by bus straight to Mwanza and catch a boat to Port Bell, Kampala in Uganda, but then we found out that we could stay in Mwanza and then catch the bus direct to Bukoba the next morning. It is 55 miles from the Uganda border and 90 miles from Masaka where we are going to stay. We ate lunch and I wrote while they took a kip and then the Belgians came and Henry fixed me some kippers and then we were off to the European Club. I really had a super time. Played dots and drank three quarts of Tusker beer (they only sell quarts!). At 11 we went to one of the Belgian's houses (he's a titled Count) and it was magnificent. Built by the Germans when they controlled Tanganyika before the First World War. The swimming pool and the rooms were as long as our whole house. We stayed there until 2 and then went home and Henry fixed cheese sandwiches and we went to bed.

July 9 The Captain came in our room at 9 am with tea. I had such a hangover I just wanted to die but was hungry all the same. I was the only one who ate and then we went to buy stamps and find out about the bus. We were invited to the Count's house for dinner and I was placed at the head of the table. Thank God I'm accustomed to continental table manners as it was very formal, but the servants were barefoot. (Now if any snobs enquire about me, just tell them I was a guest of a Belgian count in Tanzania!) I still felt terrible when we left there and went home to sleep it off. We then left at 5 because the boat left at 6 for Mpulugu. I sat on the steps watching it leave down in the bay. Then Henry took us to Ujiji, a small village not far from Kigoma. We went to the exact place Dr. Livingstone met Stanley and took a picture and hoped for the best that we wouldn't be reported to the authorities. The view to Ujiji was gorgeous, very tropical and everything is so green. Palm trees everywhere, and in some places it's a little jungle. Now listen, there has been a change in our plans concerning Tanzania so in order not to waste the stamps I'm sending these 2 pages separate. Will finish this letter. All has been good so far.

Love Barbara

<hr />

Tanzania/Uganda/Kenya

Kigoma, Biharamulo, Bihar, Bukoba, Tanzania; Masaka, Kampala, Entebbe, Jinja, Tororo, Uganda; Eldoret, Nakuru, Nairobi, Nakuru Lake, Kenya

July 9, 1965

Kigoma, Tanzania

After the Liemba left, Barb was taking a bath and John, the houseboy, came and told me someone wanted to see me. I went to the door and saw a large well-dressed African standing there. I asked him what he wanted and he said, "Don't be afraid." However, the way he looked at me, I just broke out in sweat. He kept asking me questions such as where had we come from, and where were we going. He said he wanted to talk to both of us. I told him we were going out to dinner and he asked when were we leaving. I told him tomorrow morning. He then said he would come with us! I was so scared I started shuddering – six months ago, all Europeans were under arrest for no reason at all, said they were spies. Just then, Thanos walked by with his African driver (from Salisbury) and the driver's wife. I yelled at them to come in but that I was in a hurry because I was going out, and the three of them came in. I excused myself from my visitor and he said he would be back later. Barb heard it all from the bathroom and was terrified.

I went out after John had left and locked the front door and the Captain went off with the key. At 12 we went back to the house and Barb and the Count arrived first and went around to the kitchen door. When we arrived they said the houseboy must be in there because they heard someone walking around inside. However, I told them that was impossible because I had bolted the door when he left!

They had to break down the door and John and his companion came up and helped. John's companion was carrying a long panga knife and hiding it behind him. They broke down the door and we went in. When I was in the living room, I heard a sound like a body hitting a big piece of furniture. We searched the whole house but couldn't find anyone. Thanos was supposed to be there by now but he wasn't. Everyone was so tired so the Duke stayed with us until Thanos came back and John and his friend went home. Thanos came about 12.30 and he slept in a room and his African driver and wife slept on the floor on the porch next to my room. Barb was in Henry's bedroom. Thanos' driver slept with a butcher knife's next to him. He also was afraid!

Thanos woke us at 4.30 and we were picked up at 5.15 am by the Duke and he took us to the market where we caught the bus. We got in 1st class and the ticket man was a very large old Indian with a turban. He helped us with our luggage. It was dark for about an hour and we stopped about every mile. The driver was a maniac and the road was corrugated all the way to Biharamulo, about 265 miles! When it got light I saw a rooster tied under the seat in front of me. Hell, the thing kept pecking at my feet so I couldn't spread them out! Plus the rooster was doing jobbies and on an empty stomach I felt ill. Thank goodness the bus was the size of a Greyhound Bus or we would have been rocked all over the place.

We were going all the way to Mwanza – 160 miles further to spend the night, and the next morning we were meant to catch the bus back to Biharamulo and then to Bukoba, but the ticket man informed us we would transfer at Bihar and go straight to Bukoba and be there at 6 pm the same day. People couldn't keep their eyes off Barb's fair hair. No one would help us with our luggage when we changed buses except the old ticket man. The next bus was shocking and we had to hold onto the rail in front of our seat the whole trip as it was so bouncy. Many people got on with blue plastic briefcases inscribed with the word Uhuru (Freedom). We reached Bukoba around 5.30 – what a day! A man on the bus said he would take us to a European hotel and got a taxi for us. The hotel was bad news and run by a woman who wanted 45 shillings a piece so I waited there while Barb went off in the taxi to another place. She came back and said it was only 34 shillings for both of us, so off we went! The taxi cost us $1.20 and we asked him to find out what time the bus was leaving in the morning and pick us up. We were so exhausted and I had a migraine. We went into the bar, had an orange Fanta, went upstairs. Took a shower with Dettol on the cloth, washed my clothes and went to bed at 8. Woke up in the middle of the night and a man was hollering, "Duel kiskarie!" We thought he was saying, "Two girls!" and I kept saying, "Police!" We couldn't move as we were so scared. Finally, he said in English, "He beat me, stole my medicine, and we must go to the police!" and off he went.

July 11   Woke up at 8.30 and ate some prunes (we're carrying a box with 10 foods in it) and pork and beans out of a tin and the taxi driver just walked into our room and said the bus was leaving in 15 minutes! What chaos! We finally made it to the taxi and he kept telling us that we were too late but we went anyway. When we arrived, no one seemed to know when it was leaving and others said it didn't go on Sunday. We didn't know where and what to do, so Barb sat guarding our things and I had to walk a mile to the post office to mail y'all two letters. Went back and Barb said she saw six cars with Indians driving to the border – we wanted to get out of that dreadful town so I stood on the road and a Mercedes Benz came along with an African chauffeur and an Indian in the back. We jumped in and they took us to the border and we crossed to Uganda.

Uganda is greener than Tanzania and the locals are not as poor. The national foodstuff is bananas. We reached Zabie's house which is in the back of their material shop. Zabie was at the mosque and so was her family except an older brother who let us in. Zabie's sister-in-law (whom I met in London) greeted us and we waited for the family to come back from the mosque. About an hour later, they arrived (all the women were in saris) and then we were informed if we had come any earlier it would have been bad as Sunday was the last day of a religious celebration! They are Isma'ilism with His Highness the Aga Khan[52] as their God. Aga Khan is 28 and his mother was American and is he ever a playboy! They are very religious – they visit the mosque four times a day and in the middle of a conversation will start praying on beads like a rosary. They change their saris several times a day and are they ever beautiful, with pure gold and silver weaved in the material.

When we arrived, we told the family we had posted four letters from Tanzania and what we had written in them. They said we were mad because all the letters leaving the country are opened to see if money is in them and to see if anything bad has been written about their country! Well we were nervous wrecks and knew they would open them on Tuesday as Monday is a holiday, and in such a small town naturally they would suspect and then open three fat letters to Canada and U.S. Honestly, we just couldn't think of anything else except the police coming to get us. Kenya, Uganda and Tanzania are all part of East Africa so we could be arrested in Uganda for a crime committed in Tanzania!

We talked until dinner and then we ate Indian food. Then Zabie and her cousin Asheik (a boy from the Congo) drove us around in her Mercedes-Benz – she's only 22! Masaka is very dirty with several areas that look like slums. Came back and before we knew, it was 11 o'clock. Took a bath and the three of us slept on mattresses because her two brothers and their wives and children were sleeping in the spare bedrooms. The family went to the mosque again at 11 and came back at 12.30.

July 12 National Holiday of Uganda so we went to the parade at the field grounds. What a riot! Many were barefoot and marching like crazy. The band was really good. But God I just about died when we had to stand for the Uganda national anthem. All the women were dressed in their national dresses and the head of the district gave a speech in English. At the parade we thought every policeman walking towards us was coming to arrest us! After that we were supposed to go for a picnic on Lake Victoria but it rained so we just drove around and went to the only hotel for a drink and then to the movies.

[52] Sir Sultan Mahomed Shah (1877-1957), known as Aga Khan III, was the 48th Iman of the Nizari Isma'ili branch of Shia Islam.

Mrs. Jiwa (Zabie's mother) is such a darling – she sits at the table with her legs crossed and sometimes after a meal she puts her feet on the table, which I thought was a riot.

Tuesday, July 13 Well this was the day they would come if they were going to arrest us. We couldn't eat as we were so scared. Every time the phone rang we were just about in the fainting stage. At 11 am, we went to the police station to register and we were just shaking. Asheik waited outside because he was afraid the police would ask for his passport and he didn't have one either! I think he smuggles gold and diamonds, as do many others from the Congo, and U.S. dollars are floating just like water. Asheik is 21 and has cleared $150,000 in 2½ years! I have never in my life heard of people talking such big money, but if they get caught, they've had it.

We walked in and the first thing I noticed was three large police telephones and I immediately thought they were Kenyan, Ugandan, Tanzanian police reports coming through all the time. We were taken into a small room and had to wait for the immigration officer. I just about died when he came in – he was small, dressed nicely and cheeky as hell. He looked through our passports and kept stopping at my Mozambique, South African and Rhodesian permanent residence visas and also Barb's. But everything was o.k in the end.

Later on we were picked up (Asheik accompanied us because its improper for girls to go out with a chap who is not a good friend of the family) by an Indian chap and were taken 10 miles out of town to visit an old Frenchman (God, he must have been 90!) who once was a professional hunter about 60 years ago. Boy, it was a way out in the bush right in the middle of hundreds of banana trees. He took us inside and it made me sick, it was so smelly and dusty, but he had some gorgeous lion, leopard and cheetah skins. Also had a large picture of Prime Minister Obate[53] sitting on a throne and flags all around the pictures. We stayed about a half hour. He said that four days ago there were two lions around his house. We then went to the club and played ping-pong and then went home.

---

[53] Apollo Milton Obote (1925-2005) was a Ugandan politician who served as the second Prime Minister of Uganda from 1962-1966 and the second President of Uganda from 1966-1971 and 1980-1985.

July 15   Got up at 8, had breakfast and then walked to the doctor with Mr. Jiwa so I could show him the pills for migraine headaches. The night before I gave Mr. Jiwa two and he didn't have it in the morning. The doctor gave him a prescription and then we walked home. We then picked up our bracelets and a picture of the three of us in saris. (Forgot to mention but on July 14, we went to Zabie's brother's house and all wore saris. Gee, I almost looked Indian and I just couldn't walk in it! Seven yards for the out skirt that wraps around.)

We then went shooting and we didn't do too bad. I had to lie down and aim with a Bristol 202 rifle! We had a good dinner, packed our things and we were off at 1.30 in Zabie's Mercedes-Benz. We passed the equator at 2 and were in Kampala at 3 pm, which was also very dirty. We dropped Zabie off at the hairdresser and then took our things to Mary and Sadru's house (Zabie's brother and sister-in-law) and then we just rode around town and picked up Zabie. We eventually went to all the temples and mosques. Hindus put food in front of the Gods such as Ganesh, who is half elephant and half human, and paint the palms of their hands and feet. We all went to the movies that night and I had to keep lighting cigarettes for Asheik because his sister doesn't approve of smoking. The movie was rather good.

July 16   We went shopping again and things are so expensive here. For example, Revlon compact $3.50 and everything is imported because there are no factories. In the afternoon we drove to the Botanical Gardens in Entebbe about 15 miles from Kampala. Two chaps who go to school in Pakistan went with us. Certain parts were jungle and the rest flowers and green hills. We saw some children sliding down a lovely hill on a large bark of a banana tree so we tried it and was it fun. Then we drove to a beach with lovely white sand on Lake Victoria and walked for about 15 minutes.

That night we all went to a Chinese restaurant and white men were sitting with black women. The meal was quite nice but I felt like their mother as they looked so young. After that we went to a private dance hall and none of them drink because of their religion. I was so bored because they just wanted to jive. We left at 2.30 and I was so tired.

July 18   Woke up around 10 and Zabie started hurrying us as usual. We went to see all the mosques and it started raining. At 4 pm she drove us to a park and we walked around. Everyone was staring as usual. Also, she kept telling people that she was Eastern and not Western. That night Mary and Sadru went dancing and Barb and I finally thought we could get down to letter writing and packing, but the two chaps from Pakistan came and then Mary and Sadru came back with a chap who is going to Canada, so that was the end of our letter writing! Got to bed at 12.

July 20 We got up at 6 am and I went in to make some tea but couldn't find the switch to make the burner turn on. Woke Sadru up at 6.45 and he packed some cake for us and we were off. It was pouring down with rain and the bus was a ½ hour late. When it finally came, we had to wait in line (in the rain) for everyone to make up their minds where they wanted to sit. We were just drenched and it was freezing. Poor Sadru was sopping wet. We just had time to shake his hand and the bus pulled off in the pouring rain. Thank God we paid for 1st class and no one sat beside us. It rained for about three hours and stopped with the sun shining once in a while. They call it an Express Bus – I wonder what they would call a Greyhound! It still looked like the jungle with thousands of banana trees.

It took us two hours to get to Jinja which is 50 miles from Kampala. I was so thirsty for tea but someone told me the water in the city was bad so I didn't get any. Just before Jinja we passed over the Owen Falls Dam on the White Nile. The bus was going three miles but thank goodness the road was tarred. The Kenyan border was only 90 miles from Jinja and we were really sweating the letter business and paying a bond. Tororo was the last Uganda town and then we started looking for the border post but there wasn't one. What a relief!

We stopped for 15 minutes in Eldoret, Kenya and we were just dying to go to the bathroom and someone let us use his and it was at the back of several that opened onto a patio. It was a Turkish john but at least it flushed! Went back and sat on the bus and we were shocked at the tribal scars on people's bodies. They also had large holes in their ears as you will see in my slides. We started up again (more chickens on the bus) and just outside the town the bus hit a cow (they just won't get off the roads) and it made a terrible thump. No one seemed to care about the cow and the bus driver swore in Swahili at the boy who was herding them.

So far, we had only been 150 miles on dirt road this trip. Altogether we have been on 1,079 miles of dirt road from Kitwe, Zambia to Nairobi and most of the time one couldn't really consider them roads. I fell asleep and woke up with a fly in my mouth. It started getting dark when we entered Nakuru and we could see valleys as we were climbing up a mountain. After that it was too dark to see anything as we passed Gilgil and Naivasha.

We entered Nairobi at 9.30 and when we saw the lights of the city when we were coming down the mountains, we were astonished at the size of it. As the bus was pulling into the bus station, about 20 locals were hanging on the bus hollering, "Taxi, woman! Taxi, madame!' We couldn't believe our eyes. We waited for everyone to unload their smelly chickens and then I tried to get out with my one pack on my back and tin food in my hands which Tony had given me. None of the men helped us (thank goodness) and we started walking towards the phone in the station. Barb went into call Joachim (a friend of Tony's) but she couldn't get through. I stayed outside to watch our things and then saw a large sign that said "Beware of pickpockets"! It was now 10 pm and the locals were still hanging around us. We decided we better get away from this rough place.

We met George (who works with one of the big mining companies) and he said we could stay. We got into his lovely car and his house was quiet. His wife comes to see him once a year! Our bedroom was large and clean and while Barb took a hot bath, George and I went into the kitchen to cook something. I made a large spicy omelette (4 eggs apiece) and a pint of milk and then tea. George didn't eat and told us we should not sleep with the window open because snakes can come through the window. About three months ago, a snake came into a baby's room and the snake bit it and killed it! He also told us his servant's father was a Mau Mau and he has to be so careful what he says. Hell, it's like living in a police state. We went to bed at one and just collapsed.

We woke about 9.30 and George came to take us up town to call Joachim since he didn't have a phone. Joachim was in so we waited at the open cafe of the Stanley Hotel for him to pick us up. He came within 10 minutes with Chris, another friend of Tony's. It seemed so weird talking to him without Tony. Joachim then took us to his house and it is so sweet. Seven rooms and furnished with lovely furniture and he only pays $120 a month, furniture included. He has a servant (all servants are men here) and a garden boy. He has been stationed in Ceylon, India, Pakistan and has four gorgeous Persian rugs he bought in Persia. He is a miser though – counts every penny and tells us the price of everything. However, he has said he will take us to Mount Kilimanjaro in Tanzania in two weeks and I'm so excited.

I had a Hershey bar, the first one in 3½ years, cost 38¢! We then picked up our things from George's house and then he dropped us in town at the American Embassy and there were two letters from Tony, one from you, Mother, and one from Lee Hastings (the U.S. student who had the hots for me!). We then shopped around and went into curious shops and travel agencies. Nairobi is so beautiful and continental. It reminds me so much of Atlanta except not half as large and not such high hills. I went mad and bought a leopard handbag with skin on both sides. The one I sent home from Cape Town was cheetah. Inside is a zebra change purse, lighter and cig. holder, leopard wallet, two pairs of shoes, zebra belt. Please keep them in moth balls in a plastic bag. Then we went to a different travel agency and they told us that no European women were allowed in 3rd class because the conditions were so bad and we would probably catch TB! We will have to go to Mombasa and try and hitch a boat to Pakistan, Kuwait, or any place up that way. At 4.50 we walked to Joachim's office and then we went group shopping at a lovely modern supermarket. The only one I've seen like it in the whole of Africa, real Yankee. Then we went home and had supper and talked for about an hour and went to bed at 10.30.

July 21 Got up at 7, had breakfast and were off at 8. We stopped again and I had to buy a sweater because I lost my other one, cost $8 which killed me. Bought presents for everyone so I would have something to give everyone when I get home. Have to carry them with me. Got a lift with Joachim and went home to dinner and then back into town. Came home, had supper and went to bed. We just love shopping in these shops, even if we can't buy anything!

July 22 Got up some time and went into town and came home for lunch. After lunch we dyed our hair and while I was sitting there with black jazz on my hair, an Englishwoman walked in with her little girl. I had heard Joachim speak of her. She was separated from her husband who is with the British High Commission in Lusaka, Zambia. Joachim came in and saw me with all the stuff on my hair. They started speaking German and it really infuriated us. We felt like we were intruding. She stayed until 12 o'clock and woke the child up. The poor kid.

July 23 Woke and had breakfast. We went to immigration and were nervous wrecks about the bond for $700. Walked up to the check-in line. He gave us a form to fill out and we wrote 'tourist' instead of 'transit'. He asked for our plane ticket and I said, "I beg your pardon?" and he didn't answer. Boy, I thought we had had it when he turned our papers and passports over to an official. He asked us how much money we had and I said £260 and Barb said $700 – so we got permission for a month's stay in Uganda. I've never been so relieved. Joachim drove us home. I called up a friend of Dietmar's and he said he had been waiting for us. He sounded nice.

Dietmar's friend Scottish Ian came at 8 and I almost laughed in his face, he was so British-looking and anemic. Gave all his "jolly good show old chap" – I just couldn't look at Barb, as I was so afraid of laughing. He drove a brand-new Mercedes-Benz, really gorgeous. We went to a Chinese restaurant for a drink and then to the movies. Can't remember the name but it was filmed in Cyprus and about the resistance against the British in 1957 – an excellent film. It was at the Kenya Theatre and before the show we had to stand for the Kenyan national anthem. After the show we went to a lovely coffee bar, but he didn't even ask me if I wanted a sandwich, we just had coffee, big deal! Got home around 12 and Barb was just going to bed.

July 25 Sunday, we got up at 7, had a large breakfast and were off to Nakuru Lake 97 miles from Nairobi. This is the section we passed in the dark from Kampala.

Uganda

Masaka

July 12, 1965

Masaka, Uganda

Dear Mother and Daddy,

I'm very worried about correspondence and it is very risky mailing letters from East Africa but I'm keeping records and will mail when I leave this continent. Sorry about all this, but there is no other way. I just can't say anything.

We are staying with Zabie and the family is so kind to us. If everything goes well, I should be home in eight months' time. Can hardly wait to get to Nairobi to receive mail from y'all.

I miss Tony so much but that is life. I'm hoping I will have a little money left when I arrive home to go to IBM School to learn about computers.

I have sent Bonnie a letter and present and letter to Caro. Glad you received box with books, slippers, etc. Tony is sending two more. One is an SAA airlines bag. Now there are semi-precious stones in both parcels so go through everything. Also, a bottle opener (copper) for Ruby. Will get zebra skin for Bubba in Nairobi.

All is well considering we have come 2,000 miles from Salisbury. You must let me know immediately when you receive two letters from Tanzania, No. 1 and No. 2. If you don't receive them, big trouble for me, I can't explain.

Nothing else to say so will close. This is just to let you know I'm o.k.

Love Barbara.

Kampala

July 18, 1965

Kampala, Uganda

Dear Mother and Daddy,

Our stay in Kampala was rather nice but their damn praying is getting the better of me. Tomorrow we catch (7.30 am) the bus for Nairobi and arrive there at 8 pm. We are going to stay with a friend of Tony's and from there we go to Mombasa and catch a ship to Pakistan maybe.

This is just a note to let you know I'm o.k. and will send my 20-page letter when I leave East Africa. They open letters here and I could get three years' imprisonment for what I've said so can't mail real letters.

By the way I went to the American Embassy today and they gave me a letter saying I'm a student so I can get on ships at half-price. It will only cost $26 to Pakistan from Mombasa.

Love B

Kenya
Nairobi

July 23, 1965

Nairobi, Kenya

Dear Mother and Daddy,

The leather goods here are so cheap. Leopard sandals are $2.50 so I'm buying you and Jane a pair. Also, I have bought for myself a leopard handbag with skin on both sides, leopard wallet, zebra, cheetah, leopard belts, 4 pair of sandals, zebra, Ronson lighter and cigarette holder. Came to $50 for all.

Now listen, I'm sure there's been a heck of a mess-up with the parcels, so a parcel you receive from Kenya is just for me. I'm lugging y'all's presents around because I want something to give y'all. Please keep all skin goods in moth balls. Now Daddy, would you and Bubba like a zebra belt? They really are gorgeous and super leather and only $2.80.

I'm having a hard time with zebra skins. They are gorgeous. Just wish I could afford one. Daddy, very sweet of you to say the slippers were marvelous but I'm sure they are too big. Anyway, I have something lovely when I arrive. Thanks for the offer of the flying home bit, but I would feel too guilty and that would be the easy way out, but in return you can throw a big drink (cocktail) party for me when I get home. My 50-page letter will be mailed when I leave Kenya.

Now we went to all the travel agencies here and they flatly refused to let us go 3rd class to Pakistan, because they say the condition are too bad for European women. They would only let us go 2nd class and that cost $121.80 and that's just too much. So what we are going to do is hitch to Mombasa and just stick around the docks and see if we can get on a ship (working) to Persia. I want a rug so we're going there.

I hope y'all received a large book called *Hippos Belong To Everybody*? It cost me a bomb.

I'm writing to Mrs. Kaisman [a neighbour] just now. Sent Bonnie a present and a letter also to Roz. Will write in a week's time.

Love to all.

⸺⸺⸺❦⸺⸺⸺

Mombasa

August 6, 1965

Mombasa, Kenya

Dear Mother and Daddy,

Well we made it to Mombasa but I never thought we would make it. It took two days from Nairobi, approximately 309 miles on dreadful road. Many people here are really snobs and could care less if we sat for days on end in the bush. One time we were let out miles from anyone right in the middle of a large elephant track and spent the night in a Land Rover. Will give all details in next letter. Letters 1, 2 and 3 were mailed in Nairobi, hope you received them.

We are trying to get in touch with a chap whom we don't know and if he doesn't ask us to stay at his place, I just don't know what we will do because we can't afford hotels. We will start tomorrow looking for ships. God, I'm getting scared we won't be able to catch a boat free.

Now I bought Bubba a zebra skin and I was wondering if he wanted a large drum with zebra skin top; it is used for a coffee table and is really big and beautiful. They cost about $30 but the shipping cost about $60. It really is beautiful and well worth having but if he can't afford it then o.k. If he does want it I will buy it and he can pay me later. It is about 2ft. high, round and approx. 3½ across the top. It will have to be shipped classified as freight.

Just got in touch with the German chap and he is coming to meet us so we're going to lay it on thick so he will let us stay at his place.

August 10 We are staying in a lovely flat on the ocean with the German chap. Having a ball but I'm far behind in my letter to you.

We've already been on one safari since we've been here. Hate to leave, it's so much fun. No luck so far with boats. Write soon to Mombasa.

Love Barbara

Mombasa

August 17, 1965

Mombasa, Kenya

Dear Mother and Daddy,

I have asked an American sailor from South Carolina to mail this from his ship. There is a postal strike here and mail will most probably be tied up for two months and I have two letters sitting in the post office for you. I am fine and just wanted you to know since you won't be receiving any letters. We are stranded here because there is a strike in Aden and no ships go to India, Persian Gulf, etc.

This chap will mail a parcel to you in November.

Love Barbara

⸺⸰⸰⸰⸺

Mombasa

August 24, 1965

Mombasa, Kenya

Dear Mother and Daddy,

This is just a little note to let you know I am sailing tomorrow morning for Bombay in India. We shall arrive there September 2 and cannot give a forwarding address as we don't know where we shall stay. I almost went back to Rhodesia but my common sense is making me pass on. We will definitely go to Delhi and from there will get our visas for the remaining countries.

The ship is the SS *Kampala* and we go 2nd class and have a cabin to ourselves. A parcel should be arriving in about a month's time with presents in there for everyone but things that don't have names on them are mine. Bubba should be receiving a gigantic drum in November and another parcel will probably arrive with U.S. stamps.

Must go now and pack.

Love Barbara.

[There are no letters from Callan for three months. She was in Bombay, India and was caught in an air raid in a war zone.

"I was walking down a street when a plane flew over and began shooting. I froze. Two men grabbed me and threw me into a doorway for cover. I hid my face in my arms and waited for the shooting to stop. When I looked up, I saw a hand with only three fingers next to me. I was lying next to a leper. One of my greatest fears while traveling the world was contracting that disease."

She then traveled to Ceylon (now Sri Lanka) with Barb and Susan (the American girl who had been in Madrid) and they slept on luggage racks because the compartments, which had comfortable space for 15 people, contained as many as 60. They missed the boat to Ceylon and had to wait a week. This is where Callan showed Barb and Susan basic ballet moves but later said, "That was the first time I noticed I could not do movements I had once been able to do so beautifully. I had no flexibility or extension. My muscles had no tone."

Her parents asked the Honorable Elliott Hagan, Congressman from Georgia, to help locate her as they had received nothing from her and were extremely worried. See letter dated March 3, 1967.

Susan is now traveling with Callan and Barb.]

Nepal

Kathmandu, Kilimanjaro

Nov. 24, 1965

Kathmandu, Nepal

Dear Mother and Daddy,

We passed into Nepal 6.30 am by rickshaw and went up the road to where all the Indian trucks were; they had all sorts of strange decorations on them. We went through customs with a breeze and just couldn't get over the whole scene – fascinating! We waited until 8.30 and finally got a lorry for $1 and had to sit on the back that was piled up to the top with flour sacks, with no top or sides to the truck. We were with two chaps from Israel and one English chap and two Australians that we met in Delhi. We then waved goodbye to them and were off towards the mountains on the shabby, narrow straight road that leads to Kathmandu. I was already cold and the sun was very hot. We kept stopping – don't know for what – and we were so happy that we were going to arrive before everyone else.

About 10 miles past the border, we pulled into a small village and the lorry driver said we were just stopping for 15 minutes to have the lorry checked. The four of us started playing bridge and just didn't realize what time it was, and at 11.45 the Israeli yelled at him in English and gave him the devil. He promised to have it finished in one hour… four hours later, we pulled away from the small village of small wooden doll houses. During the last four hours, we walked around the dusty cobbled streets and saw the three other trucks had also broken down. We were so thirsty and bought some lemons, which we thought were oranges and they were just dreadful and sour when we were so thirsty!

It was turning dark and really getting cold when we started up the mountain and was the road ever narrow. It was built by the Indians with U.S. money and it is the only road into Nepal, except the road from Tibet which the Chinese are building. It kept getting colder and we all huddled up together to keep the wind away from us and I kept thinking when I was very young how Daddy told us he rode to Atlanta in the back of a truck and had to put newspaper in his sweater to keep warm, and how I wish I could get hold of that paper now and put in on me! It was dark and we kept climbing and climbing and we just couldn't watch how close the lorry was to the edge of the mountains. I was so cold I decided the minute I got to Kathmandu, I was flying back to the border!

We arrived in Naubise, a small town, at 9 pm and we just didn't know what was happening. Finally, we realized we were going to stay all night because they are not allowed to drive at night. All the shops were still open. I got so annoyed because no one could speak English and we were freezing in the back of that darned truck. I yelled out, asking if anyone spoke English and a young chap dressed in Nepalese clothes said yes. We climbed down from the truck and walked through the small streets with candles and gas lamps shining from the stores; there is no electricity in the town and I only wish it had been light to see all this.

We walked to a Nepalese restaurant, and I had my first introduction to their low doorways! The room was so small and the ceilings were extremely low. It was really the most exotic strange scene I've ever seen. We sat down at short tables and the owners were sitting on the floor cooking on a large clay stove; chickens were all over the place and two women were sitting in a corner on the floor making candy. We ordered rice, tea and omelette and they cracked eggs and threw the shells on the floor. Men were sitting on the cold clay floor smoking their "hubbly bubbly" pipes. Everyone was barefooted and the children were smoking cigarettes! I found out later that they start when they are four! I'm sure if Marco Polo had come through here, it must have looked the same. Nothing has changed – including the cooking instruments! If I hadn't observed them being used I would have never known what they were for. The food was fantastic and the best rice I ever had. I was very cold in there and there was no glass in the windows; in fact they don't have glass in this country.

We left after an hour and got all our gear out of the lorry and walked up the steepest stone stairs that were between two buildings and slept in a schoolroom. The students sit on the floor and there is only one blackboard covered with algebra. Actually, the room looked like an attic in an old German house. We opened the small wooden windows and the cold fresh air smelled so nice. We awoke to the sound of our driver hollering to us in Hindi up from the street telling us to get up as it was 4 am! So we carried all our stuff down all those stairs and nearly killed ourselves in the process; it was pitch dark.

Climbed into the bus and we were off climbing up and up with the icy wind blowing all around us and were we cold! There were people walking up the road carrying large baskets with sticks through them by a long cord which fit across their foreheads and the basket slumped on their backs and their heads were almost touching their knees; that was quite a load. Up and up we climbed and the villages we passed were fantastic and some of the oldest things we had ever seen. The countryside was so clean and neat the way they whacked their rice paddies; from any view it looked like lovely uneven green stairs leading up to the top of the mountains and hills. We all held tight when we turned corners; I never saw such wild driving! Then all of a sudden, we saw the beautiful high snow-capped mountains and were we ever thrilled; Kilimanjaro was our first snow-capped mountain. Three hours after that, we broke down and we were really above the clouds. The people gathered round as usual. We came to a police point and we all had to get out as it was too dangerous for anyone to stay in the bus because at this point cars go over on an average of one every couple of weeks or so – only last week a car went over and 12 people were killed.

When we entered Kathmandu, I was quite shocked to see it was so large and had a few relatively modern buildings; we were let off at a garage on the main street and were we so surprised to see so many Europeans. We caught a rickshaw to a place everyone recommended. Barb went in to check it and said "No", so we left our things there and went walking trying to find another place; we went into a dumpy place down a disgusting lane cluttered with garbage etc. and had a bowl of rice and an omelette which really did the trick.

We had to walk a long way with a Nepali chap to the Peace Corps. to see if we could stay there. We passed the King's palace and couldn't see much as it was set so far back. However, the Peace Corps. said we couldn't stay there but one chap was nice enough to give us a ride to the Tourist Corner which used to be a palace and there we decided to stay at 5 rupees (42¢). We were put in a large room with two Finnish and two Danish girls; I had to take a shower in the small cement and clay shower room and I just about died when the icy water hit me; if anyone had a bad heart I'm sure it would have killed them!

We got up next morning and it was so cold, but we washed our clothes on the front steps in a bucket of hot water, which was brown – they had boiled it for us over an open fire. Went to the Globe for lunch, it is run by Tibetan refugees and had hot cocoa, rice, liver and onion. I thought it was good and all the young travellers eat there. I really like these Tibetan people and think they add to the scenery of these streets. In front of our place was a large courtyard with a fish pond in the middle and corroded water where we rinsed our clothes. We looked in all the shops which one literally has to climb up to on knees, and then take off your shoes and stoop to look at the junk that they sell!

Five of us rented a Jeep and went higher into the mountains on the one dirt road; it went through several villages and I guess no one ever drives through there because the streets were littered with rice drying in the sun and women shifting it to separate the grain – they had to move as we drove over the cobblestones. It was very dusty on the road and rice paddies looked beautiful with the sun shining on them and people planting rice. We reached the tourist bungalow at dark and were greeted by a very nice Tibetan man, who showed us to a precious room with a fireplace and bathroom with a flush toilet; we paid him to get us some firewood and he lit the fire and the darned chimney didn't function right and all the smoke went into the room and we had to open all the windows and doors so it was cold. We ate in a separate part with chickens running around and the stove was the typical clay one on the floor. The meal was dreadful!

We all slept on the floor in our sleeping bags and after an awful breakfast we started to walk up the mountain. We thought we would never make it but when we reached the top, we saw the eclipse of the sun over Mount Everest and it was breathtaking! This only happens every 72 years in Nepal and that is why we made such an effort to get here. Everest looked very small because it was so far away and a little bit of the bottom is in Tibet. We just sat there by the huge fire and drank in the beauty of it all. We finally tore ourselves away and then walked down. It was nine miles and we took the mountain paths the locals use and my boots were rubbing against my heel so I took them off and walked barefoot. My poor feet were cracked on the heels and were bleeding and the pebbles were going into the cracks and I was in pain! Thank God a rickshaw came along and gave us a ride down into the village!

Next day we rented bicycles and eight of us cycled up to another village. We went to a Hindu temple but the guard wouldn't let us in. He had a gun and slammed the little wooden door in our faces; non-believers are not allowed to go into their temples. Walked around through all the small streets with the wooden carved little 'doll' houses that look as if they are about to fall down. Women were spinning their yarn and others were washing their hair; the whole scene was so unusual and so different. The ride back was so much easier because we went downhill!

I'm two weeks behind in writing so will generalize. A German boy came next day and all of us went on bikes and then walked up 500 stairs of stone to a large temple with painted eyes on the steeple (in fact most of the temples have these eyes on the doors to show that the gods are watching). We walked into a Buddhist temple and peeked in a large room and saw the monks praying. It was quite fascinating! I couldn't see myself walking down 500 steps so I slid down the steel bannister! Rode back and had buffalo and lemonade for supper.

The next day we all rode out to the Tibetan refugee camp and I bought a gorgeous handmade sweater for $5.50. Everyone was dressed in traditional Tibetan clothes which I really liked and they were wearing handmade boots. We watched them making rugs.

We then went to see the Living Goddess[54] who is only 14 years old. We walked into a palace courtyard and she came to a balcony and just stared at us; she's Hindu and apparently, if she ever scratches herself she isn't the Goddess anymore. Once a man was painting a picture of her and she made a servant take it from him. The King asked her to give it back but she said the gods told her to take it and the painter never got it back. About four years ago, a foreigner ran over a cow and he was lying in the street. A wagon rolled up, picked up the cow and left the poor man in the street! They rushed the cow to the hospital and he finally got

[54] The Living Goddess, also known as Kumari Devi, is the tradition of worshipping a chosen virgin as the manifestation of the divine female energy, the goddess Taleju. She is usually a prepubescent girl from the Shakya clan of Newari Buddhist community. The best known is the Royal Kumari of Kathmandu, who lives in a palace in the Kathmandu. The current Royal Kumari is Trishna Shakya, who was installed in September 2017, aged three. When the girl begins to menstruate, or if she suffer major blood loss from injury, the goddess leaves her body.

there too. He had to pay for every day he and the cow were both there. He couldn't leave the country till they saw that the cow was o.k. He was never allowed back into Nepal.

Will run on now but you will hear from me real soon.

Love you both B.

⸻⸻⸺◦﹛◦﹜◦⸺⸻⸻

Nepal/India/Burma/Thailand

Kathmandu, Nepal; Nepalese border; Calcutta, India; Rangoon[55], Burma; Bangkok, Chiang Mai, Thailand

November 30, 1965

Kathmandu, Nepal

We were up at 5.30, had some hot milk and rice pudding which Barb makes and were in the rickshaw at 7.15. They confused our tickets so we had to wait for the 8 am bus. We got on the old wreck and our first-class seats were a giggle; I kept putting my feet in the oil on the floor which had leaked out of a tin. The locals were spitting as usual but the drive was beautiful, if very tiring. Our driver couldn't stand the thought of the other bus passing him so every time the other bus overtook us he had to pass him so we were playing little passing games all the way down the mountain, which scared the Dickens out of us! His horn wasn't working properly and this just drove him crazy so we had to keep stopping to fix it. Ate peanut butter sandwiches and bread made by the cook at the Marine House and it tasted like cake. (Marine House is where we spent the night, remember).

Went through the town that we spent one night in on the way up and did it ever look grubby! Reached Birgunj at 4.30 – it is on the border and we caught a rickshaw to the train station on the Indian side. There were loads of carriages and very small covered wagons; no cars at all and one would think the gold rush was on with every wagon loaded with people.

[55] Now known as Yangon, Myanmar

A train was coming so we had to wait at a crossing and a cow kept licking my feet, but I didn't dare do anything about it because I was afraid of being told off by the locals. The cow was behind us, pulling a heavy wooden cart that had huge wooden wheels.

It was a riot of confusion; everyone had pulled up on both sides of the road and on the other side of the crossing and there was a bus and a steamroller side by side so when the gates opened no one could move! It took over half an hour to get organized and everyone was yelling and screaming; we were in convulsions because we weren't in any hurry. We messed around the train station looking at the stage coaches, and our train finally came hours later. But from then on, it was simply dreadful! We changed trains four times in the night and had one and a half hours at each stop; we didn't dare sleep for fear we wouldn't wake up. We went into 3rd class because it was empty and climbed up on the luggage rack and went to sleep! We woke up hours later and couldn't believe our eyes and ears when we looked down! We had changed onto an electric train, and didn't believe what we were seeing – it was so modern!

Arrived in Calcutta and caught a stage coach which was beautiful with the gas lights on the side and had lovely wheels. Went to a hostel for women – what with all our washing and bags, it now looks as if 20 people live here! We couldn't wear our shoes or smoke which just about killed us for sure! We have a crazy clay stove on the floor where we cook, as everything is done on the floor. Then went to the Burmese Airways and booked for Friday which will let us stay in Rangoon for 24 hrs.

Walked all over the city looking for material for Jane and Mother, finally found what I wanted, some 45in. raw silk but it still isn't as lovely as the silk that I bought in Bombay. We all had supper with a couple that we had gone around with in Kathmandu; they had come back before us.

December 11 Bar, Susan and I caught a taxi to the Union of Burma Airways (UBA) and were taken out to the airport in their bus. The plane was nice and the food very good and the hostess wore a typical long skirt and the national blouse. We flew low so we saw the coastline of India and the rice paddies. I took out my film of Nepal to put in a new one so I could take pictures of the Golden Pagoda in Rangoon and forgot to press the safety catch and the film was wound up in my camera, so no pictures of Nepal!

Arrived at Rangoon Airport and they took us to the Strand Hotel, their best, at $12 dollars per day. We had a lovely large room, and three meals that UBA paid for. We caught a rickshaw to the Golden Pagoda[56] and although it is the eighth wonder of the world we weren't that impressed! Had to walk up many stairs with tiny stores on both sides all the way up. Finally reached the temple – it was crowded with smaller temples surrounding it and thousands of statues of Buddha in different positions. The people were not very friendly, very hostile and no one spoke to us. It was late to take any more pictures so we left and caught an open cart back. None of the drivers would stop for us until a Burmese chap clapped his hands.

Went back to the hotel, had a steaming bath (what a treat!), had a wonderful dinner in the magnificent dining room – glazed duck, coconut, ginger, bananas fried, tea, the best! Tourists are not allowed to go outside the city and can remain only 24 hours in Burma. I really wanted to know more about the people and customs but it was impossible.

We then arrived in Bangkok and were shocked to see all the U.S. planes at the airport; all the prices were in dollars, and the U.S. soldiers had different booths. We all caught a taxi to the Thai Song Greet Hotel and the highway was terrific – all American cars but no one speaks English. Our hotel was rather good and only 50¢ per night. We tore around this town, catching buses or rickshaws to get visas and TB checks – our boat was in the harbor so we had to get our things in order. Went to a Philippine Embassy party and it was dreadful – no one seemed to be having any fun in comparison with other parties of this kind that we were lucky enough to be invited to. Met some American chaps who are sending a parcel home for me; a sari, the handmade Tibetan sweater from Nepal, plus material for Mom and Jane.

It is December 21 now and I just sent a very few Xmas cards – I never seem to have enough time to do much of this. Received the wonderful Xmas checks from both of you, and you just can't know what that means! Please have my films developed and mounted soon as they come because they are my prize possessions. I still haven't written about the trip from Bombay to the Nepal border but will try to do it sometime.

---

[56] The Golden Pagoda or 'Shwedagon' is the most sacred Buddhist pagoda in Myanmar, and is said to contain relics of the four previous Buddhas of the present age.

Tomorrow we go to Vientiane in Laos, and maybe we can see Bob Hope who is only 100 miles from there! Be back in Bangkok on January 12 then on to Cambodia!

We were up at 5.30 and caught the bus and were on our way to Chiang Mai (524 miles from Bangkok and also close to the Burma and Chinese border). The road was good and nothing but rice paddies and canals on both sides of the road and all the cute wooden houses are built on tall stilts for the monsoon season. Mostly Chinese were planting rice and we noticed they wore nothing but blue or black clothes with hats, quite different than the ones they wear in the movies. At noon we stopped at Nakhon Sawan (known as the Heavenly City) and had a typical Thai dinner which consisted of watered soup with roots, shrimp and lettuce, plates of fish, and separate plate of cauliflower. The shrimp was really good but it does not stay with you very long – soon you are hungry again. We now started hitting semi-jungle and there were plenty of elephants working along the roads. Next stop was Yanhi Dam where we stayed in a lovely new house made of wood. Our bedroom was nice with pink sheets. Took a shower and went to the dining room which was packed with newspaper reporters. Talked with them for a long time and then went to bed.

We saw Yanhi Dam, which is almost a miniature of Kariba Dam between Zambia and Rhodesia – you will know it because I sent many pictures of the week we spent there and Zambia in general. You also told me, Mother, that you are saving everything from the newspaper of interest concerning countries that we have been in and that in itself is quite a project it seems to me; what a time I'll have going over those scrapbooks and things! All along the way, there were the most fantastic temples with small tiers of three on the side of the roof and two large tiers in the middle with figures on the top of the front and back with bells hanging from them that tinkle in the breeze; the archways to the inside are beautiful and the cut glass and stones make it a sight to behold. These temples are in the middle of nowhere, no villages are in sight. The people in these villages are so poor and simple but seem very happy.

We had lunch in a small town called Lampoon and about two hours later we reached Chiang Mai. We were expecting to see a small village but it was a growing city. We went to the U.S. Consulate and they called up a school and they said we could stay there so we went on over and it only cost us 45¢ a day. We stayed in a dormitory with ten Thai girls from 12 to 18 years old; they were so curious and watched every move we made; we were not allowed to wear our shoes in the building which annoyed me, as I could just see my feet getting full of all sorts of germs and then eventually falling off my poor body! There was a sunken tub in the bathroom of white tile which was always filled with water to throw on yourself when taking a bath, used huge copper containers for this purpose. The sink was really modern except for the fact that the hole in the center didn't have a pipe and the water went straight onto the floor through the hole and splashed one's dress and feet!

We caught a Thai cycle – a small canopy wagon for two pulled by the front part of bike. We went to the market and looked at material, which is cheaper than Bangkok, and that nearly killed me! No, I guess I can't say that either, because the Thai silk just isn't as good as the Indian, and you always hear so much about Thai silk. This place is dead, not even a coffee bar open at night. The girls entertained us with their singing and playing, it was such a lovely different sound, the soft plinking and the sweet soft voices. They sang in Thai to Buddha. When it was over, we felt a little sad. They wear sailor-type dresses and their faces are so delicate and their skin is such a soft light brown nut color. There are so much smaller and more delicate than Western women.

We had breakfast and then off to see a beautiful waterfall where the royal family sometimes vacations. After that we drove way out to a very small village where most of the Thai silk is made and watched them hand-loom it. It made me a little ill to see those young pretty girls weaving in their wooden looms; they only make 35¢ per day! We drove up the mountain on a dirt road to the King's summer palace but it was closed to tourists so we peeked through the gates and it looked so lovely and was typical Thai architecture. We continued to climb into the mountains on the most dreadful road for an hour until we reached the point where one can park a car to climb down the mountain. The path was awfully steep and we had to hang on to bushes in order not to slide down; I never thought we would make it!

Most people here came from China 60 years ago and have no written language of their own. The men wear crazy clothes and the richer they are, the more silver, large round rings they wore around their necks. The women wore short pleated skirts with slits way up the sides. They live in little shacks and never below 3,000 ft. Before 1959 their survival depended on growing opium but the Thai government is teaching them to grow potatoes.

We looked into one of the houses and was it ever gloomy! And they had a corner reserved for a spirit and a Chinese man told us not to go in because the spirit of the mountain was inside and would be offended. They get their water from a brook far away up the mountain and it trickles down and supported by bamboo cut in half. I thought it pretty clever but the bamboo halves were green and slimy. There were four men completely out of it from smoking the opium in "hubbly bubbly" pipes and another man was lying down in seventh heaven! The place reeked of this odd smell and I was glad to get back in the fresh air. Some little boys were playing with tops that I'm sure their ancestors played with thousands of years ago. They don't use money and their diet is herbs. I did notice several horses tied up. We started back up the mountain and was it a climb! On the way down, we came across a French couple and gave them a lift. They had walked up the entire way and it took them seven hours! When we came in after supper, the Thai girls danced for us (classical) which was fantastic; it looks as if they have no bones in their bodies!

Cont. of this letter will be mailed in Laos and I have to wait until Thai to mail this. Love B.

1966

Thailand/Laos/Thailand/Cambodia/Thailand

Chiang Mai, Nong Khai, Mekong River, Thailand; Vientiane, Laos; back to Nong Khai, Udorn, Khorat, (Bangkok again??) Aranyaprathet, Thailand; Siem Reap, Angkor Wat, Cambodia; Krabi, then Hat Yai, Thailand

December 24, 1965

Chaing Mai, Thailand

The girls woke us at 5.30 and we packed and were off again, saying goodbye to the pretty girls. They hated to see us go because by now we were good friends, and they thought we were the greatest. Got the bus then stopped at Tak (where Bob Hope performed three days before) and had a big dinner. Then on to the next town. Although Thai is a strictly Buddhist country, they put Christmas decorations up everywhere and all the Thais wish the Europeans Happy Xmas. We then went to an ice cream parlour and had delicious homemade vanilla ice cream with canned milk on top. They have a marvelous custom – when one sits down in a restaurant or café, the waitresses hand each person a face cloth with Dettol (disinfectant) on it and it's very cold from being in a refrigerator and after the meal they give you another one for your mouth, hands and face.

We are only about 120 miles from Bangkok now and we see the strangest sights; hundreds of TV antennae on the shacks which are on large stilts because of the monsoons. The temples seemed even more beautiful with the sun shining brightly on the rooftops. We were headed for Vientiane, the capital of Laos. We were now on 'Freedom Highway' and it is infamous; there are killings and robberies every week or so and were we scared! But not so scared that we would turn back! The police just can't catch them because they just disappear into the thick jungle. Each person who got on looked like a highway robber to us but just figured that if they were, there wasn't anything that we could do about it, so don't worry, and we finally fell asleep, in the most awful position and woke up later when we reached a real dump. Won't go into detail concerning the gang on the bus because they are the same as on all other buses and trains. A woman directly in the seat behind us was screaming and shouting and showing the juicy red of her mouth from betel nut and really didn't really mind where she spat! But no one paid any attention to her!

Arrived Nong Khai at 5 and saw hundreds of GIs but seemed they were all going in the opposite direction. Finally, we arrived at the border town and went to immigration where the officer only spoke French and Thai. We finally got our papers stamped and then he sent us across the street to another officer but I started to get nervous because we had already been in the country one week illegally; he started giving me the devil and said I was fined $10. I told him I didn't have it and I got by without paying!

We went down to the landing of the Mekong River and were informed that all the boats had stopped running at dusk, but a man told us he would take us over for 50 Baht. We said we only had 20 Baht which is $1, but he refused. We were getting desperate, when the customs officer called down and told him to take us on over for 20 Baht. It was cold and choppy and we held on to our packs as we darted along in the rickety boat. When we reached the Laotian side, they kept saying "Taxi" and we knew they would get a cut in it and still insisted we had no money. The old wooden stairs we were on just about fell to pieces. We didn't even get stamped into the country or go through immigration. This was the first time in any country this had happened to us.

A taxi took us to the one house that takes guests and it wasn't bad at all. We went to the best place in town to eat and it compared to our second-rate hot dog stands in the States. There are lovely tall coconut trees everywhere but no nice residential section; the Europeans live in large houses with Laotians as neighbors in nearby shacks. The water is pumped out of the muddy Mekong River and although it goes through a filter process, it's still vile and my gums are bleeding from washing my teeth. Every time I wake up in the mornings, someone is climbing the coconut trees and the neighbors' children hang at the gates all the time when we sit out on the porch. It's extremely tropical here and there are plenty of banana trees. The country is neutral and has a king and queen; although Vientiane is not the royal capital, it's the administrative capitol and everyone is represented here. The North Vietnamese have a hospital here just down the street for their wounded. It's like being a prisoner here because one can't go outside the city limits due to the Pathet Lao[57].

Now, don't quote me as saying this but this is the way I see it. They are the rebels who live in the jungle and I imagine the Red Chinese inspired them. It seems they want to take control of the government and if not, they create a riot. These riots take place about every six months and in the last one, the police were fighting the military for control. They really have gun battles in the streets of the city and one of the police stations is covered with machine gun holes; every household and business keeps many flags handy for when these coups start; they fly the flag for whoever is winning on their particular street! I understand from several chaps who work here that they were sitting on the balcony of one of the houses drinking beer and were placing bets on who was going to get mowed down next! Quite a few were killed and they have a really pathetic hospital and the wounded were laid out on bamboo racks. All the police and military wear U.S. uniforms, labelled U.S.N. or U.S.M.C. [US Navy or Marine Corps]. They say it is just about time for another coup, and everyone says we are mad to stay here any longer.

We met some U.S. chaps who have rented rowing boats and keep them hidden in the bushes down at the river. I figure the Viet Cong probably has something to do with it because why would they go to all the trouble of renting these boats? For sure it's that they want to get out of Laos when the next coup starts and row across to Thailand.

---

[57] The Pathet Lao (officially the Lao People's Liberation Army) was a communist, political movement in Laos formed in the mid-20th century. They ultimately conquered the whole of Laos in 1975 after the Civil War. The Pathet Lao were associated with and dependent on Vietnamese communists.

There's so much going on here and when you ask someone, they all clam up, including the Yanks. For instance, there are 13 marine guards at the Embassy and the Ambassador's private house is guarded 24 hours a day.

The French were kicked out of Indochina which was Laos, Cambodia and Vietnam in 1954. The Japanese put in electricity and sewage when they came through during WWII. Vientiane has not much to offer and is the most underdeveloped capital of a country that we have ever seen; there are no newspapers, not even a Sunday edition, and no telephones. The Yanks put in telephones connecting the base with the Embassy and U.S. AID and that's the only connection here. The city is spread out with only about six paved roads and no trees at all except around the houses and shacks. The French started building a very large Arc de Triomphe and didn't finish it when they were kicked out – the Laotians have been working on it for eight years and it is still not finished. All the Yanks call it the Arc de Defeat! The streets are dirty and the government buildings are whitewashed a dreadful yellow as is everything else in this place. There is trash in front of all the buildings and no sidewalks anywhere! It's a ghost town, only with people in it. Believe it or not, but there is nothing to take a picture of! By the way, that highway that I spoke of was not Freedom Highway, but Friendship Highway (out of Bangkok). Only hope this letter gets to you.

January 9, 1966 Packed and went out in the street by the house and waited for Air America people to come by and give us a lift, stood there just a few minutes and an Air Van gave us a ride out of the city limits. Caught a taxi to the boat landing and just waited for the boat to fill up. The river was smooth this time and kept thinking how much it looked like the Savannah River; kept looking back from Thai to Laos and what a difference; all the little Thai shacks with their TV antennae and telephone wires and poles whereas the Laos side was nothing but palm trees and shacks.

Back on the Thai side of the Mekong, we went through immigration in Nong Khai again. The officer who had given me heck for being in Thai illegally before took us to the Honda dealer. He argued in Thai with the owner for half an hour and translated for us into French; the bargaining just wasn't succeeding so we walked out. The officer followed us and talked us into going back and we bargained for two hours for three scooters. We were there all day, going through registration, taxes and learning to drive the Hondas. We left Nong Khai at 5 pm and drove to Udorn[58] on our scooters at 40 kl. per hr. and it was really fun with very little traffic; we arrived just at dark and went directly to the Officers' Club.

Jim (our marine pal from Cyprus) had a friend there and his wife called Ek asked us to stay at their house for the night; she looked a lot like Claire (our New Zealand friend who is still with us). Ek is terrific and is driving through Savannah in March so will call y'all. Up early with Ek cooking us breakfast and singing songs with her guitar. We then left and started through the heavy traffic – a truck stopped right in front of Barb and she fell off her scooter, and went crashing to the ground. When I saw what had happened, I froze and then I went sailing off mine and my poor camera went flying across the road and was all smashed up. It happened so fast – Barb was bleeding all over but I didn't even get a scratch. We drove to the infirmary on the base, they bandaged her up and gave her a tetanus shot. Off again, drove straight to Khorat just stopping once in a while for a cigarette and rest. The sun was extremely hot and was I blistered. Arrived in Khorat at 5.30 and we were just exhausted.

Earlier we had been driving on the wrong side of the highway and a large truck was behind us and kept honking but we didn't want to go on the other side because it was fresh tar. When he kept honking, I got nervous and was pulling over when that swine passed us on the wrong side and I almost pulled right in to him! We left Khorat at 6 pm when it was dark and was it ever cold and the trucks literally pushed us off the road at times. The only thing that kept me going was the thought of meeting our friends in Bangkok.

January 22, 1966 Up at 4 am and rushed around like mad women trying to get our food organized; called for a car but it didn't come and we were in danger of missing our train. Finally one came and we reached the station just a few minutes before the train pulled out; that cheat of a driver tried to overcharge us for the ride but we wouldn't pay and he was screaming in the station and collecting a huge crowd that didn't know what it was all about. I told him to get a policeman and he finally left.

[58] Udorn was one of the bases for the United States Air Force from 1960-1975.

We bought our tickets and ran for the train and some chaps helped us on with our food and gear. Third class was paradise compared to many trains in other countries, except that the seats were made of wood and the backs were so straight and high, one couldn't sleep on them. We sat like this for six hrs. One hour before the border, we hid our Cambodian money. We arrived at the train station three miles from the border with Cambodia and then caught a bus right to the border to a town called Aranyaprathet.

The ride from Bangkok to here was nothing; very flat land, small houses of wood and grass were on both sides of small, narrow canals. We crossed a space rather like No Man's Land. The U.S. Embassy advised us not to go as we have broken off diplomatic relations with Cambodia and have no embassy there to help citizens who get into trouble. The Germans didn't even have visas but they got in without any trouble at all. We waited in a small café for the bus and when it came, we didn't see how all of us could fit in it as was so crowded, but the ticket collector made all the Cambodians sit in the back! It was a wild bus and so cold, I just didn't see how we could take it. We were cramped in there like sardines; the benches are made for three people but there were six of us squeezed on one! The trip lasted about four hours and then we arrived at a city called Sisophon and we all felt ill and had sick headaches and we wondered if it was worth it!

We changed buses here. It was larger than the first but was also not built for comfort but to squeeze in as many as possible. Reached Siem Reap and went hotel hunting. We all found rooms – the Germans, two Swedes, and one Danish – which weren't much but we have stopped looking for comfort. The water was so bad, we nearly vomited every time we brushed our teeth. We were given a hot pot of tea and it was good but the pot didn't look very clean. We all for dinner had steak, which was buffalo and not very good.

Up very early the next day and the bicycles we all had ordered were waiting outside for us and we all rode to a café and had breakfast which was expensive. We then rode out to the ruins; the whole area is called Angkor Wat and there are about 80 temples spread out all over the area. We didn't go to the main one but cycled to all the others and was it rough going but worth it. It was a fantastic empire at one time; right in the middle of the jungle and half hidden by it. Some of the walls were being smothered by the growing jungle and it was so peaceful with the stillness of the ruins, with no civilization around. The only sounds were the birds and different strange sounds from wild beasts; a great place for meditation. It took us all day; we had a marvellous good, free feeling, knowing that we were right in the middle of the beautiful, lonely, treacherous jungle! Went back to town and knew we would come back tomorrow to see and climb the main temple called Angkor Wat.

Today we did just that, climbed to the top of the temple where Buddha is kept and could see way over the jungle. It was an eerie sight really – looked like a small city surrounded by a moat. When it was built, the stones were reddish ink and carvings and patterns were engraved in almost all the walls and pillars. It was probably built around the 12th century at the height of the Khmer Empire. The Cambodians still call themselves by this name. There were loads of elephants in this area, working.

January 26, 1966 I have been in bed for a week now with dengue fever caused by mosquito bites but the girls have not complained about it at all – strange. Tomorrow we leave Cambodia and will be back in four days and go on to Singapore, catch a boat on February 21, come back to Bangkok where we will pick up our things and then to Manila. (I was going to stay there to meet Seig, your friend, but figure if he wants to see me he can come to Hong Kong.) We arrive in Hong Kong on March 2.

Have heard from Mr. and Mrs. Sarthou in Hong Kong, and it looks like he will have jobs for all of us in his company! Hope we will be able to stay for at least six months.

February 7, 1966 Before reaching Penang, we had to change at Chumpan and go on a dreadful road on the west coast next to Burma; most of the road wasn't paved and we thought the bus would literally fall apart at any moment. The scenery was changing and becoming very jungly (if there is such a word!) with palm trees everywhere. Parts of the road were in the process of being built and sometimes the bushes would come right in the windows. We were glad when we finally reached Penang. We had Khao pad – if I haven't mentioned it before it is rice with several different things added but not nourishing at all. We then boarded another bus (that's all we do these days) and sat next to a middle-aged Buddhist monk dressed in his orange Greek-looking robe; he immediately got up and sat across from us. When I took out my gas cigarette lighter and used it, he took a fancy to it and motioned to see it so I had to hand it to one of the German chaps to hand to him, as monks cannot touch anything a female touches directly unless a man touches it after her. Most monks have a little boy travel with them so that the young boy takes the charity food from women and hands it to the monks. He asked how much he could buy it for from me – when I told him it wasn't for sale, I don't think he liked it very much. Anyway, monks aren't supposed to own material things!

Finally arrived in Krabi, and got the last room left in the only hotel. 75¢ per night. Did I tell you that in all the restaurants, they sit on the floor and cook at a clay stove? This letter finds us in a small town named Hat Yai.

Love B.

Hong Kong
Hong Kong

March 5, 1966

Hong Kong

Dear Mother and Daddy,

I have not yet written about all our trip in Malaysia and Singapore but will do so as soon as I find a job. The day we arrived here in Hong Kong, Dr. Sarthou took Barb and I out to dinner and introduced us to the people in the office. He is helping me to get a job but I'd rather find one on my own because I know if I don't do well, they would wonder what kind of a nut he sent over to them! He flies to Japan tomorrow and is going to pick up our suitcase which has been at the U.S. Embassy for 1½ years! I am mentally and physically worn out and in no hurry to find a job but will start Monday when some of the tailors are finished with my clothes. It is chilly here and rained all day today which really put me in a bad mood. Rent is fantastically high and I just don't know what to do when Barbara leaves for Australia on March 14. We are staying in a hotel/guest house, one small room with one bed, and we pay $13 a week apiece. Shopping is fantastic here but not as cheap as two years ago. I think I shall really have a ball when I meet some young people and the city is just beautiful.

I want to buy a $150 (in U.S. $350) tape recorder, wig, strand of pearls, hair oil treatment machine and a lot of other junk then I can lam out[59] of here whenever I want to. The only problem is I have 11 suitcases now and just wouldn't know how to get everything home. If I meet someone off a U.S. ship like before, he can take home my 144-piece bronze dinner set! Received letters in Bangkok with Valentine and two $25 checks; thanks ever so much but really you are spoiling me.

Haven't heard from Tony for four months now, and I'm sick with worry. So sorry about your arthritis, Mother. If nothing else works, the Chinese have a cure for it and they practice it in Singapore. If you want me to find out more about it, I shall. Don't forget we in the Western world still practice some of their remedies. Must go to sleep now.

Love Barbara

<hr>

Hong Kong
Kowloon

April 16, 1966

Hong Kong

Dear Mother and Daddy,

I'm really sorry I've only written once since arriving in Hong Kong but honestly I just haven't had time to write anyone with seeing Barbara off

---

[59] To 'lam out' is a U.S. phrase meaning to hide or flee from someone like the police and authorities.

(she's now in Australia), trying to find a job, and keeping up my social life. I worked for 2½ weeks at Dr. Sarthou's place redoing some of the filing and God they now can't find a thing I've filed away! Let's face it, that type of jazz just isn't my field but he did give me a chance which I didn't live up to.

I bought a tape and have been waiting to use a Chinese girlfriend's tape recorder to send y'all the tape but she is going to Saigon – of all places – to get away from the hectic life here in Hong Kong, so when she returns I will get it off to you. I live in Kowloon[60] which is across the river from Hong Kong on the Chinese side, so actually I guess geographically speaking one can say I live in China. It's where all the action is such as nightclubs, shops, etc. I live in a real small room in a house with a Chinese woman whom I'm very fond of and it's right on Nathan Road (the road where all the riots took place last week). It was really funny and rather exciting watching it from my window until they started throwing tear gas at all the open windows. Actually, apart from shopping, and going to the different nightclubs/restaurants, there really isn't anything else to do like horseback ride, because they just don't have clubs like that and every day it is foggy or raining so that cuts off the beach.

I went to a Buddhist fortune teller and he told me March was a bad month for me and April would be even worse, and with all my bad luck I really believe it! He said that May would be much better so don't give up hope. Will tell you on the tape all the other things he told me about my future. I am applying for teaching jobs and I am hoping to get one because not too many people know English and everyone is dying to learn it. No degree necessary, so that saves me!

There are just so many fantastic things to buy here like material, ivory, linen, beaded evening sweaters, gold, pearls, stones, etc. Let me know anything y'all want. They have gorgeous beige tablecloths, handmade of lace and linen; boy are they beautiful for only $30. Does Harry want an ivory chess set? I will start looking around for pierced earrings for you Mother, maybe emerald from South America. I eat nothing but Chinese food and I'm really getting good at using chopsticks! I'm not in the best of health and must take it easy for a while and gaining back all my

---

[60] At this stage, Kowloon was an enclave of China.

strength so for the first time in my life I have rosy cheeks. It seems so funny since I have always looked so pale when I wasn't sunburned. Had six rolls of film developed and are they ever good.

Bubba owes me $75 for all the things I bought for him. I deducted it from the money he sent me and the $75 was out of my own, so could you ask him when he could send it to do so, because if I can't find a job pretty soon I just might be coming home and I want to buy everything I can here. Let me know what everyone would like, I will do my best. Daddy, you are the hardest one to go shopping for. I was going to get a pair of silk pajamas, then thought you would never wear them, a silk shirt with your initials on the pocket but didn't know if it would be too hot. Ask if Jane or Ticky want a beaded cocktail sweater, which would cost a fortune in the States; I can have them made up for next to nothing and they are really beautiful with silk shirts to match. Y'all think it over and let me know.

The people here are rude and I'm really beginning to dislike them. They just push the hell out of you when you're getting on a bus, but I shan't take that jazz anymore because they think you're showing weakness. I will clobber the next person who pushes me!. Honestly, I just didn't realize I could be so violent but you can just take so much.

Had a charcoal painting done of me in Malaysia by the artist we stayed with. When I get some extra money, I am going to buy a wig of human hair and have it styled for me so I can just put the bloody thing on when I want to go out at night. They're really great and the best ones only cost $45. The same wig in the States would cost about $200! My best friend is a Eurasian girl and is she ever a darling. She is so good to me and was introduced to me by Dr. Sarthou.

By the way did you ever receive a large blue suitcase, not the one I sent from South Africa, but from Japan? Barb and I had the Terre'Blanches deliver it to the U.S. Embassy in Tokyo over a year ago and when Dr. Sarthou went to pick it up, they didn't know what he was talking about. I thought maybe they had sent it home since I put the return address on the outside. It had a red coat, olive green suit, skirts, sweater, handbags etc. – they were Barb and mine together. I'm just sick about it because all my good clothes were in there. Let me know if you remember it, I remember you received the blue suitcase back with all my things in it – the one you sent me in London, but this one is a very large one.

Tony will be here next month. The fortune teller told me a man was looking for me who needed me very much and would find me in Hong Kong but I must not marry him because it will never work out. He said I can't marry until I'm 29 and then I will marry a person from Europe, not an American, and will be very happy with him. So, I think I'm going to listen to his warnings. It's Saturday and I think I will go see *The Sound of Music*.

Love B.

―――――――⋘⋙―――――――

Kowloon

May 20, 1966

Kowloon, Hong Kong

Dear Mother and Daddy,

Never received an answer to my last letter and still don't know what to do about presents. I might be kicked out of the colony at the end of the month as I am working without a permit and they won't give Americans one. If anyone official writes or wires you asking if you will send me money to leave the colony, say no because they will make me fly $550 to San Francisco and if no one will send me money I can catch a boat at half the price. Just say you have disowned me!

I bought a tablecloth for $50, 72x108, beige bush linen with beautiful handwork in it. I remembered you always wanted one, Mother, and I got him down from $70. It is gorgeous. I have started sending my 144 pieces of bronze in show boxes with 13 pieces in each box, marked as gift and will put several names on them, so don't go giving the parcels away that I send. Just don't have a clue what to buy the children and can't remember their names or ages. Will probably buy Jane and Ticky and you pierced pearl earrings, and don't know what to buy Daddy, Bubba or

Harry, unless it be watches. Anyway, I will have to send them by separate names too. Was going to buy a pair of emerald earrings for you, Mother, but the stones weren't pretty and they were rather expensive. If the men would like crocodile belts instead of watches, let me know and also if the girls would rather have evening beaded sweaters which are gorgeous, let me know. Please tell Bubba I need the $75 he owes me and let me have it as soon as possible, before I leave Hong Kong.

I am living in a gigantic flat in Kowloon with three Australian girls and I sleep in the servant's room. I pay $27 a month and make $72 a month teaching but I have to quit that as the government knows I am teaching there. I want to stay here about three more months then I shall be ready to come home. Have still been trying to make a tape for you because every day I lose my English accent more.

Kowloon

June 7, 1966

Kowloon, Hong Kong

Answer to question. I still live in a large flat with two Australians and two New Zealand girls. I have my own room and sleep on an army cot for U.S. $27 a month and electricity and gas are about U.S. $6 per month for my share. It's really lovely and the bathroom is very modern, well, modern compared to what I'm used to! I eat at the hotel (lunch and supper) at a large round table in the dining room. I am really good with chopsticks and I eat 1½ bowls of rice at each meal including octopus heads, chicken claws, ginger, bamboo shoots, bean sprouts, shark fin soup, fish eyes, etc. I never eat Western food and when I do, I get a runny tummy. I walk everywhere I go. The hotel is owned by a Chinese family, 100 rooms, small, air conditioned. I work from 9 to 12, and then 5 to 10 so my social life has ended. I want to go to Japan from here, but I don't know what to do with my tape recorder. Afraid to ship it home for fear it will be broken. I still have many slides. Barbara lost every one of hers. I've had many clothes made by a tailor out at the airport. I had nine fillings fixed – god was it expensive. I didn't work on a junk, applied for a job but they wouldn't let a girl on board. Will go to President Lines next week to see if I can work on a ship back home.

∞§∞

Kowloon

June 30, 1966

Kowloon, Hong Kong

Dear Mother and Daddy,

It was marvelous hearing your voice again after three years! I'm sitting in the bar of the hotel drinking Chinese tea and learning how to add on the abacus (Chinese adding machine made of wood). My hours are from 9 to 12 and 5 to 10 pm but I always seem to arrive an hour late am to pm. I am public relations manager, salary H.K. $900 a month without commission and drinks (U.S. $162). If I can only hold out for another month, I shall just about have enough money to pay for my passage to California. My main job is to talk to all the U.S. chaps from Vietnam and try to keep them in the hotel bar instead of them going to all the bars across the street where they pay U.S. $2 to buy a bar girl a drink. I'm not allowed to date any of the hotel guests, but occasionally I meet them down the street and we go for dinner. I haven't met anyone I fancy and I must really say my ego is way above normal since I am the only female in the hotel and the first these chaps have seen for months.

Now as far as they earrings go, Mother, I took the picture into several jewelry stores and the cheapest price I could have them made for is U.S. $45 and they refuse to make them pierced because they are too heavy and will pull and make long holes in your earlobes. I have been all over looking for these earrings and just haven't found any but will keep trying. But they are not worth $45. I would never get jade through customs. Have bought Daddy a watch and will also buy him a crocodile wallet.

I bought an outstanding present for Bubba and nice ones for Jane and Ticky. I will buy dolls for the children and a toy Chinese junk for Little Harry, but please don't let anyone know that I'm bringing these things. I refuse to arrive home after four years with no presents. You mentioned on the phone you would be coming to Hong Kong – if so, when? I don't know exactly when I'll be home, but I have my bags packed so I'll be ready when they kick me out of the colony. I never hear from Tony and he has two large bags to ship home for me. Barbara is in Vancouver now, she flew from Hawaii.

It's so hot here now, that three of us sleep on the floor of one of the girl's rooms which is air conditioned. You must start making a list of everything in the boxes I send. In all you should receive 12 or 13 boxes (shoeboxes) of bronzeware, 144 pieces altogether.

The hotel gave a gigantic party on a boat which is like the ferry boat which crosses the harbor. It was given for Captain Tom Taylor who is General Maxwell D. Taylor's[61] son. I was hostess and most of the people were from the U.S. Consulate. I rather fancied Tom as he was ever so good-looking and what a build! I couldn't understand why he paid no attention to me, when all the other chaps did! Later I saw him with a Chinese bar girl and was he ever embarrassed – I don't blame them at all. Everyone was quite shocked to learn I was an American, in fact everyone wanted to know when I was going back home to England! We went to Picnic Island to swim and had a ball. Everyone was getting drunk and when the ice was finished, we went cruising into Aherdene where all the sampans are (these are small wooden boats that all the refugees live on) for more ice. It was a riot as everyone was looped and they kept yelling to the those on the boats, "Vote Republican! " Then on to Repulse Bay for swimming again. There was so much food and booze. It was so much fun and I met so many nice people. Must go now.

Love Barbara

---

[61] General Maxwell Davenport Taylor (1901-1987) was a senior U.S. Army officer and diplomat. He was the distinguished commander of 101st Airborne Division in World War II. He was appointed by President Kennedy as chairman of the Joint Chiefs of Staff. He is the father of biographer and historian John Maxwell Taylor and of military historian and author Thomas Taylor (mentioned above).

Kowloon

July 19, 1966

Kowloon, Hong Kong

Flat 22, 8ᵗʰ Floor, No. 22 Wing On Mansion, Hankow Road, Kowloon, Hong Kong

Dear Mother and Daddy,

Went to see Dr. Sarthou the other day to give him a wallet for Daddy. He said he might not be able to get to Savannah, but would mail it. By the way, I showed my flatmates the part of the letter which said y'all didn't approve of me working in a bar. Let's face it, I think you both realize I have too much respect for myself to do that. I am Public Relations for the International Hotel which is a first class hotel and was chosen by the U.S. and British governments for R&R and government officials to stay in due to the hotel's good reputation. I just go around talking to the guests from 5 to 8 and my job is envied by all the European girls here. So, stop worrying. I enjoyed reading Jane's letter so much. Shame little Harry probably doesn't remember who I am.

I leave for Japan on August 11 on a French ship called the Vietnam which is the same one I took from Singapore to here. Will arrive in Yokohama on August 15 and will be met by a chap who lives in Tachikawa Air Force base outside Tokyo. He flies in here a lot. He and his friends are taking all my gear there for me and the 65 lb. tape recorder is already there. Seig flies in there a lot so I have written to him asking him to pick it up for me and take it back to the States. I have booked my place on the ship but can't pick up my ticket until I show them my passport, which I can't do and also, I'm really afraid I shall get into trouble with the British government. Things are just working too well for it all to go well.

I have to hang around Japan until October 1 when I plan to get in touch with Dr. Sarthou. He said he can get me on a ship back to the States for free. Now look, I know I could write y'all for the money to get home, but it is such a waste of money because I can get home free. Just think, that money could be spent for something else. Will go up to the northern islands of Japan to stay with some Japanese friends of mine.

I love doing things on the spur of the moment and I'm really excited about getting out of here. Will let you know in a few days' time whether I am in trouble or not. Please give me the ages of the children again.

Love B.

———⌘———

Japan
Kobe, Kyoto, Yokohama, Tokyo, Hokkaido

August 24, 1966

Hokkaido, Japan

Dear Mother and Daddy,

Arrived in Japan on August 18 at Yokohama but before that we stayed in Kobe for two days and three of us caught the train to Kyoto for the fire festival. Kyoto is a booming city but where the people actually live is just beautiful, with small cobble streets going up and down hills and lovely little houses (all made of wood) with beautiful little rock gardens. The little stores are so neat, it's incredible. Mother, you would go mad looking at the beautiful delicate little china bowls and plates and they put each bowl in wooden slots on the wall. Never have I seen any place so neat and clean! Shoes off all the time and usually places have slippers to step into. If one buys a bottle of Coke, every time you drink from it, the sales girl wipes the space where it was standing. Truly it was like walking through a fairyland Disney created!

Yokohama is a suburb of Tokyo and just a large harbor. Not too many women wear kimonos in the summer but winter time they all do. I guess you have heard about communal toilets. Well, the first time I walked into a toilet (bathroom), a European man was going to the john and I just about died and went running out and all the Japanese thought I was mad! Now I am used to it and think nothing of it.

I caught the train with an English chap and an Australian girl to a youth hostel in Tokyo. God, we spent so much money in taxis. For two days I tried to get in touch with Seig's friends and finally did. He should be in Tachikawa any day now. I also found out where all my stuff is in Tachikawa. A Canadian girl who speaks fluent Japanese came to the youth hostel to put up an advert for a roommate, so I moved in and won't have to pay rent until next month. I will try to get a job in Japan because I shall be able to save $250 a month and then after three months I will have more than enough money to get home.

Tokyo has a population of 11 million. It is terrible expensive – like 28¢ for a half cup of coffee – really. The people are extremely clean but not hygienic as far as the toilets are concerned. The Japanese men are quite smashing looking. The train and underground system are fantastic, the people very honest. I don't know if I ever mentioned Ron – a Lt. Commander in the navy stationed in Saigon? Well he sent me $60 before I left H.K. so I wouldn't starve in Japan. To see the performance of bowing is a riot. All the men bob up and down and might bow six or seven times to one person!

As of now I am in Hokkaido – the northern large island of Japan. Have been away from Tokyo since August 21 and have spent $70 just on trains (sleeping in the aisle), youth hostels and eating. No one can understand how the locals can afford to live with the small income the Japanese make. In next letter I will write about my trip all around Hokkaido. Hope Seig will be able to take some things back to the States for me.

Love Barbara

Sapporo, Aomori, then Tokyo

September 1, 1966

Tokyo, Japan

Dear Mother and Daddy,

I hope you received my letter from Sapporo in the northern island of Japan. Somehow, I think I forgot to put U.S.A. on the address, so if I didn't, it won't get to you. I traveled with a darling Australian girl who is a pacifist. Spent around 60 dollars for a week but most of this was for trains, buses, etc. which is very cheap for Japan. Naturally we stayed in gorgeous youth hostels which were 60 cents a night but I just couldn't take the Japanese food so existed on chocolate, Cokes, etc. – you know, all the good things for one's health!

There were no tourists and hardly anyone spoke English. All the students would come up to us and ask if they could speak an English conversation with us. There really isn't too much to tell about the landscape, as it looks so much like the pictures one sees of Canada. The trains and buses are very clean and whenever we arrived or were leaving a town, they would play sentimental Japanese music on the speakers. All the buses had lovely girls in uniforms telling the history and legends of each place, but naturally in Japanese so we didn't learn a thing from that angle! Occasionally they would sing a song. They are so shy and cover their mouths with their hands when someone says something to them. They are so delicate, very softly-spoken, dainty, and always bowing. I'm really fascinated by them, and I have even started bowing!

Many times, we couldn't get 2nd class sleepers on the train at night and ended up sleeping in the aisle on the floor. When we were in Sapporo we went to see a Shinto (mixture of Buddhism and another religion) temple. It was so beautiful with lovely rock gardens and brass doors – all the wood is the natural gray shade. They don't believe in coloring the natural because all their philosophy is based on nature. It was just so peaceful and beautiful and what amazes me is they use hardly anything to create such simple beauty.

Off in the woods we saw blue and white material tied between the trees to make an enclosure and women in beautiful kimonos were walking back and forth. We went over and all of them were sitting on a large mat on their knees. It was a tea party or ceremony and one woman told us we could buy tickets across a small little road. When they informed us it was 50 yen ($1.40), we said we couldn't afford it so another lady took us across so we could see. My God, you would not have believed the bowing and such delicate time they took just to fold a napkin! Everything has to be done just right, like twisting the large tea cup three times and then sipping with a loud noise three times. The tea was a dull green like the green on top of water, and was it ever dreadful to taste! We were invited to sit with them for the next session and when it was over, we could hardly walk from sitting on our legs for so long. I don't know what all the big fuss was about but photographers were taking pictures of us right, left and center. No one spoke English but with our little Japanese phrases we understand what they were trying to tell us. It was really an experience and I loved every moment of it because it was so different and fascinating.

In the temple, there was a priest who wore an outfit that made him look like one of Genghis Khan's men. Boy, I thought he was tough. Mostly all of the people traveling on the buses through Hokkaido were students who all wore Huck Finn hats. Apparently, the families were the rich ones because it is rather expensive traveling in Japan, and the cost of living is just as expensive as the States. People who have been living here 20 years still cannot figure how the locals on average can exist with such high prices and low salaries, and mostly all of them say the more they get to know the Japanese, the less they understand them.

One night we stayed in an inn which had no Western customs, slept on the floor and had our first public bath with just females. I was rather embarrassed because it's quite obvious all the Japanese girls are observing you from head to toe to see the difference. The people take a bath every day which is very refreshing and even the poor ones go to public bath houses. In one youth hostel, they had a bath which was the size of a swimming pool with columns all around. It was really gorgeous and there must have been 50 girls in the pool! When you enter, you just carry a towel and soap then you sit down on a little round plastic box, soap down and rinse yourself off and then get into the pool which is

恋人はライオ

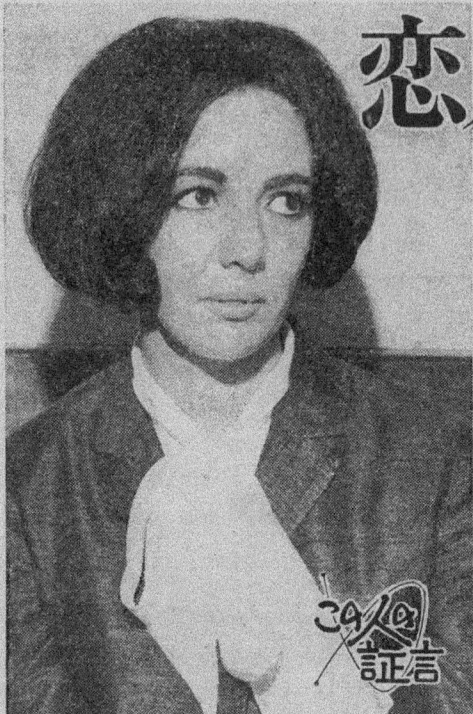

〈ゲスト〉
バーバラ・ピンクニー さん(26歳)

"なんでも与えられる生活"に退屈して世界漫遊に出たバーバラさん

この人の証言

道路工夫からハイ ソサエティまで

ジョージア州にささげられた生活だったの。

バーバラ パパの職業は?

チンペイ バーバラ 建築家、メードが三人いて、わたし専属のメードもいたわ。十四のときにはすでに車を持っていたし、ヨットも持っていた。

チンペイ ほしいものは何でも手にはいったんだね。

バーバラ そのとおりよ。

チンペイ なんでも与えられるという環境に、わたしは退屈しちゃったの。

チンペイ さいしょの恋人はいつごろ、与えられたの?

バーバラ 十六のときにね。

チンペイ カレすらも、キミをアメリカに認めておくことができなかったの?

バーバラ カレは結婚してましたし、まずアラブ諸国へ飛んだのである。ヤンキー娘そのままだったのである。

チンペイ なんだい、じゃ、結ばれっこないね。

バーバラ わたしは、恋を積極的に忙しいと思ったことはないわ。日本の男性は、まちがった考えをもってます。女性はつねに男性を求めると思ってるらしいけど、恋よりも冒険が好きな女の子も、たしかにいるの。わたしみたいにね。

――バーバラの無銭砲裁旅行は、こうして始まった。懐中に六百ドルだけ持った二十一歳のヤンキー娘は、ヤンキー娘そのままだったのである。ヤンキー娘たちは親から独立するのはあたり前だが、それでもやはり、冒険に踏みきる勇気の持主は、たくさんいない。安全な生活をまず第一に考える。男だってそうだ。バーバラは、なにをやって食べていたろう、という世界漫遊か。文字どおり、フラリと家を飛びだした。出たとこ勝負の世界漫遊だ。

バーバラ・ピンクニーさんのメモ

一九三七年、「風と共に去りぬ」で有名なアメリカはジョージア州アトランタで生まれた。二十一歳と二十二歳のとき、これといった目的もなしに世界旅行に出た。日本へ来るまでに、もう五十カ国以上歩いて来た。

(彼女と英語でデートしたい人は大使館は東京都港区麻布2の0の8、日本外国語商品サービス=電話(4)一〇〇四に連絡してみるといい)

バーバラ すいぶん、いろんな仕事やったわ。ロンドンでは、道路工事のシャベルもにぎったわ。下層階級の生活が知りたかったの。でもすぐそのあとで、上流階級のパーティーにも出席したのよ。マーガレット王女のPR。南アフリカでは、広告会社に勤め、お役所の秘書もやったわ。ローデシアでは林木会

社の秘書、南仏では映画のエキストラ。ローマでは映画のエキストラ、ブドウ狩り、東南アジアでは?

バーバラ インドで田植えをやったけど、一日五十円しか稼げなかったの。

チンペイ そりゃ、安いね。

バーバラ 十時間働いて、五十円よ。でもわたし、貧しい女の人に百円あげちゃった。お金稼ぎじゃないもの、わたしの仕事は。

チンペイ きれいな仕事ばかりやったわけじゃないんだね。

バーバラ ええ。サハラ砂漠では、キャラバンにくっついて、ラクダの世話もしたわ。たとえば、ラクダのフンを集める仕事。ラクダのフンはね、あとで食べ物にまぜて食べるの。

チンペイ ほかにどんな仕事?

バーバラ ホンコンではホテルの

チンペイ ラクダのフンを食べた?

バーバラ 知らずにね。おいし

チンペイ 胃袋もゴウケツだね。

extremely hot. The place is steaming and when I tried to take a picture, my lens was steamed up so it won't come out!

An old man of about 70 came in to check the water and I hid my body and all the girls looked at me as if I was mad. I couldn't believe my eyes when he walked up to the girls standing in the nude and was asking them if the water was too hot for them. They weren't at all embarrassed and just stood there facing him carrying on a conversation; I was shocked but when it happened again, I just exposed my back to him so I wouldn't go against their custom (they're fanatics on customs). I could think of many chaps that would pay a fortune just to have that man's job!

We managed to get a 2nd class sleeper all the way to Tokyo from Aomori which was great. I arrived back in Tokyo with 20 cents. The boat from Aomori to the island took 4½ hours and they played "May old acquaintance be forgot" and people were crying – so sentimental! We stayed in the ladies' compartment which was a gigantic room with gold carpet on which we slept with all the Japanese women. Some of their customs I think are marvelous.

I honestly don't know when I will be home and I am afraid my slides will get mildewed here so will have to get them off along with all the presents I have for everyone.

Love B.

Tokyo

October 15, 1966

Tokyo, Japan

Dear Mother and Daddy,

Honestly I'm so sorry it has taken so long to write, but it's the same old story. Met Dr. Sarthou for breakfast Saturday morning and had a most enjoyable time with him. He was ever so nice and I told him all about Michael, my Japanese friend, and he said he was dying to meet him.

Michael came to the hotel at 10.30 looking as white as a ghost. I have never seen him so nervous, he even stuttered when he spoke English to Dr. Sarthou. Really, I couldn't believe it and God only knows what Dr. Sarthou thought. Later on, Michael told me he was frightened because a friend of my parents might get the wrong idea about our relationship.

Went to see Seig yesterday and he is sending some more things home for me. They are to be given as Xmas presents from me – the large man's watch is for Daddy. I will type a list of the winter things I want so you hurry and send them to Seig and he will bring them to me the next time he comes here. As to my morals, I have done nothing I am ashamed of and the reason I only date Michael is because he has proved he would never try to get me in bed which is more I can say for the American men who travel through or live in Japan. I have too much respect for myself to associate with such people even though they have money, and no one is going to exploit me, so I think that takes care of the moral issue.

Winter List: Underarm pads which can be pinned on with small pins, not the type that have straps. Cheetah and Ostrich handbags – the Ostrich is black with little bumps on it. Revlon deodorant – not Hi And Dri but a special formula one which one only has to use every third day in a roll-on tube. Short coffee-brown whole slip that was sent from Rhodesia along with a wool purple, sleeveless dress; bed socks, wool; Camel colored wool slacks sent from Rhodesia. Black boots sent from England along with duffel coat, with hood, wool and wooden looped buttons. If I have a pair of loafers (shoes) send them also. I remember I had a red and greed plaid blazer along with a white one, send those along with any skirts (especially a gray pleated one) and sweaters, cardigans, and there is a red wool long-sleeve pullover sweater that I want. There was a black wool suit left in my closet with a white mink collar, take the collar off and send the collar. Fur coat and try to have it glazed, that is if it is in respectable condition. Go through my drawers and see if there are any Bermuda slacks and send them. Black stretch slacks with a loop at the bottom which fits on the feet which were sent from Rhodesia – these will be for skiing this winter. Honestly, I just can't remember all the stuff I have, but Mother, I know it will be quite a hard job but go through everything and pick out the stylish things and send them to me. Also, blue wool Tahitian sweater that was sent from Bangkok, also zebra handbag and white soft wool underpants and T-shirt sent from Rhodesia.

Please do not buy anything except deodorant and underarms pads. Send them to Seig's address and he will bring them to me the next time. I have been doing some modeling, teaching, working every night and lost 10 dollars by staying at Yokota with Seig but he bought me 10 dollars' worth of things at the PX [Post Exchange]. He is very nice to me but he judges me just as others do and thinks he understands me but doesn't have a clue how I function or why I do the things I do!

I am terribly happy now in Tokyo and wouldn't think of leaving, not even if someone gave me a free first-class ticket to the States. Michael thinks I'm a perfect lady and I have never showed him my mean nature because he makes me so happy. Don't worry, I'm too realistic to marry him, and being from one of the old Japanese families, he is committed to marry a wealthy Japanese girl. I have not even met his family because they would not approve of me being a gaijin[62], an outsider and Westerner; how's that for a switch! Must run to the British Embassy, don't know why they want to see me, then to work.

Please don't let Seig know I feel this way but I think he is rather conceited and I just don't have time to waste on people who exist on their ego.

Now, honestly please don't buy anything because it will just be a waste of money. Tokyo is becoming more pleasant since I am learning how to catch all the different subways to different sections of this gigantic, over-populated place. I was going to come home for 12 days in December because I could get a round trip from Yokohama to San Francisco for 20 dollars, but I think the mental strain would be too much just for 12 days so I am not coming. I might go to Russia from here via Siberia, but this is still in the vacillating stage. Now hurry and get these things to Seig as soon as possible because he will probably be coming back in three weeks' time.

Sorry I can't write more about my life in Japan but I am just too busy with all my jobs.

Love Barbara

------⊶⊷------

[62] Gaijin is the Japanese word for foreigners and non-Japanese citizens in Japan. Some feel it now has a negative connotation, while other feel it is a 'neutral' word.

Tokyo

December 6, 1966

Tokyo, Japan

Dear Mother and Daddy,

Sorry again for the delay in writing, but it's the same old story, running here and there accomplishing nothing as usual. Received last letter with $5 check, which I thank you very much for.

It is very cold here now and terribly depressing without the sun, and the flat has the typhoon shutters drawn closed which doesn't let one see the outside, so it is rather like a prison. I never get to see Michael and he realizes how depressed I am, so he is going to break it to his 70-year-old mother that I shall come live with them for a week, just for a change.

I got in an argument with the people I was working for and since the President who liked and hired me had quit, the other people don't like foreigners, so out I went. They would have done the same to the other American girl but she is going home on December 20 so they knew they were getting rid of her anyway. It's very difficult to understand these people – they don't like hurting people or should I say, it puts them in a difficult or unpleasant position to tell a person what they want to say, so they are for always making their inferiors tell a person the bad news!

I had agreed with the ex-President the rate of $11 for five hours and then he asked me to work six hours. When I received my pay check at the end of the month after the President (the one who hired me) had left, they had only paid me $8 dollars for six hours, and I had to pay 58 cents for a taxi every night for working the extra hour because the subway closes at 11.30 and I got off work at 12.00. So when I complained about the salary, they gave me the story that business was bad (which it wasn't) and they couldn't afford to pay me more than 2.50 an hour. I told them that was not fair as I had been told something else concerning salary and anyway that is less than the Japanese girls are making that were employed the same time I was. They said I could work there for 2.50 an hour if I wanted to but I just told them I had too much respect for myself to be in a place where I'm not wanted. They are very anti anything that isn't

Japanese, they don't speak English and they just can't seem to understand that Japanese men like to practice their English with foreign girls.

The ex-President is furious with them for doing me so dirty, but he can't say anything since he has left the place. He is opening a new place on January 1 and wants me to come work for him, so now I have one month of doing nothing which is terrible in a way. This isn't the first time I've been done over. Meanwhile, I don't get any of the money they owe me, and really, I just don't want it anyway, because it is very cheap now. Michael is also disgusted. There is no use having a contract drawn up, because it means nothing. God, I'm really fed up with this place – I just can't compete with their lack of respect for people who are not family members.

Michael promised me he would take me skiing for New Year's and if he lets me down, I will be so disappointed and really fed up. I think Seig is rather fed up with me but I really could care less since it's a real bother going out to Tachikawa and I really don't fancy him. Really, I just don't know what's the matter with me these days, I haven't even bought Xmas cards for the family and Michael thinks I'm very naughty. I still have the remainder of the dolls for the children but can't even concentrate on wrapping them. As for one of my flatmates, Allison, she is driving me crazy, and everyone who has met her thinks she is so vociferous, rude, and very unfeminine. Eileen, the lady next door, said she is very jealous of me, although I can't believe that.

1967

Tokyo

January 5, 1967

Tokyo, Japan

Dear Mother and Daddy,

Again, I apologize for waiting so long to write. Daddy used to always say to me, "That's all you're capable of, saying 'I'm sorry'". I have been unemployed for a month waiting for the chap to open a new club. I shall start next week after I have an operation on my ears. Remember, I always wanted them pinned back flat against my ears, well that's what I'm having done.

New Year's is a big deal in Japan and for days literally everything closes and all the Japanese stay with their relatives. I didn't see Michael except once; the rest of the time I stayed home reading and freezing to death. Yesterday Michael took me walking all over the Ginza (main street). He wore his kimono, carried a silk fan and wore wooden shoes three inches high. He looked so handsome and aristocratic. I looked ever so funny walking behind him in my miniskirt, black flowered stockings, with my handbag over the shoulder and sunglasses on. The Japanese couldn't believe their eyes! You know he comes from one of the oldest families in Japan and for the four months I have been dating Nichidasun (Michael's Japanese name) I have never been allowed to meet his family. However, the other day he informed them he was dating an outsider (Europeans are referred to as red-headed barbarians!). Michael is teaching his

70-year-old mother to say, "Yes, just a moment, please" in English for when I telephone!

Each day I just exist thinking of the day Allison will leave which will be January 31. I really loathe her; she is common, loud, rude and very unfeminine. Michael dislikes her very much.

I bought a kimono for Seig when he returns and I hope he will take the rest of the things home for me.

I'm very unhappy here but shall wait until summer, go to Russia and then home.

January 14 I had the operation on my ears on January 10 and was awake during the two-hour operation. I was a nervous wreck during the sawing and stitching process. One of the best surgeons in Japan did it. Stayed in the hospital one night and have been home in bed ever since. The bandages come off January 16. Michael said I look like a blood awful American football player. Don't tell anyone I had the operation on my ears, you know how they are.

Tokyo

January 17, 1967

Tokyo, Japan

Dear Mother and Daddy,

Like Mother, you forgot to put in the rest of the letter you wrote me! Thank you very much for the $40 and I also received $20 from Bubba, but don't say anything. Will write everyone you mentioned, also received a St Christopher necklace from your friend Constance – she thanked me for writing her a letter, heavens I don't even remember. The large watch is for Daddy – the other three are for Jane, Ticky and Mother. The two prettier ones are for Mother and Jane. I have worn one of them and they are great. Three year guarantee. The tie tack (brown star sapphire) is for Bubba – the dolls for the children. I still have four more here. So, Mother, you give the dolls to the children before they get too big.

I was operated on a week ago – it took two hours and I was awake. Nothing they gave me made me sleep. I still have a bandage on my head and it was very painful for about four days. Cost me $150. Michael has not been able to come see me for his mother (70 years old) has pneumonia. Allison has gone skiing with her husband-to-be – he's Korean (terribly nice) – but she's stupid. Meachan has moved out and took her oil heater. Last week the plumbing was all messed up and when the people upstairs flushed their toilet, it all came into our tub! Couldn't even open the bathroom door as was afraid the odor would knock me out. I have been in bed a week and the flat is just filthy and God I can't begin to tell how cold. The electricity went off yesterday and something is wrong with the geyser so I have not had hot water for two days. Ice is in the sink from the dripping water and every dish in the place is dirty. Can't get in touch with the landlord so don't know how much longer this will go on. Thank God I borrowed an electric blanket but the girl is furious with me for not returning it.

Now my boss has informed me I cannot work until I find two more foreign girls so when I get better, I have to find two and that will be the hardest thing to do. So, you see I'm just here feeling sorry for myself but I become more mad each day and will come out of this somehow. Michael really gave me a lecture and told me I was the stupid yet most sensitive person he had ever met. His technique worked for he knew I would get furious and show him I wasn't. Hope you don't get upset but if I came home it would be admitting defeat.

I shall try and write more especially about the Japanese people. Michael should be coming soon to clean up for me and buy some food. You know it's very funny that we are from different races but I have never known anyone that understands me so well.

Hope all is well. Xmas I went to Mount Fuji but could hardly see it as it was so cloudy, but had a marvelous time with Michael.

Love Barbara

Letter From Mr. & Mrs. Pinckney

March 3, 1967

Honorable Elliott Hagan, Congressman:

Our daughter Barbara is this spring visiting in Tokyo and has hopes of touring portions of the interior of Siberia and Russia, bordering the Pacific Ocean. She has traveled extensively in Europe, Africa, near East, Middle East, and Asia and so is experienced in traveling in areas that are non-American but we are alarmed by her intentions of traveling in that particular area, since it is probably not a scheduled tour. She may not have companionship.

Therefore, we would appreciate your comments and advice on such a trip, which we will immediately forward to our daughter.

Thanking you in advance for anything that you can do to help us in this matter. We want to thank you again for having the State Dept. in Bombay, India locate our daughter Barbara last summer when war conditions became acute and interrupted her communication with us.

Tokyo

March 12, 1967

Tokyo, Japan

Dear Mother and Daddy,

Again, I must apologize but so much has happened, such as Allison returning from Hong Kong and bringing every bum she could find to eat all our food and sleep on the floor! I am still working from 8 until 11, not far from the house. An English girl lived with me for a month and has left for South America. She was so adorable and looked like Julie Andrews. A German girl is living with me now and I am about to lose my mind. She never takes a bath, doesn't shave under her arms, doesn't use deodorant and never washes her clothes. She puts all her dirty, smelly clothes in the closet with all my clean clothes which I wash every day. The place is really beginning to smell and I am getting embarrassed when company comes. Her brother stayed with us for a week and he had not taken a bath for over a month and had not washed his socks for two weeks. God, he smelt like garbage. I have done so much hinting but she gets annoyed with me and tells me I'm like a cranky old grandmother. I will have to ask her to leave if she does not start being clean.

Cherry blossom time is around the corner and today was the first warm day. I'm so sick of Tokyo and will be more than glad to get out. Everyone drive me crazy. As far as Russia goes, I just don't know where you got the idea I was going to work there. It is the cheapest possible way to get to the States from here. From Yokohama to New York, it only cost 550 U.S. dollars. I will be on the train across Siberia for eight days, stay in Moscow two days and then on to Helsinki by train. It is costing me 260 U.S. dollars to Helsinki, all expenses included. I might go down to Italy from the Scandinavia countries to visit a girlfriend of mine, or I might just head on to New York. I leave here June 2 and hope to have $1,400 to spend, that is if I don't get fired from this job, which I almost did last week because a Japanese man hit me and naturally, I flattened him!

I met the head of the dental society here and he is letting me have all my teeth fixed for free. I am really lucky because doctors are rather expensive on the salaries people make. The pictures of Bubba's children were adorable but I must admit the cowboy outfits were so typical American. There really isn't so much to tell about my doings for I sleep until around 12, tidy up the house, eat something and then take a bath and get ready for work or for my students. Everyone I have talked to says the Siberia trip is terrific and I might even go to Poland from Moscow. Honestly the propaganda the people in the States are fed is so bloody ridiculous and disgusting. So please be relieved.

Des Brown will probably come to see me next month on R&R from Vietnam. Also, Seig telephoned Saturday but I couldn't see him because they were going to leave very soon. Will catch him again and hope he will take home some statues for me.

If anyone asks you what I am doing in Japan, just tell them I am teaching English, naturally British English. Someday I will really write you about the customs of the people. I have to get a new passport next week and then I will have to ask the Japanese government for another extension. I don't know if they will give it to me; if they don't I will have to spend 50 dollars to go to Korea for a re-entry visa to Japan. I must go teach my horrible little children and then a scientist at a hotel restaurant, then I see Michael for an hour, and then to work until 12.30 tonight.

Will try not to wait such a long time for writing.

Love Barbara

Tokyo

May 17, 1967

Tokyo, Japan

Dear Mother and Daddy,

As of now, I am really saving the money, $1,500. I still have six students a week and that is what I pay the rent with. Also, I get my dental work done free and now I am working with five other European girls selling peanuts on top of one of the largest hotels, the Nakkatsie, in their beer garden. We wear old peasant Japanese men's clothes and really look ridiculous! For two hours (6 to 8 pm) we just walk back and forth for $9.20, tax free. I do this five nights a week and will eventually do six nights. I earn $168 a month from that and I change to my other job in Shibuya from 8.30 to 11.30 and clear $336, so now I am able to save $500 a month.

I am planning on staying here until August but I think the government is getting annoyed with me, since one is only allowed to stay here two months on a tourist visa and I have been here for eight. But man, I am going to have one of my Japanese girlfriends whose father is in Parliament ask the officials to let me stay. I just know something will happen and I will have to leave since I am making so much money. I would like to walk out of here with $3,000 but nothing ever goes as one plans. Will send you some pictures of the beer garden job. I might go to

South America instead of Russia. I wish I could afford to keep the flat by myself for Wally, my roommate, is so dirty. Really, I just about throw up at the filthy habits she has and she gets really angry when I tell her to be cleaner. I hope Jane and the children got to Savannah alright. A late happy Mother's Day.

Love Barbara

—————————⸘⸘—————————

Tokyo, Japan

July 10, 1967

Tokyo, Japan

Dear Mother and Daddy,

Can't remember how long it's been since I last wrote, but things are as usual except for the rains which have made me lose over a hundred dollars since June 22. The peanuts job at the Nakkatsie Hotel pays $9.20 for two hours, except when it rains. I still have the same job at night in Shibuya and now I'm no.1 and make $14 for three hours. I have an old Japanese friend of 65 years old, who is very wealthy and already he has given me a $100 bill as a tip, one 18cc gold ring with a beautiful jade stone which cost a mint and I lost… He has also given me another opal ring, six bottles of French perfume, a large cameo pin, a lovely pink French hat and several other things.

I must admit the Japanese men are the most boring men I have ever come across but a foreign girl is treated like a queen. Michael would be considered a weak man by American standards but is a 1st class man in Japan. So gentle, reserved, witty, delicate and speaks with a classical tongue in Japanese and English. When he came over here on Sunday, he cleaned up the whole flat and gave me a massage and then I cooked for him and he washed the dishes. I am really on the cooking spree and yesterday we both got sick from chicken I had soaked in white wine for 30 hours. God it was dreadful, and I'm afraid he is terrified of my cooking now!

I usually sleep until 11 every day then put the bedding on the line until evening, tidy up the flat and then read until it's time to go to the peanut job.

Vergie, an American girl, comes over here once a week to take a bath and I fix dinner. Food prices are ridiculous as well as everything else. She wants me to go to Spain with her to the University of Madrid for a year which I would love to do. I was thinking of going there on the Trans-Siberian train which would only cost me $200 from Tokyo to Spain. Then from there I could go to Rio de Janeiro and then home but that would take two years from now before I reach home, so what I think I shall do is work here until October and save $3,500, go home for two months then catch a boat to Spain. So, I shall probably be home November but you know how I change my mind.

I went to Korea about two weeks ago for three days. Flew there and I must admit I thought the Koreans were ever so nice and very friendly. The riots broke out the same day I left! There was literally nothing to do so I just shopped all the time. Bought a 24cc gold bracelet 37.5 grams.

I go to Ikebana, the "art of flower arranging". My teacher is a lovely elderly lady who always wears a kimono. She keeps telling me my arrangements look like a jungle! Japanese taste is to strip nature and re-style it to simplicity. They will cut more than half the branches and flowers off, which they have been paid for – to me this is cutting off money, so I want to stick everything in. Michael goes into hysterics every time he sees my arrangements.

One of the chaps I dated from Beaufort Air Station [South Carolina, so when still in Savannah], John Czerwinski, came here last week and bought so many lovely things from the PX. I had a lovely time but he was rather shocked by my accent. Remember Dez Brown? Well he should be coming soon, and I'm terribly excited as I always did rather fancy him!

I bought a beautiful kimono for Daddy which I shall send sometime. The magazine pictures enclosed were taken at the beer garden on top of the Nakkatsie Hotel. I always hide when pictures are being taken for I don't want immigration to have proof that I am working. The one girl in the picture resembles Jane. Someday when the sun is shining, Michael will take some pictures up there on the roof.

Wally has left, thank God. It took me three hours to clean up the bathroom after she left!

I have lost so much weight in my face and my bones show. My hair is in shocking condition and I am letting the dye grow out of it.

Did you give Bubba the tie tack? It's a star sapphire from either Burma or Ceylon. Also did Harry and Daddy get their crocodile wallets? You never mentioned it.

I must wash my clothes and get ready for the peanut job.

Love Barbara

Tokyo

September 2, 1967

Tokyo, Japan

Dear Mother and Daddy,

Sorry I did not get to speak to Daddy on the telephone, but never mind, I shall be home soon. Immigration has not left me alone since August 3. Michael has been out of town in New Zealand and so I have had no advice as to what to tell them. As usual, I rubbed them up the wrong way so naturally they want to kick me out of the country. I was fired from the peanut job because the officials keep saying that I was being paid. It will close on September 15 anyway, but I am still losing $145. They also know I work at the 'Hi Dick' so I haven't been there for three nights, losing $45 in the process. The only problem is if they ask anyone there if I am employed. The Japanese will panic and say yes. Really, they are nits at times. God am I fed up! Michael will arrive tomorrow night and then I shall discuss my next move with him.

The article "Hello, Richard" is about 'Hi Dick' where I am a hostess. In the Social Scene article, read "The Nepalese Ambassador" and see my name in the middle! As I hope you know, HRH means His Royal

Highness. He will be king when his father passes away. They won't have to change pictures when he becomes king for he is the spitting image of his father! Princess Mikasa pronounced (Mc-ka-sa) is the Japanese Emperor's daughter. This is the second time I have been invited to a reception for royalty in Tokyo. The first time was for Princess Chichibu, the Emperor's sister, in December. Try to get Rick at the paper to write something about it.

I have saved $3,000 but if only I could stay until November it would be $4,000. Barb is coming here and taking over my flat in November. I really would like to see her again. I'm trying to work on a free trip home but these things never happen.

What is the style in Savannah? Do people still wear miniskirts? Please let me know for I don't want to arrive looking like a country bumpkin! Will let you know soon enough if Michael shall come with me.

I shall go now.

Love Barbara

Tokyo

November 8, 1967

Tokyo, Japan

Dear Mother and Daddy,

I shall arrive in Savannah on December 21 by Delta at 7 am. Vergie and I are leaving Tokyo on December 18. Will stay in Hawaii a day and a half and then to San Francisco by Japan Airlines arriving December 20 at 7.30 am. I have to wait all day in San Francisco because the other flight I catch would put me in Savannah at 2 am on December 20 and I wanted to arrive in daylight. So, I have booked on Delta, leaving San Francisco 10.20 pm, arriving Atlanta (I THINK) 5 am December 21. One hour wait in Atlanta and arriving Savannah 7 am December 21. I can't remember if it is dark at 7 am in December or not. I don't want to arrive at night time – I'll be too depressed. So, if you can please find out if I can catch a plane for Atlanta and Savannah on the morning of December 20 from San Francisco. During Xmas time there are extra flights.

Let me know as soon as possible so my agents here can change my schedule for I have paid my fare all the way to Savannah in Tokyo as I was able to pay in local currency $41.00 then I have to pay to get back to Europe for I'm not staying in that crazy country for long. I shall really be out of circulation so ask Jane to put the word around and set me up with friends so that I can show off my evening clothes.

So, that's all for now. I can't afford any Xmas presents, for yesterday when I was mailing parcels home and I left my wallet on the counter with $33 in it.

Love Barbara

TOKYO, JAPAN

December 11, 1967

Tokyo, Japan

Dear Mother and Daddy,

Please don't encourage anyone except the family to come to the airport. I will have been three nights without sleep and shall be in no mood to see anyone. I shall stop in Hawaii for two days and shall stick to my original plan. Arriving in San Francisco on December 20 and arriving Savannah on 21st at 7 or 8 am from Atlanta. God, I shall be exhausted. I would love some chocolate cake when I arrive home if possible with pecans and chocolate frosting, homemade! Plus potatoes and gravy, I am very thin so don't be surprised. I just can't bring anything home for Xmas. Only for Page and Harry, that's all. As of now, I shall have to pay well over $200 to customs on the junk I am bringing with me.

Please, I want nothing for Xmas. I have got nice day clothes but Japanese things are rather large for me. Everything here is medium size.

Delta flight number: DL 892

Can you ask Steve Grady if he received all my letters, and what about the Thompsons?

Love Barbara

⸻⊶❋⊷⸻

[There are no letters for 1968 and half of 1969. Callan returns to Savannah for a flying visit Christmas 1967, spending some time planning the next leg of her trip. She even appeared on the cover of *Savannah Magazine* in January 1968 with an interview about her travels.]

𝕾𝖆𝖛𝖆𝖓𝖓𝖆𝖍 𝕸𝖔𝖗𝖓𝖎𝖓𝖌 𝕹𝖊𝖜𝖘
SAVANNAH EVENING PRESS

MAGAZINE

January 14, 1968

1969

Spain

Madrid

August 2, 1969

Madrid, Spain

Dear Mother,

Really sorry I haven't written but honestly my social life has been too much since Daddy and you left. First of all, I am now getting $135 more from my job as I had enough common sense to check what my rights were which they hadn't informed about. One day after work I went horseback riding out at a ranch with a cowboy who trains horses for the movies. I rode much better than Paul Newman[63] or so Corkie the cowboy told me! I went riding twice with George Peppard[64] and a week with his girlfriend Judy Geeson[65]. Do you remember when we saw *To Sir, With Love* with Sidney Poitier? She was the leading girl. Anyway, I spent two weeks with her in Madrid and I must admit I used to get very embarrassed when the limousine would pick me up with a bar and TV inside. Christ, it looked as if Jackie Onassis were in it! Shirley, my flatmate, was very jealous as she was not invited, and since then we are not as friendly.

---

[63] Paul Newman (1925-2008) was an American icon who starred as Butch in *Butch Cassidy and the Sundance Kid* which was released in 1969. His horses were probably trained by Corkie.
[64] George Peppard (1928-1994) was an American actor who starred opposite Audrey Hepburn in *Breakfast at Tiffany's*.
[65] Judy Geeson (born 1948) is an English film, stage, and television actress. Her film debut was in *To Sir, With Love* She starred alongside George Peppard (above) in *The Executioner*.

I went to dinner in George Peppard's suite at the Hilton, and had a ball. For extra money I have been washing two chaps' clothes from the movie *The Horsemen*[66], for the laundry refused to do their clothes as they were so dirty. I make $10 a week by sticking their blue jeans in the twin-tub and letting them soak.

I have also gone to watch Chapandaz (Afghanistan men) play Buzkashi (the national game of Afghanistan where men on horses use a dead goat as a ball). They have been kicked out of four hotels for cooking on the living room floor and burning holes in the center of the room and also, they went to the toilet in a corner in the living room and just left it! The fifth place they moved to, someone showed them the toilet and their comment was "a built-in spring"! Five places in three weeks – not bad! I got some beautiful presents from them, two oriental rugs etc. for I was the only one who would be seen with them. There were seven of them and the shortest was 6'2"! The Spanish fled with fright when they saw these giants walking with crazy ropes, hats and whips! They finally moved to 42 Dr Fleming – the same building Conchita's hairdresser lived in.

I took them to Galerías Preciados (a famous Spanish department store) and the sales clerks were coughing as they smelt so bad – I put cotton wool up my nose! Do you remember the extremely large, round, colored glasses the Spanish girls wear? Well the men went wild over these and even slept with them on! God they even looked more frightening with the glasses! They have gone now.

I had a party here at the flat with Don Gordon, John Russell[67] and George Peppard. Gorgeous ham and turkey from the base! Have not spent one cent except for $42 for rent the whole month of July. Shirley and I have been offered to stay in a house on the beach for free so we will probably be leaving next week. Will send the negatives, picture enclosed. Will buy five plates and have a friend send them through A.P.O. I did not receive anything from Jane (no receipt) for the candlesticks. I am going down to American Tourist Bureau this afternoon, I have the receipt for that. The painting I am sending you is still at American Express, for I need certain documents before it can be sent. The reason I am sending

[66] *The Horsemen* starring Omar Sharif was finally released in 1971 It took two and a half years to film.
[67] Don Gordon (1926-2017) was an American film and TV actor who starred in *Bullitt*, and *The Towering Inferno*. John Russell (1921-1991) was an American film and television actor.

it through American Express is because they will insure it for full value at a cost of $40. If it is sent through A.P.O. it can only be insured for $200 and you paid $385. I can still send it through A.P.O. for $3 but if it is lost you only get $200 back – but it's very rare that something is lost in A.P.O. I shan't send it until you let me know which way you want it.

Enclosed is a list and receipts and articles. Let's just call it even for I have $1,000 saved from work. Too late now to go to American Tourist Bureau for I spent all afternoon getting receipts organized. Shan't write for a while – you know me. I'm taking the film around now. Ask Jane what size American dress she takes. Conchita was very excited to receive your letter. Have been offered three jobs but wasn't interested. Didn't get to see the men land on the moon. The Spanish don't care who is the leader as long as there is peace.

Love Barbara

⊸◦⊰⊱◦⊸

Madrid, Spain
Madrid

November 3, 1969

Felix Boix No. 9, 4oA, Madrid 16, Spain

Dear Mother and Daddy,

Ever so sorry it has taken me so long to let you know what is going on. I have been doing secretarial jobs except for the last month. Thank God I'm not the type who spends much money for I would be broke now. The Spanish government is really cracking down on foreigners working. I live in a terribly formal flat around the corner from Shirley's place.

Madrid is very cold now and a drag. Sixty foreigners in this neighborhood were thrown in jail for six years for smoking pot, or so I read in the newspaper.

I am dating an Scottish producer who is very kind to me and gives me the attention I have always needed. Conchita just arrived back from Mozambique and I shall go see her this afternoon.

I really would like to get married now and have children before my body becomes too old but I just can't marry for the sake of marrying – I'm too much of a romanticist.

January is when my lease is up and since I can't afford $100 a month for rent I shall probably go to Ibiza – an island off the coast of Valencia. It is supposed to be cheaper and warmer.

The children's little cards were precious and I appreciated it. Hope Jane received my large get-well card which I sent when she was in the hospital.

Remember Susan, the American girl I traveled with in India and also was in Madrid? Well she is engaged to a viscount in England – he has a 300-room palace! God, why couldn't that be me. I shall be at this address until January 4. Hope all is well with everyone.

Love Barbara

P.S. Bob Burnette's painting has been sent and I still am trying to get the plates off. Please write all information about American Tourist Bureau. Have you ever heard from them? Let me know everything before I leave – should I go down there again?

―――――∽◦⧉◦∾―――――

Madrid

December 15, 1969

Madrid, Spain

Dear Mother and Daddy,

Susan – Mother, you met her – is really in with the jet set and was engaged to an English viscount but he drank ever so much that she has spilt with him and is arriving here today! She will stay with me for a while for her girlfriend lives around the corner. I shall stay in Madrid until the end of January to see if there is a chance of me going to Afghanistan with Columbia Pictures. If not I will go to Malta and Conchita wants to go too, for the new Spanish government is cracking down on people who own businesses without a licence. I am so glad to be out of that flat upstairs for the language was tiring me and I never met anyone but bums and that crazy Vivian next door was too much. I can't mind admitting but for three months I have been in a terribly depressed mood which is why I haven't sent your plates, Mother. I shall send them after the Xmas rush for I am snapping out of this mood. Will put all my things in storage when I leave.

I am dating a producer who is very kind to me. He's Scottish but I only want to get serious for an American. I love traveling but I really feel it is time to get married while I can still have children.

My flat is so beautiful, I hate to leave it. The rent is outrageous – $100 a month – but that's this neighborhood. I must tell you I cannot afford to send any presents and I feel very bad about the children but I don't even have money for rent. I forgot to tell you I worked for a man typing contracts and he left town without paying me, which is why I am broke and I can't do anything about it for I don't have a working permit. Angie, an English girl who was Hayley Mills' double in the movies for a long time, is coming to see me next week but I can't let her stay for long. She is a true hippie and I must avoid that scene – their life appeals to me but I know it's not good for me.

Actually, what I want now out of life is an education, but it costs money. Did I tell you I wrote to the British Museum asking them if they needed secretaries on digs in the Middle East, but I have not heard from them as of now. The government is making it difficult for foreigners to work here now so that's another reason for leaving; Madrid to me is not the city to meet nice people.

I might be depressed here but if I were in Savannah, I would be put in a mental institution! Hope everything in the family is all right and you have a lovely Christmas. Sorry I don't write more but that's me for I seem to always be very spiteful when I write.

Love Barbara

1970

Madrid

January 23, 1970

Madrid, Spain

Dear Daddy,

Christ, you won't believe what I'm going to say, but Conchita and I are planning on opening a steak barbecue and Kentucky Fried Chicken combined restaurant in Malta. Conchita is going to finance it and I shall be half partner. It will be just a dumpy place which we will more or less construct ourselves (can you imagine!) and will work hard for two years, for that is all the time we will have before the government nationalizes everything. We will go at Easter so until then I will get a job as a waitress – what a drag! We also have to have a Maltese owning 10% of the business, to please the government. Now what I need desperately is a recipe for a barbecue sauce for steak and how to fry chicken. If Bubba will write me up some recipes in his free time, I will pay him $100 but only if the business is a success.

I also need legal info about an American opening a business in Malta and how it is done. I am going to the Embassy today and also writing to my Navy lawyer friend in Washington D.C. See if you can get info from Chamber of Commerce or maybe they can tell you which government department can give you advice. I have nothing to lose, so I am going into this wholeheartedly. Also, two young friends of mine have started a suede factory and I have found many connections for them so I should be getting a handsome commission when the business gets going – but I never count now until the money is in my hand.

I am associating with a friend of Susan's, MJ Designs, who does designs for Paris Vogue and is drawing up a color chart for me and also designing the most fantastic clothes for a dressmaker to make up. She is so fantastic for she has actually convinced me I am beautiful! I went to a psychiatrist and he told me my only problem is I know what I want in life and refuse to take less. And that I am a product of my society which has really screwed up my thinking with guilt complexes. Daddy, if you have any info or advice to give about the restaurant crap, I will be more than willing to listen. When it comes to making money, I always listen for I am inexperienced and ignorant. I feel life is opening up to me again. Write soon.

Love Barbara

Madrid

March 23, 1970

Madrid, Spain

Dr. Fleming No.44, C/O Apt. 918, Madrid 16, Spain

Dear Mother,

Just a short note to let you and Daddy know that I am finally coming out of my depression and feel life does have a meaning, but one must be strong to survive. Now I am about to have a fit because Roz is coming. Don't worry, I shall be charming, but also don't forget she has always liked me because I am different.

I am not going into business with Conchita and I told Roz on the phone I work for a director.

Moving out of the flat April 4 into a flat at Dr. Fleming. Corkie, the chap who trains horses, is letting Angie and I have a room so I shall not have to spend money on rent and can reimburse you for goods. I didn't even know it was March so I shall send Harry a card and some stamps for his birthday.

I am much happier now so don't worry. Hope everything is all right. God only knows when I shall write a long letter. Might call if I can find way.

———— ⋘⋙ ————

Madrid

March 23, 1970

Madrid, Spain

Dear Mrs. Frame,

Just a short note to let you know how excited I am you're coming. I'm ever so much looking forward to seeing you again.

Now I just talked to my boss in Rome and he shall be in Madrid April 1 to April 5 or 6. Since my future in Europe depends on this job I really can't leave Madrid until the 7th. Also, an apartment is free on April 6 but not before. After the 7th I am fancy free so if you can make it around the 7th it would be better but if you can't, don't worry as you can go to the Valley of the Fallen on a day excursion and tour Madrid on a tour while I am working. Also, I have to be out of my flat by April 4 and I am terribly confused about that for I am there half the time and at another flat (my girlfriend and I are staying with a friend) the other half at Felix Foix No. 9, Madrid 16 Tel. 457-3976. From April 4 onward I will be at Dr. Fleming No.44 Madrid 16, Tel 250-5800 Apt. 918.

I shall enquire about renting a car but as of now I can find no information on Garabandal[68]. Please inform me at Dr. Fleming address when you shall arrive and what flight so I can try and be there, can't wait.

Love Barbara

———— ⋘⋙ ————

[68] The Garabandal apparitions of St Michael the Archangel and the Blessed Virgin Mary are said to have occurred from 1961 to 1965 to four young schoolgirls in a rural village community in Cantabria.

Madrid

March 29, 1970

Madrid, Spain

Really, I have just had it. I am not very pleased with Roz coming, for right now things are just too confusing. I have to be out of this flat on April 4 and can't do anything about it until then because another girl is helping with the rent and she will stay here until the 4th. Then I have to be here on the 5th to check the place over with the landlord and I am sneaking things out as I don't want any trouble because I am living on the fianza (deposit) and I am in the country illegally now. Angie and I are moving into a flat but Corkie is not leaving until April 6. My Jewish director friend from Rome (Mel) does not care for me associating with Corkie as he says he's too stupid to appreciate my presence and I can't leave town with Roz while he's here for I might have a chance in Rome through him. He is a Zen Buddhist.

I don't want Roz to know we are moving in with a man, for you know how East Coast think. Anything innocent can be made filthy! I have been very sick for the last four days with fever and terrible eye aches and am extremely dizzy. I'm just trying to pull myself together to get out of Madrid and I'm in no mood for the responsibility of renting a car for Roz and all that crap. God, my nerves just can't take anymore and I don't want to see any of Jerome's [her uncle] children for I refuse to play any silly little U.S. games and I refuse to be a hypocrite, so FUCK the lot of them. That is not a bad word in modern English – it's like saying darn.

Don't worry about my nonsense for I have never in my life been so mixed up. I don't know what I am or who I am, and shall never find out until I either go under treatment or get out of Madrid.

As soon as I find someone with A.P.O. to ship your plates home, I will. They are packed. Monday, I go to American Tourist Bureau and fight with them. After that I just won't be able to argue anymore.

This is an article on Mary Joe. She's fabulous and gave me two children's paintings she created for Hallmark, two cost $150. Will send them to the children.

Love Barbara

Madrid

April 8, 1970

Madrid, Spain

Dear Mother and Daddy,

Roz arrived and is driving me crazy. If I see much more of her, I will be in a mental home with a breakdown. My God, she really believes God ordains marriages. She can't believe my clothes (my entire body is clothed) and I look so straight it's unbelievable. She's trying to make me a puppet of the U.S. in dressing habits.

Forget that. I told her don't change me because I'm happy. Boy, I've had it with all societies. Feel like going to Israel.

Just seeing her has made me realize I am an outcast and I must search until I find my type of people.

How dare anyone try to teach me how to think or judge me for my thinking?

Love Barbara

Madrid

May 22, 1970

Madrid, Spain

Dear Mother and Daddy,

Whoever packed the cosmetics for me did a marvelous job. Only had to pay 15 cents for customs so thanks a million! The dishes were sent yesterday but for some reason I don't trust the chap who said he mailed them so give them two weeks – if they have not arrived by then write to this address and let me know for I will track him down. I went to the insurance company and they were extremely nice and showed me three letters they had written to you at the Generalisima address. They gave me a form to fill out for the claim and said many times that it is customs who break things. Now if you want I can go to Macloa for the candlesticks and also to the Rostro flea market for the mirror if you really want them. Insurance co. had only $15 marked for candlesticks. I shall send you the form and claim even the glass on the pictures because he said he could pay me in pesetas here (which would not show a record of money in the U.S.) or he could pay you from the States which would show. Write and tell him you cried for weeks over the things and all the glass I sent home arrived safely.

Mo Jo went with me, as she was afraid that I might lose my temper. I will learn if I have the job or not by Sunday. If not, I am catching the train to Marrakesh and then come back to Madrid for a week and then off to Ibiza where all the hippies are. Please try and get everything to the insurance co. so when I come back I can go down there and know if you want me to collect the cash and buy the mirror and candlesticks, and send them on, or whether you just want the cash. Put the price of everything higher and you can get more money (except the candlesticks), claim the plates at 300 ptas a piece = $4.35, the mirror at $45 and the glass at whatever. Will send form this afternoon and tell them how they were wrapped. Have you met Roz's husband-to-be? Ain't he a right fascist pig? Bonnie wrote to me!

Love Barbara

Morocco

Marrakesh

June 20, 1970

Marrakesh, Morocco

Great to be in a groovy country again! Will be back in Madrid next week. Bus ride was exhausting from Tangiers. Will try to fly back to Madrid but afraid that's out of the question. Having a ball here and really don't want to leave. Existing on bread so my stomach's all right.

———————— ⊶⦿⊷ ————————

Spain

Madrid

July 12, 1970

Madrid, Spain

Dear Daddy,

Well, how shall I begin? Let's say this is serious letter which I do not want Mother to read for she will not understand that I am all right, but this is the way things are.

I fell madly in love with an American man, who was very wealthy but a sadist and after I was associating with him, he had a complete charge of my mind. He was slowly destroying me and telling me I was old and ugly after I fell for him. I had to forget him and build up strength to resist his power over me so I turned down a job dubbing in the movies $200 for three weeks' work and split to Morocco, since I needed to re-enter the country as well. I came back two weeks later after the money he gave me for the trip was stolen. Angie is still in Marrakesh since there was only enough money for one of us to get back. Went for two days without eating – not even a cup of coffee – and saved the rest of the money to fly from Malaga to Madrid, $15, so I could be with this jerk.

Anyway, when I returned he said he was going to take me traveling with him and since Corkie's wife was coming, my American friend said I could keep Angie's and my stuff in his flat. He called me up a Saturday night when he got off work and said he was leaving for Copenhagen on Monday and the landlord would not let me take over his flat. So I had to go over hysterically crying, start packing Angie's and my things including three large boxes which have been mailed to Jane and home. (Jane can use – borrow! – anything she wants in the boxes and although one was addressed to Jane, the articles are still mine and things like a candelabra parts are in different boxes, so all little screws etc. are in the boxes for a purpose plus half of a chair which the other part has not been sent yet. So, keep all wood pieces together.)

I am throwing up with nerves and hating myself for not being calculating and getting into the romantic stage. This is what frightens me the most – I used to be a realist now I am a romanticist, which is a slow destruction. For two days I was in a state not knowing where to keep the luggage and not having a cent to my name. He sat and read a book and didn't even help me pack! He loved seeing me hurt and in need of help. He knew I had turned down the job to be with him and he had $8,000 cash in his wallet which I almost took $200 for 'cruelty to Barbara' money. I was afraid when he realized it he would turn me into the police, even if he were in another country.

Monday morning at 7, I had 18 suitcases, 3 large boxes, plus bags and bags of things as there were no more suitcases to put them in. He left me standing there scared stiff and he jumped into a chauffeur-driven car for the airport. So now the only person who would help me is a chap who has left his wife and child, called John O'Brien. He helped me in three taxis with the junk and now I am staying in his flat with an American girl who is married to a crazy Spaniard who is running around town looking for her and her child to kill them with a switch blade. She received two airplane tickets from her parents for the States but her husband alerted the police and said it was a kidnapping, so now she can't leave the country legally. The police are looking for her to drag her back to him after he tried to kill her and the daughter – a woman has no rights in Spain. Some friends of John's from Italy are hiring a boat to collect her and the child (who both have U.S. passports) from a particular beach in Majorca. If the police don't find her before she leaves Madrid, she can make the boat.

This is not exactly the environment I need right now. Angie owes me $50 which I hope to get back plus I had to find someone to take care of her 6-month-old Afghanistan dog, Keisha. People are coming in and out all day and already two dresses of mine are already missing.

Daddy, what is the matter with me? I know I'm a very difficult person but this is because I've always been extremely insecure and at the age of 30, it is worse. I mean I don't seem to be able to handle it anymore. I want a child so badly while my body is still in condition, actually I just want a man to love me for what I am but they always seem to take advantage of me for I am not a strong person anymore. My gypsy way has destroyed me mentally and physically and I can't continue my life as it is. I am out of the terrible depression state I was in and hate myself for being so weak and getting into such a state in the first place. If I ever get in that state again, I will definitely do myself in and really the only thing which prevented me from doing it was thinking that Mary Joe would have the responsibility of shipping my body home and what the family would go through and always asking why. But that is morbid and the past so let's forget it, and take an objective look at things. No, I haven't flipped, I'm just mixed up.

Now this is the real reason for the letter. I want money, big money and I am willing to work very hard for it, for never again shall I be pushed around especially by men. The only way to do this is have enough money to buy what I want and not rely on anyone and false people always judge by materialistic wealth instead of inward wealth. Daddy, I'm tired, oh my God I'm tired and the only thing in life I want is just to have one man adore and love me but it seems this is impossible so I shall again join the capitalistic system of being hard, calculating and only think of myself.

Daddy, I leave it up to you to convince Mother I'm doing the right thing. Remember Susan, the girl I traveled with in India? She has had an offer to open up schools in the U.S. – a combination of ballet and yoga and she needs an assistant. So now I have to get $1,000 to send me to school to get in condition. The yoga might be extremely difficult for me for I am such a daydreamer and have never trained myself to think for a long period of time, which yoga requires. I will have to go to school for three to six months plus I want to go to a psychiatrist there. I have to get in touch with Susan by phone to see when I have to be in London to train with Lotte Berk[69]. I hate London for it is expensive. I will have to live under grubby conditions and no fashionable clothes to wear but I can stick it out. I've got to. Now I have sent in my income tax in, I will receive $300 back. I was planning on $600 back for some reason, so now that's out. I can use my director friends Mel's operator from Rome for long-distance calls free but his operator has not called for days and for calls to the States he has to be given one day's notice. This is why I don't think I can call you. Now I still have $500 left from the Navy which no one knows about so I shall probably be writing you from London for $200 out of my stock. I must admit I am very proud of myself for not touching any of the money in stock by the way as since I only made $2,684.08 for a total year, I did not fill out about stocks. I filled out the 1040 short form.

I shall try and go to Ibiza for a few weeks for I need the sun, wind and ocean before I reach cold London. So I shall probably have to write for $300 instead of $200.I know it's very hard for you to understand but if nothing else has happened, you must realize that it has taken me 30 years to accept you as a friend instead of an enemy. I only hope you are capable of understanding that statement and feeling the beauty in it and this is why I shall never hide or have to lie about anything anymore. I have finally accepted you the way you are and it is your duty as a father, and most important as a friend, not to condemn me but help me in any respect, no matter how silly or ridiculous it may seem to you. This is helping each other and giving without measure and whether we admit it or not, it is everybody's responsibility to help each other and understanding and not judging. How can we judge our neighbors' actions when we don't even know our own actions? This is true Christianity and a true human being. Oh boy, you can really see in this letter how Madrid affects me. The phone number I am at now is 270-4684. So anyway, that's been my life for the last two years.

Now Susan said she might have to borrow a $1,000 from me on my stocks. I don't mind if I can be protected legally, that I can definitely get the money back so can you think of that and if there is a risk then you

---

[69] Lotte Berk (1913-2003) was a German-born dancer and teacher, who lived in England from 1938. In 1959, she developed her own method of exercise, drawing on ballet moves and positions, that concentrated on the idea of building core stability.

will have to think of a good excuse when she phones you, like maybe you are borrowing on my stock and yours so there's no loose money. Remember she is offering me a future if everything goes alright so be very tactful and use an excuse which can be verified for she studied the stock market and worked for a firm in New York so she knows how it works.

Must go pack my mirror to send home.

Love Barbara

P.S. Mother can read this but she gets so upset and worried which doesn't do her any good. But man, I've got to find myself and I know a doctor can help. Also tell Susan I wrote for money but you could not even send me any.

Madrid

July 25, 1970

Madrid, Spain

Dear Mother and Daddy,

God, you caught me at a bad time for my mind was really confused. I talked to Mel about what you said and he agreed with you completely, except he thinks I should go to London and really check things out. He knows my disposition and he knows I need something to work on for my own salvation and to become a better person. He does not think an office job is the best thing for me for I have to be around people who stimulate me so that I work to be as good, if not better, than them. Apparently since I am so complexed, I could never get along in a society where people expect things, a narrow-minded society. Mel also wants to check into this school for he is quite familiar with all types of schools in London.

Mel is a psychiatrist (or should I say he has a doctor's degree in that and quite a lot of other things) and dubs and directs films and the theater. He was the one who pulled me out of the state I was in and said I have a long way to go but at least I'm laughing at the state I got myself in. I think it was for the better for it will be a long time before I shall let myself get in the same situation. Mel has connections everywhere but since I can't act, dub or really do secretarial work, he's rather stuck. Anyway, it was because of him that I have a job typing out scripts for a dubbing studio 9 am to 11 pm every day including Saturday. God I'm exhausted but feel it has done me good. Don't tell anyone but I only make $23 a month but that doesn't matter as much as the fact that Mel does dubbing for the same firm so I get to have my usual pep talks every day.

My teeth are really killing me – I mean, like every one of them around the gums and the infection is back again in my gums, so if this school is not what I hope it is, I can at least get my teeth done free, with only the expense of staying in London and that is much cheaper than dentist work in the States. I'm working very hard for as soon as I finish these scripts I am off. Meanwhile I have to move out of the place with all of Angie's things and mine for I am not paying rent and the couple who are letting me stay there are leaving. Must find a place for Angie's things, send a few boxes off, find a place free for myself for a week or so and that's about it. Mary Joe, the artist that I sent you the article on, is being given a showing at a hotel in London, thanks to Mel and his connections, starting September 1. So, it will be sort of a reunion with M.J., Susan and Mel.

I went to 44 Dr. Fleming and the portero (doorman) said all letters have been sent back so I did not receive your last three letters. Please once more let me know how many parcels you received and more or less what was in them for I sent three boxes with three different sets of curtains; two red and one green set. That's really it.

If Mel doesn't think the school is legal or if there isn't anything in it, he will let me know immediately by phone or wire, for he does not want me to spend any money unless I will benefit from it – after he approves or disapproves, I will let you know. He is trying to find me a place to stay so I won't have to pay rent but it is very difficult for everything in London is very cramped and a house guest is a drag and usually in the way. If he had the money he would give me $500 but he's in terrible shape financially with a wife and five children and a wife! God, if he wasn't married he would be the ideal one for me. He's referred to as everyone's father and really, I don't know how he even gets a chance to breath, for everyone leaps on him asking him to help them with their problems. He's 46, looks like Orson Welles with a moustache and beard and a very Jewish look about him. Actually, he looks like what I would think Moses looks like! His biggest gripe is people exploiting others for any reason. Anyway, I love him dearly and he shall always be a friend of mine. Well that's just a little about my friend Mel 'Welles'. Oh, by the way he had the highest IQ during the Second World War and he went on special missions in Germany right when Hitler was at his peak. Has written several books and plays.

Angie is still in Morocco doing her thing. I expect to see her arriving back with tattoos on her face and dyed hands and feet. Angie is really lovely but a real sad case – in fact, it was because of Angie that I realized I must pick myself up or I would be exactly like her. Her problem is she will not admit the truth about herself. Anyway, if she's happy to be living in poverty with the hippies, that's her business and I really am glad when she is happy. The poor darling is so mixed up with life and the most irresponsible person I've ever met!

I was complaining to Mel the other day how she had inconvenienced me with the dog and luggage and he really became upset with me and more or less told me I had some nerve, for I was thinking of myself and lying in self-pity, that I didn't even realize the nice things people had done for me. When I accept someone as a friend then I should accept them as they are, not what I'd like them to be. He's right, so now I have to find someone who is honest and will keep her things. I've got to go now for I have to get out three reels in the course of the afternoon for all the dubbers are here from London and Rome and they want them to finish as soon as possible so they won't have to pay out so much money. By the way, Susan is a very reliable when she is interested in something and very intelligent. God, I can learn so much from her and she was very annoyed with me when I stayed in Madrid for so long.

Love Barbara

England

London

August 12, 1970

London, England

Dear Mother and Daddy,

Arrived in London on the 10th. Susan met me at the airport with a car. I am staying in a big flat by myself in Lowndes Square, one of the most expensive areas in London. I don't pay rent and can stay here until August 16. A Greek ship owner and his wife are sponsoring the school in New York with Susan as the head and me as her assistant. Susan paid $750 for a course at a particular school in London for she has to have a degree for the New York school. She talked the Greek out of making me have one so I go to the school September 1 to January 15 every day, for $200. On September 15 I enrol in another school so that will be two schools I'll be going to. Susan has told everyone we are both terribly wealthy so were in with the big people. She has made an appointment in Paris for me for a mini facelift which I'm scared to death to do. I've got to get out of that one for I know nothing about it. Now if I don't have to pay for a flat I've got more than enough money, but if I have to pay for one I'm not in such good shape. Susan has a dentist friend and so I can have my teeth done free.

The weather is lovely here – have been to three movies since I arrived and I'm on my way to another after this letter.

Clothes and food are cheap and I went to see *Hair* at the Shakespeare Theatre last night. God it was marvelous. People were running around the stage naked!

I feel great now and full of energy. Mother, I know what you are going through for when I was in Madrid my neck and shoulders were almost paralysed from pain. The pain was so great I would take sleeping pills to get rid of it. I'm sorry for any worry I've put you through but I'm great now and feel like life has meaning. Anyway, as plans go Susan and I should both be in New York end of January.

Now Mother, if you're not capable of writing then have Jane or Daddy write for you to Conchita. Just a short note to tell her you think about her all the time but have been in the hospital for a long time. You see, the thing is Shirley has talked Conchita out of liking me, but she adores you, Mother, and would do anything for you. Conchita is coming to London September 1 to stay with her friend, a terribly wealthy English woman who Conchita helped by stopping the Spanish government from confiscating her land. She is indebted to Conchita and several of Conchita's friends have stayed there for free. I asked Conchita if she would ask her friend if I could stay there for a month and she said agreed but I know if she receives a letter from you, Mother, she will make an effort. Ask how her father is. Please do this for me for it will save me around $200. When my income tax returns to your address, let me know and I will tell you whether I need it or not.

I am enclosing two checks which can't be cashed so could you renew them? Received your last letter in Madrid. Don't worry about me. I'm straightening out. Write to Conchita immediately for she will be driving to London soon with two of my suitcases. Write a list of things which arrived home. Did my Persian rug arrive? Went to the insurance company again – case closed. That's what they wanted.

Love B.

<hr>

London

August 23, 1970

London, England

Dear Mother and Daddy,

Susan never explains things. A Greek shipper and his wife are going to back a school in New York with Susan as head. Now the school where Susan is learning a special technique and the school in New York will be the same name. The woman who started this particular school is called Lotte Berk and she said all people who were going to teach under her system would have to get a degree, at \$750. Now the Greeks think I'm very wealthy and they (Susan talked them into it) decided they wouldn't let the teacher know I was the one who was going to New York, for once she got the \$750 she wouldn't pay any attention to me. So now I have to hide my identity and pay every 10 days (\$200 for four months) so she will work with me. It starts September 1. On September 15 I shall start at London Contemporary School of Dance for \$100 for four months. Susan will leave December 1 to set up school in New York. I shall follow but will be home for this Xmas.

My God, it looks as if I'm finally going to be doing something I want to do. I feel great and I'm very happy in London right now. The weather is great and the clothes are wild, wild, wild. Do you remember Judy Geeson, the young English movie star who I met in Madrid? I have been with her most of the time and I have met the most fantastic people. The man who wrote all the score for *Oliver!*[70], and the actors Laurence Harvey and Peter Sellers[71].

Judy is a fantastic, lovable girl whom I am terribly fond of. Mary Joe, the artist, is having an exhibition of her paintings at some Royal Hall which Mel, my ex-boss and psychiatrist, is coming to. Susan is probably going to marry the Head of Revlon for the whole of Europe. I went to Paris for the weekend, compliments of Susan's boyfriend. As soon as my income tax check comes in, please send immediately for I have to pay for schools. Listen, you can stop worrying about me for I can find my way now and I'm very happy with my true friends Susan, Mary Joe and Judy.

Will write again when I get time.

Love you. B.

—————⊸◦{}◦⊶—————

---

[70] *Oliver!* Written by Lionel Bart, (1930-1999), it won the Tony Award for Best Original Score in 1963 and in 1968, the film version won six Oscars, including Best Picture.
[71] Laurence Harvey (1928-1973) was a Lithuanian-born actor and director. He was known for his cut-glass accent and debonair persona.
Peter Sellers CBE (1925-1980) was an English actor and comedian. He first appeared on *The Goon Show* and was a global star in many films, such as *Dr Strangelove* and *The Pink Panther* series.

London

September 19, 1970

London, England

Dear Daddy,

Please read this letter to Mother. First of all, thanks ever so much for the 50. Received the three checks. I don't understand about the one for $117.12, I was supposed to receive $300 from my income tax form I sent from the Navy to the Income Tax Office in Georgia. If that is the $117.12 from them, how could you cash it? I can't tell you how upset I am to hear about Mother, poor darling, has suffered all her life. Will write her a separate letter. Now to relieve both of you, I shall go into detail of what I am doing.

First of all I am living with Judy, who is doing a movie next month as Dustin Hoffman's partner. She lives in an Italian village right in the heart of London with flowers, gardens and fountains for the grounds. Her cottage is darling with two bedrooms, a small dining room, kitchen and a gigantic bright living room with half of the ceiling glass. We have central heating and wall-to-wall carpets. She has been marvelous to me but I don't know how long I can stay – my God, if only I could stay until December 1.

Things really look good for the school in New York. I go to school every day with Lord Harlech's[72] new young wife (he's the one that Jackie Kennedy was supposed to marry) and Peter Sellers' ex-wife Britt Ekland[73]. Before I moved in here, I was living at the Earl of Sondes' flat while he was in New York. So far, I have met Peter Sellers, Laurence Harvey, Irish author Edna O'Brien, and was invited to a party which Princess Margaret and Lord Snowdon attended but I didn't go for I would have had to stay too late, anyway I didn't know they were going to be there. So, you can let the snobby people in Savannah know that, just tell Jane. I am extremely happy now for I have a roof over my head

---

[72] William David Ormsby-Gore, 5th Baron Harlech (1918-1985), was a British diplomat and a Conservative politician. He was the British Ambassador to the United States. Once Kennedy was assassinated, Harlech asked Jackie Kennedy to marry him but she did not accept. His first wife died in a car crash and he then married Pamela Colin, a Manhattan socialite.

[73] Britt Ekland (born 1942) is a Swedish actress, model, and singer.

and to be surrounded by people that really care for me. Mary Joe and Susan came over to meet Judy and see me and they couldn't believe how I had changed for the better. Mary Joe saw me laugh for the first time. Susan and I shall be in New York for six to eight months then we go to California. I shall be home for Xmas then I fly off to New York.

Judy has a parrot called Benjie who flies and lands on my head in the morning. He is full of personality and I really love him. He kisses me in the mouth and he smells gorgeous. I was planning on the $300 from the income tax people which has thrown me back a little so I will have to have about $200 from my stocks but I will give you advance notice.

I love going to my classes and next month I shall double the time I go to be in great shape. This has really changed my life and I feel so great. I'm up very early and excited about the whole day. All the tension has left my body with no more neck or back aches, and I'm eating well. The first three days of class I couldn't move, I was in agony from using my muscles. My modern ballet class is a drag but I'm don't miss a class. I literally can't walk when I get out of class and I have to sleep before and after classes for I am so exhausted but it's a great feeling. My Russian teacher told me it was incredible how well I could do everything only after a few lessons. Susan just phoned and said she and Greek shipper's wife were really pleased with me and that the Russian teacher looked forward to my coming to class!

Daddy, I can't explain how happy I am. It is like God has put his hand on my shoulder and said, "Now it's time for you to feel happiness!" My God, now I am glad I had such a bad, sad time for two years for if one does not experience sadness, how can one feel happiness?

Please let Mother know how I am for she is really the only one who has known my depressed moods and it will make her very happy that I am loving life. London is very warm and the flowers are still in bloom.

Must go to class now.

Love you Barbara

London

September 19, 1970

London, England

Dear Mother,

Just a wee note to let you know I love you more than anything else in the world and I pray you shall be alright without pain. Someday, Mother, I shall repay you for all the understanding and love you gave me. I am living with Judy and have met several famous people. I was invited to a seated dinner party where the guests included Princess Margaret and Lord Snowdon! I am doing marvelous in my classes and shall be in Savannah for Xmas and maybe Judy will come with me. After that I go to New York and after a month when I am settled in, I shall send you a ticket and I shall have bread to buy you nice things which you deserve.

I am very happy now, Mother, for Judy is marvelous to me and she has a lovely bird called Benjie whom I love, and a darling little dog named Tara. I see Mary Joe and Susan almost every day and I have only met nice people since I have been here. Life feels beautiful now and the sun is shining every day. Now hurry and get well, Mother, for I have traveling plans for the grooviest Mother of all time.

Love you Barbara

London

October 8, 1970

London, England

C/o Judy Geeson, Chelsea Village, 416 Fulham Road, Studio B. London

Dear Daddy,

Things are going marvelous for me in school. I never miss a class and work ever so hard each day. I am literally exhausted after each class. Judy is so marvelous to me and is literally supporting me. I shall not forget. As soon as I get my check in New York, I shall send her some money. Only eight more weeks of work and surviving and all my worries will be over.

Buy the October issue of *Vogue* magazine. Lotte Berk's school is in it! I go under the name Bif Brimacombe because if they find out I'm the one for New York, then I'm out. Judy is supposed to get to New York next week and then to California for a cowboy movie and then on to Jamaica for Xmas. If this happens, I shall look after Benjie and her house. If her boyfriend decides to come home from New York in two weeks' time, I'm in trouble for I shall have to find a flat for two weeks and it's impossible in London for one can only rent for a month and you have to give key money.

Daddy, what happened to the money I was supposed to get from my income tax?

Love Barbara

London

October 25, 1970

London, England

Dear Mother and Daddy,

Great to hear from you by letter and marvelous speaking to you on phone. Received $600 in checks and that will be all I need, for I got on a special flight for $120 to New York by jet. Leave London Sunday, December 18 and shall arrive in Savannah the 19th instead of December 21. Judy might fly down and see me but I don't think she will make it. If you or Jane want a pair of suede boots which fit tight and come up to the knee, let me know. Colors Royal blue, ox blood, grayish pink, beige, brown, black, unbelievable price of $21.00. They are so expensive-looking. Susan said they would cost $70 in New York. Send American size.

I am really excited about coming home. Mother, ask your doctor if you can do stomach and leg work. No back work – if not, don't worry. You can help me with errands and all that jazz. Now, are you ready for this? In about two weeks, the Earl of Sondes will call you from Atlanta to tell you he is forwarding a book to you from Lydia Bach (this is Susan!). It will be a small book on the exercises – show this to your doctor. He is also forwarding you *British Vogue* magazine with Lydia (Susan) doing the exercises.

The garbage strike has been on in London for a month and the entire city is beginning to smell. Only seven more weeks and I'll be home. I only have Benjie the cockatoo now in this large house. He is so adorable and plucks all his feathers out when he is put in the cage. He has complete control of the house and sleeps at the head of the bed – last night he crapped right on my nose! I screamed at him and the poor little darling was shaking. He knew I was angry with him. I think it is marvelous Jane can come to New York but I want to be all organized. She can take the class for free.

Anything I can get for anyone, let me know. Clothes are so cheap here and gorgeous.

If Judy calls you from New York, don't let her know you believe in what I'm doing. Just say you can't understand me going to exercise class because of my bad back and you wish you could help more but money is terribly tight now but easing up. So, I don't think I shall have time to write anymore for I shall be extremely busy.

London

October 31, 1970

London, England

Got the flight for $120 to New York but they don't know what time the plane arrives so I can't make a reservation to Savannah. Find out for me how much it cost on the train from New York to Savannah on a sleeper day and night and also flights from New York to Savannah. Usually nights are cheaper, well in Europe they are. Next week I have that terrible wart removed from my foot and have to go under local anaesthetic (God, do I need a dictionary), all for $8.00. If I had known I had to be in the country a year I could have saved that and got it free, but who cares? In Savannah, Jane's doctor said it would be around $100.

Well shall see you soon. I am having the same trouble in London. Clothes don't fit me.

The school opens January 21 in New York.

Love Barbara

London

November 19, 1970

London, England

Dear Mother and Daddy,

Don't ask me where the devil the money has gone but I don't have enough for my fare home! Could you borrow $200 more for me – as soon as possible. It is so cold and rainy in London now and the blowflies are crawling outside the kitchen window now because of the garbage strike.

It is really incredible how the money goes in a big city. Do you remember Wendy? I'm supposed to fly to Ireland the weekend after next; she will pay half the fair. My stomach is so hard now – if someone hit me in the stomach with a board, it wouldn't hurt! Since I'm now on a chartered plane I shan't know when I leave on the 18th until a week before. I will just have to take my luck and try to get to Savannah any way I can during the Xmas rush. I think I shall just stay in Kennedy Airport until a seat is available to Savannah or Atlanta. God, with all the luggage and everything, what a drag.

I shall really miss Benjie the bird. He is so darling. I get up at 7.30 to let him fly around the house before I leave for school. He sings and coos and sometimes when I don't put him in his cage at night, he flies upstairs and sleeps on the head of my bed. I put a piece of paper on the floor, so no worry there. One time he crapped on my face and said hello. I just can't get angry with him for when I had my foot operated on, he never left me and stayed on my stomach while I was awake and when I fell asleep he would jump on my stomach and perch next to my head.

When I woke up it was as if a little white eagle was protecting me. I never realized it but even a little bird responds to love, but when I get angry with him, the poor little darling starts shaking and waits for the hit on the beak. That's when he eats a sweater on the living room sofa!

Love Barbara

London

November 27, 1970

London, England

Dear Mother and Daddy

I wrote a brief letter about a week ago but don't know exactly if I mailed it or not. I have teeth trouble again plus I am going to Ireland for a week to stay with Wendy.

Mother, write technically exactly what is the matter with you physically for I have a physiotherapist friend and he said if he knows exactly what is wrong with you, he can tell me exactly what and how this will affect your body if I show him all the exercises. Please do this for the day I arrive you and I shall start working immediately. If you don't let me know, I shall have to go to your doctor to show him all the exercises, pay him and he will then send me to someone else. I will not work with your body until it has been approved by a physiotherapist for I know nothing about anatomy. This will save time so send technical information of what happened to you, and why you were in a cast.

See you soon.

Love Barbara

London

December 8, 1970

London, England

Electricity strike, garbage strike still on. Milk strike, newspaper strike. House freezing and afraid Benjie will die on me.

Need rest of money so can I borrow on stocks? If not possible, please send money from saving account – $275 as I have to pay for dentist and the rest of money is for the flight. God, I don't have money for my ticket because of dentist. I shall arrive in New York on December 23 and will make my way to Savannah, anyway possible. Please do not plan a party for me for I couldn't take the strain.

Love Barbara

HOME

When I got off the plane in Savannah, I looked like a wild woman. I was hunched forward; my hair was almost entirely gone and my teeth were so bad I needed gum surgery. My mother fainted when she realized it was me. My father was filming me get off the plane and I could see the look of horror on his face. I hope he destroyed the tape! I was a mess – I looked awful. All in all, my travels ended up lasting a decade and took me to more than 120 countries on nearly every continent

I think it was in Marrakesh in the summer of 1970 where I started to realize how much damage I had done to my body whilst wandering around the world. My muscles had lost all their tone and I had no flexibility or extension. The ballet exercises I had done as a teenager were now impossible. I was also suffering with a severe case of malnutrition and my third bout of amoebic dysentery. Then a friend who I had met on my travels told me about an extraordinary process in England by which the human body could be dramatically renewed and reformed through exercise. She persuaded me to return to London to try it. As soon as I arrived, I saw two doctors. One said I needed surgery on my back and knees. I was told that if I didn't have the surgery, I would probably be in a wheelchair in two years. The second said my back would never recover and also needed surgery. It got to the point where I would cross a street and I would have to ask someone if I could hold onto them. It kept getting worse and worse, and I wasn't willing to admit it. I couldn't move anymore. That's when I knew it was finally time to go home.

But when I met the teacher, Lotte Berk, I was sure I had found my cure. She was a 57-year-old, half-German, half-Russian dancer who had seriously injured her back dancing but now had the body of a 21-year-old girl. She held her classes in a little basement room called the Rehabilitation Exercise Studio on Manchester Street in the center of London. Her classes were brutal, and with my bent spine and travel-damaged knees, it was a slow and painful process. But she helped me reconstruct my body back to health and youth. I spent about four months with her and also attended daily classes in Martha Graham technique at The Place dance school. Those few months in London were the most important of my life and helped to start my body healing.

My friend had bought the franchise rights from Lotte Berk and was opening a studio to teach the classes in New York. She saw how fast I learned the exercises and the dramatic changes they were having on my body and asked me to teach in the studio when it opened. So, I landed back in Savannah for Christmas, and three weeks later I was teaching my first class in New York! I didn't stay there long. I left because I didn't approve of the way clients' bodies were being treated. I was told to change the way I had been instructed to teach the exercises, supposedly so we could handle more clients in the salon. I was prohibited from asking the women I worked with if they had back problems, yet my back hurt when I did some of the exercises. Other people might have been hurting as well. This was extremely upsetting for me. Lotte Berk was a master in this field and we had studied this program personally with her. I believed in my teacher's program, and, in all fairness to her and to myself, I could not continue the way things were going. I couldn't take the strain on my back and so left the studio to experiment with my own movements.

When I came back to America, I had never seen Saran wrap, push-button phones or refrigerators with ice-makers. I thought, *These are the creations of superhuman beings. These are the creations of Americans.* I wanted to be a part of my own wonderful culture. I wanted to do something special in America. I wanted to be a success. But I thought only men were successes. However, I also realized that I could have been a woman bent over a rice paddy, working all day, with her baby strapped to her body. Those were the two extremes, the pull to be an achiever and not having the push to know how to go about it. I couldn't relate to having

a home. I couldn't relate to being a part of a society again. I identified with the street people, the shopping bag ladies. I wanted to know what they carried in their bags, if the contents resembled what I had carried.

After leaving the exercise studio, I stayed in New York and said to myself, *If I make it, it's got to be in America's toughest city.* I had a door that closed with a lock, a bed, running water. I had protection. If anything happened, I could call the police. It was a culture shock. I was a happy woman.

In 1972 I went to a numerologist in New York. He said, "Lay low, nothing is going to happen in your life."

I said, "Can we cheat!?"

I was desperate then. I wasn't accomplishing anything and I wasn't happy with myself. I wanted another name. I told him, "Give me a nice name that's not going to hurt."

After many calculations, he said, "Callan."

By now I looked terrible and was in constant pain. I got to the point to where I couldn't even get out of bed in the morning. I had a mattress on the floor and it would take me maybe 25, 30, 45 minutes to roll over to get on the floor. And then, how do you get off the floor up to standing? That's why in my Callanetics exercises I talk about *How to get off the floor without using your back or putting pressure on your back.* I learned all these things myself, just through my own ailments. I started experimenting with the exercises I had learned from Lotte Berk in London and with motions taken from ballet and Martha Graham technique, plus my training in judo at the Kodokan School in Tokyo. I incorporated intense disciplines I had experienced on my travels, including belly dancing and Tai Chi. That's how I developed what I then called The Callan Reconstruction Method. It was impossible for me to make big or sudden movements – my body just couldn't do it. That's where the little tiny pulsing movement that you see in all my exercises comes from. I physically couldn't move more than that.

Doctors later said to me, "Callan, that was so clever of you to come up with the $1/16^{th}$ to $\frac{1}{2}$ an inch motion."

And I just looked at them and said, "I'd love to take credit for it, but it really wasn't intended that way. It was the only way I could move my body. I couldn't move it anymore."

What I was really going for was to stretch the spine. And what I was thinking was if I can stretch the spine at the same time as contracting or strengthening the surrounding muscles, it seems like – and I'd never spoken to a doctor about this – it seems like those muscles are there for a purpose. If I kept them strong enough – including the inner thigh muscles – then those muscles could take over, and take away putting all that pressure on the back and overloading it. And I didn't know whether it was going to work or not. But it did!

That's what I did. I got myself into certain positions to where I could contract the muscle very, very deep – always, always, always stretching the spine – to where there would never be any pressure on it. And by getting into these positions, by stretching the spine, it actually made the buttocks muscle or whatever muscle I was using at the time, work deeper. I didn't care at that particular time what my body looked like, I was in such pain.

Pain was always my motivation. I would modify the motions so much in order that my body could begin to do them. Most of them became entirely new exercises. Others I made up completely. I didn't really understand the human body. I only knew that when you turn a certain way, you're pulling a muscle or you're contracting a muscle – only because I could feel it so intensely in my body. If I had studied under a doctor, I would never have put Callanetics together. I would have been terrified, because it goes against a lot of the old teaching.

Every day I did my exercises, even as little as 20 minutes, my body started getting more erect and straighter. I could actually start moving my neck! People would look at me and say, "My God! What are you doing? You look incredible!"

So, I started showing my friends and then teaching classes. My students became my best advertisement. They'd say, "If you do what I do, your body is going to look 10 years younger in 10 hours," because they didn't know what else to say and that was the experience that they had with my exercises. I didn't create the name Callanetics – my students did! We didn't know what to call it. People would ask what they were doing and they'd say, "I don't know. Some type of a body motion."

And they came up with the name Callanetics because my name was Callan and they didn't know what else to say!

I would teach out of my apartment. Word got around New York that my exercises worked. I created exercises that tightened the buttocks and slimmed the thighs. My students said, "You've got magic. Sell it. Write a book."

"Don't be crazy. I can't spell," I said. "And you've got to know somebody in publishing!"

One of my students said that her husband was always talking about so-and-so agent and looked up the number in the phone book. However, I refused to make the call. But another student got the agent on the phone. Finally, the agent said to me, "What's your name?"

"Callan Pinckney."

And she said she'd been trying to locate me because she had friends who'd heard I had incredible results. She asked for my exercises. And I told her I'd give them to her if she sold my book!

I believe in destiny. I was destined to write my first book. I know that. I don't search my soul trying to figure out why. I just accepted that an opportunity had happened. When I was in Hong Kong, a Buddhist fortune teller told me I could have an impact on the world. I thought it was rubbish then because I had so little to eat. But that impact happened. It wasn't easy. I'd rather fight people in the desert than deal with shrewd business people. At one stage, my book wasn't being properly promoted. So I became a nuisance, I made demands. More than once I heard, *Who do you think you are?*

Remember, I was still full of anger. My anger had taken a different turn, though. What maddened me was that you had to be a celebrity to write and sell an exercise book. Anger can be a positive force. It galvanized me. I borrowed $70,000 and went on the road, promoting myself in city after city. That $70,000 was for traveling expenses, press kits and thousands and thousands of dollars' worth of telephone calls.

I got so nervous that my face twitched. I thought *What if I can't pay the money back?* I had no money for myself – I ate cat food!

It has all worked. When I first started out on my trip, my philosophy was: *Do something to help yourself or get out of the universe.* I survived 10 years on my own. That was Part One of me. In a sense, I was a daydreamer then, someone who stared at the world going by. Now I say every day is a new beginning. I don't accept old age. Absolutely not. I'm going to be buried stark naked with red high-heeled shoes and a gorgeous hat with the tightest sleekest body in the entire world, so nobody could ever say,

"That old bag, what did she know?!"

Callan Pinckney

ABOUT THE AUTHOR

Callan Pinckney was raised in Savannah, Georgia. She trained in classical ballet for 12 years and studied other forms of dance, movement, and exercise. She had to restore her own body to health when, after a decade-long backpacking odyssey around the world, the rigors of travel, combined with a congenital back defect, led to physical collapse.

This was the beginning of CALLANETICS. She experimented with various exercise techniques, using her early ballet training to develop the program which finally solved her physical problems. Callan taught her revolutionary exercises to thousands of students, celebrities, royalty and distinguished clients worldwide, all of whom testify that Callanetics is a unique, safe exercise system for transforming body shape.

She published 11 bestselling books and was inducted posthumously into the National Fitness Hall of Fame in 2016 for her contributions to the fitness industry. Her 1986 video *Callanetics: 10 Years Younger in 10 Hours* reached record sales and earned the title of top-selling fitness video of all-time.

So huge was her impact on the exercise world, the word Callanetics was added to the Collins English Dictionary, Cambridge Dictionary, and the Free Medical Dictionary.

Callan Pinckney passed away in 2012. She left behind an extraordinary legacy that will continue to inspire future generations of health and fitness enthusiasts.

9 781068 617423